## PALETTE KNIFE PAINTING

# DEEP IMPASTO®

Paint beautiful masterpieces using a palette knife and the impasto technique

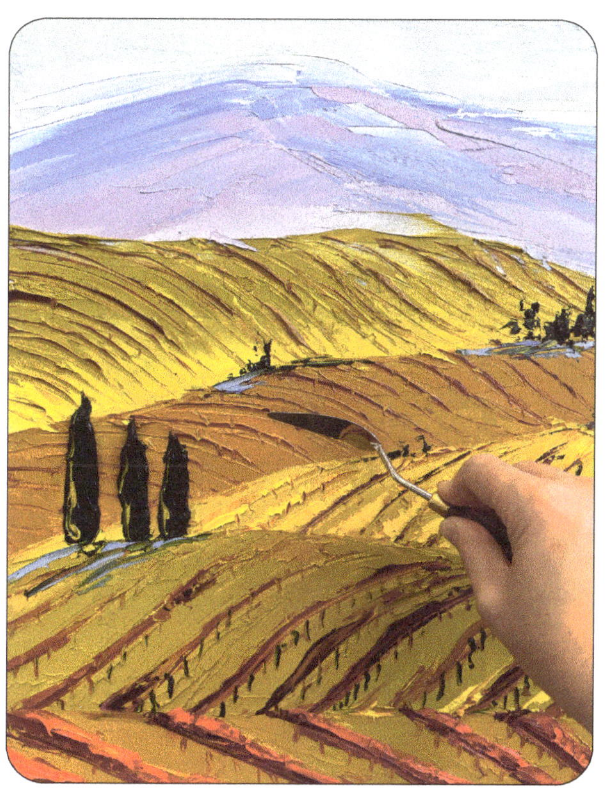

Palette Knife Artist
**LISA ELLEY**

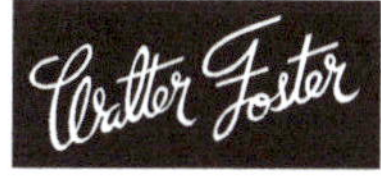

**Quarto.com | WalterFoster.com**



First published in 2023 by Walter Foster Publishing, an imprint of The Quarto Group.
100 Cummings Center, Suite 265D, Beverly, MA 01915, USA.
**T** (978) 282-9590 **F** (978) 283-2742

EEA Representation, WTS Tax d.o.o.,
Žanova ulica 3, 4000 Kranj, Slovenia.
www.wts-tax.si

---



Walter Foster Publishing titles are also available at discount for retail, wholesale, promotional, and bulk purchase. For details, contact the Special Sales Manager by email at specialsales@quarto.com or by mail at The Quarto Group, Attn: Special Sales Manager, 100 Cummings Center, Suite 265D, Beverly, MA 01915, USA.

ISBN: 978-0-7603-8216-5

Digital edition published in 2023
eISBN: 978-0-7603-8217-2

Design: Cindy Samargia Laun
Copyedit: Leah Noel
Proofread: Tracy Wilson

## PALETTE KNIFE PAINTING

# DEEP IMPASTO®

Paint beautiful masterpieces
using a palette knife and the
impasto technique

Palette Knife Artist
**LISA ELLEY**

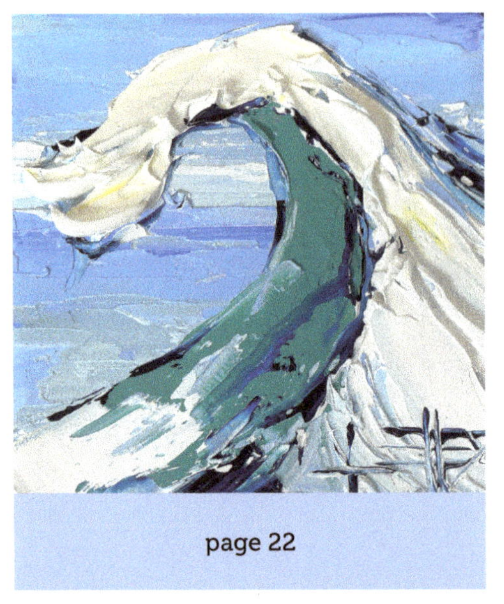
page 22

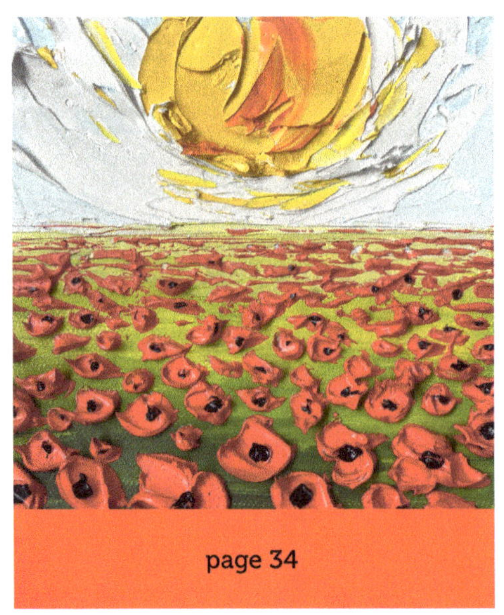
page 34

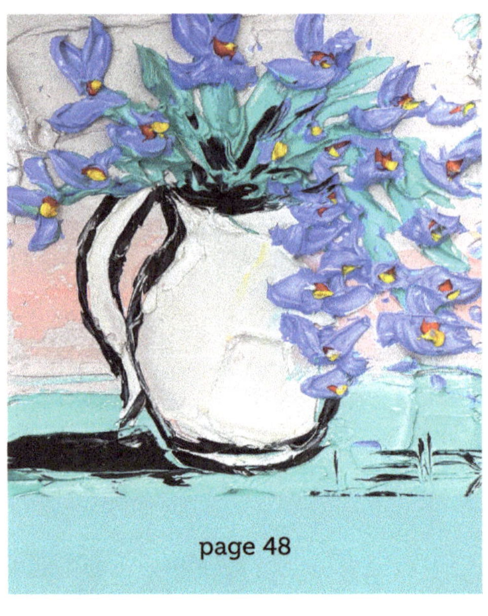
page 48

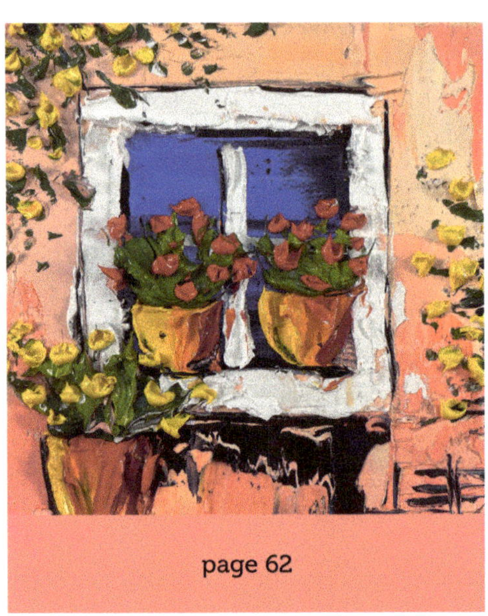
page 62

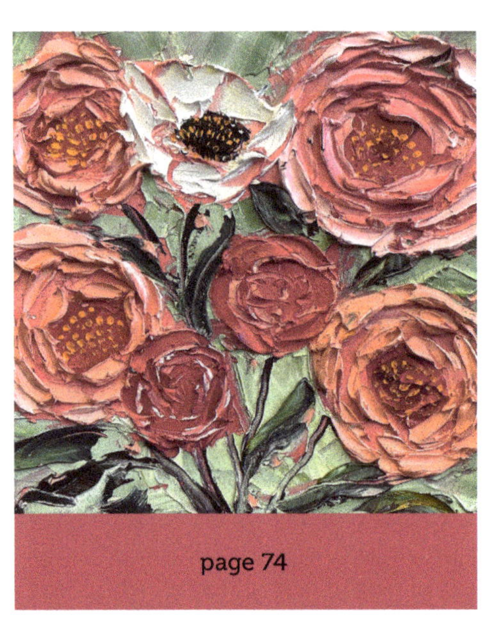
page 74

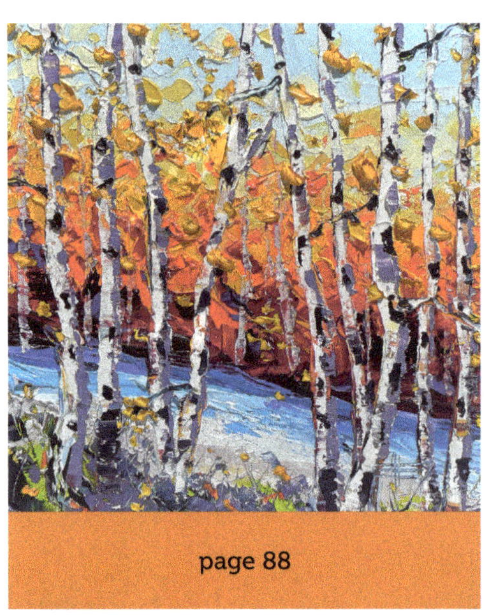
page 88

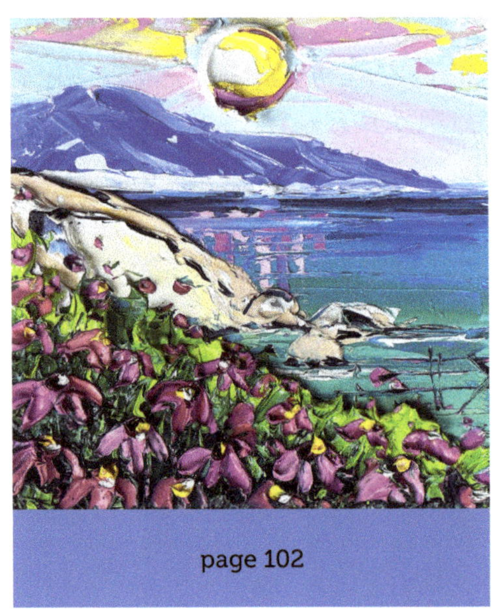
page 102

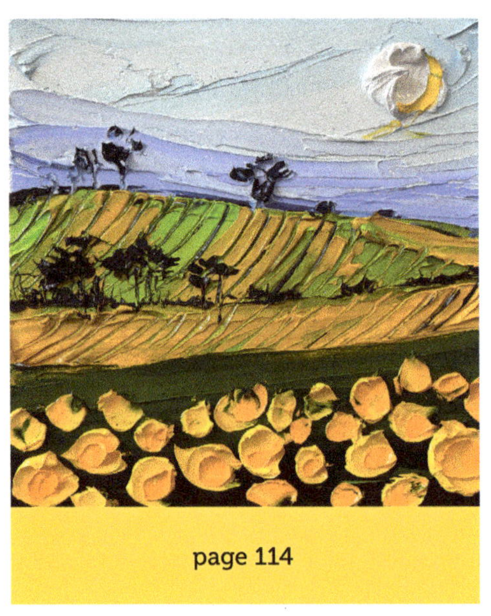
page 114

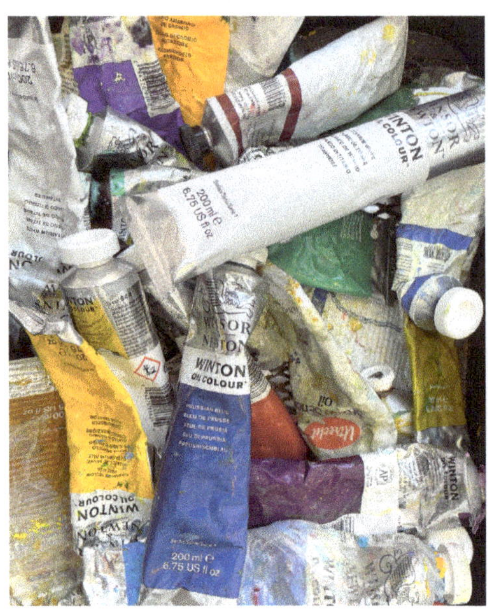

# Contents

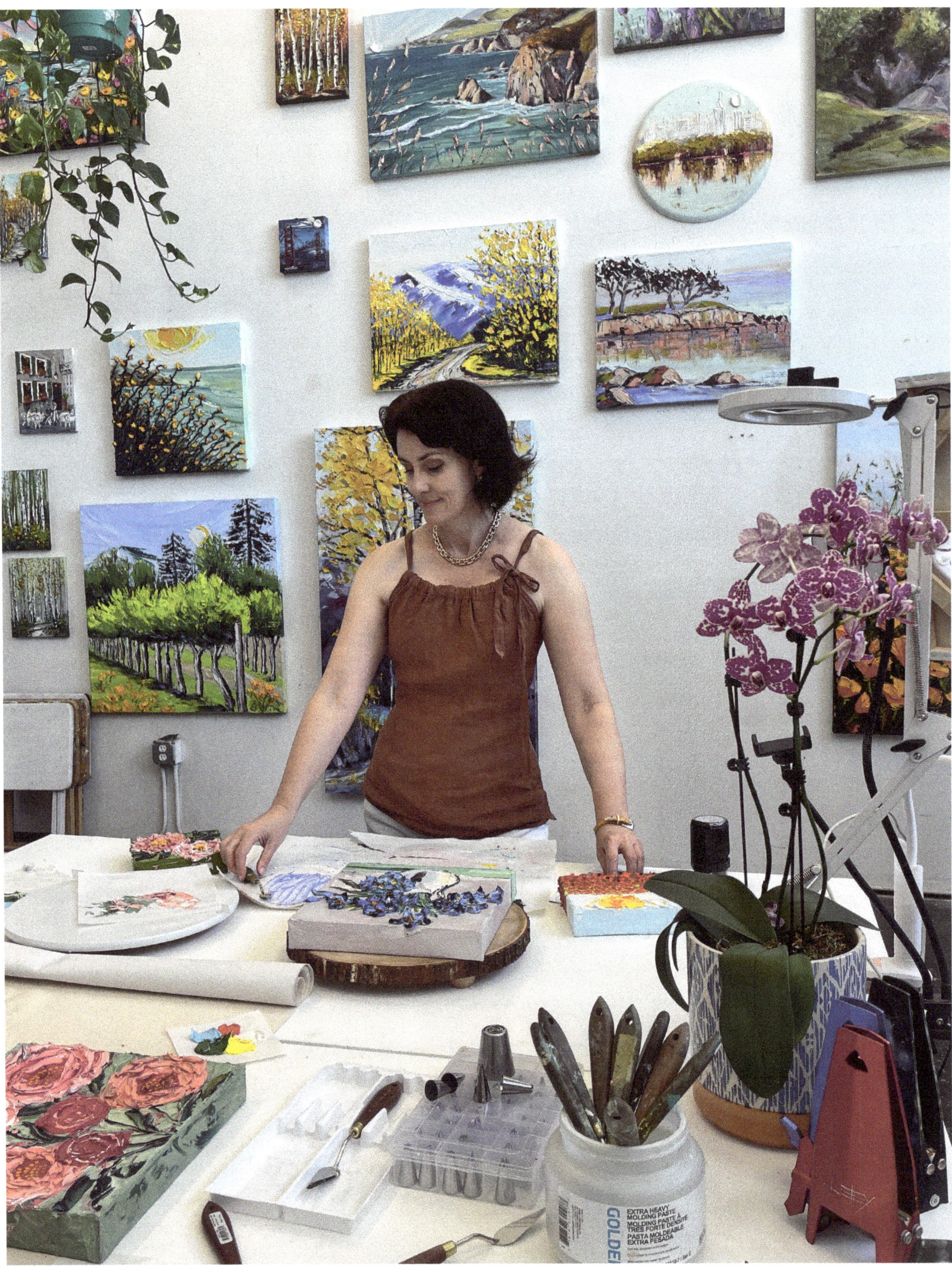
GOLDE
EXTRA HEAVY
MOLDING PASTE
MOLDING PASTE À
TRÈS FORTE DENSITÉ
PASTA MOLDEABLE
EXTRA PESADA

# INTRODUCTION

Hello and welcome! My name is Lisa, and I'm a professional palette knife artist with a studio in the San Francisco Bay. I've spent over a decade painting almost entirely with a palette knife, honing my skill and experimenting, and I'm excited to share my years of experience with you!

In this book I really wanted to focus on bringing you a variety of striking, technically strong, and bite-sized projects that you can complete quickly and just have lots of fun with. In our busy, modern life, it's hard to find the time to create, and I've been intentional over the years to carve out a slice of daily painting time. This keeps me feeling creatively nourished; plus, you'd be amazed at how just 30 or 40 minutes of practice a day can really build up a skill set.

Palette knife painting is harder than it looks, so I've devised a series of tutorials where I break down every stroke. We'll start with the basics of how to handle the knife and what tools to choose, before moving on to the layering process, color blocking, blending, different knife effects, and how and when to apply texture. With this knowledge, you'll be able to progress quickly and skip the mistakes I've made, gaining a solid understanding of the palette knife painting technique. Whether you go on to incorporate knife painting with your brushwork, which is a more painterly effect, or paint entirely with a knife like me, you have another solid skill in your artistic toolbox.

Overall, my goal with all my palette knife painting is always to balance technique with texture and uniqueness, making paintings look good enough to eat.

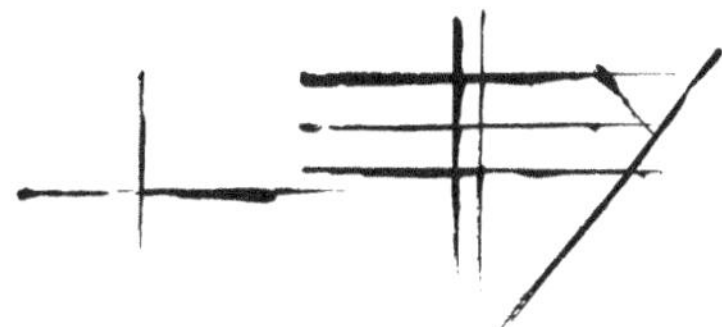

# WHY PAINT WITH A PALETTE KNIFE?

Why should you paint with a palette knife? Great question! Why make it harder? Well, when I paint with a brush, which I do occasionally, I tend to focus on the details. With a palette knife, I can't focus on the details too much, so my paintings are looser and more gestural, with bigger sweeps and strokes. Also, spreading thick paint with a palette knife has an amazing feel, not unlike spreading buttery frosting on a cake.

Let's think about the big picture here too. Art is emotion. Art is a memory, a desire, a person, a thought, a taste, a sound, an experience, a place, or a feeling. My main goal with my paintings is always to convey emotion. I feel like I can do this better when I add texture with a palette knife, as it tells a story, invites the viewer in with interesting light and shadows, and sends the eye around the canvas. My collectors and followers are often left with an "I want to eat it" feeling, due to the sumptuous texture and color! If I can evoke an emotion, and my art resonates with someone, I feel like I've done my job.

**Here are some advantages and uses for the palette knife:**

- Cleanup is a breeze! Just wipe and you're done.
- It's fast! Remember those mesmerizing 25-minute Bob Ross paintings?
- They're a onetime purchase that lasts forever, and they are reasonably priced.
- Palette knives are great for mixing paint, as well as scraping and cleaning your palette.
- Scraping off mistakes or excess paint is easy, without weakening the overall effect.
- Adding another clean layer and pure color notes is possible, without blending or disturbing the wet layer underneath. This creates a dramatic effect, which is hard to achieve with a brush.
- You can create a variety of different edges, crisp or blended.
- You also can create crisp, sharp lines for buildings and architecture, bridges, fences, furniture, lamp posts, boat rigging, cables, and power lines.
- Carving out details is fun and so is building up a relief, such as extremely textured flowers on a smooth background.
- By angling the blade and applying pressure, you can create curves, fan shapes, ovals, angles, circles, and zigzags.
- You can apply large patches of color quickly.
- Dabbing in highlights in the final stages of a painting creates a more dramatic piece.
- Bold palette knife strokes can complement a brush painting for a more painterly effect.
- Skimming layers right over the top of the wet underlayer leaves a speckled effect great for fog, steam, clouds, snow, shadows, rain, water, and tree foliage.
- You can quickly enhance the textured effect of already-textured subject matter, such as rocks, cliffs, mountains, snow, tree bark, tree leaves, sand, and stone buildings.
- Palette knives are shiny and beautiful!

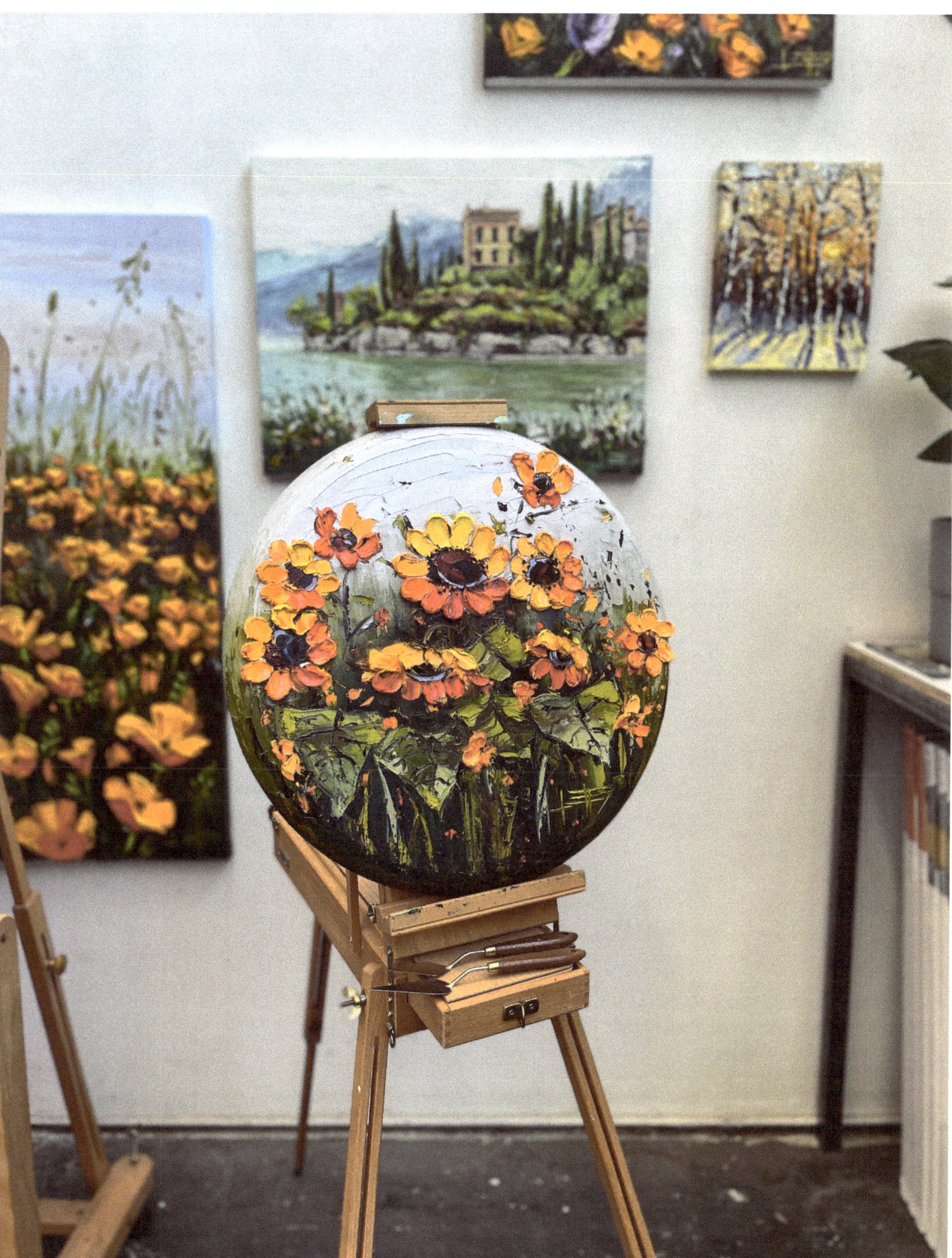

# GETTING STARTED

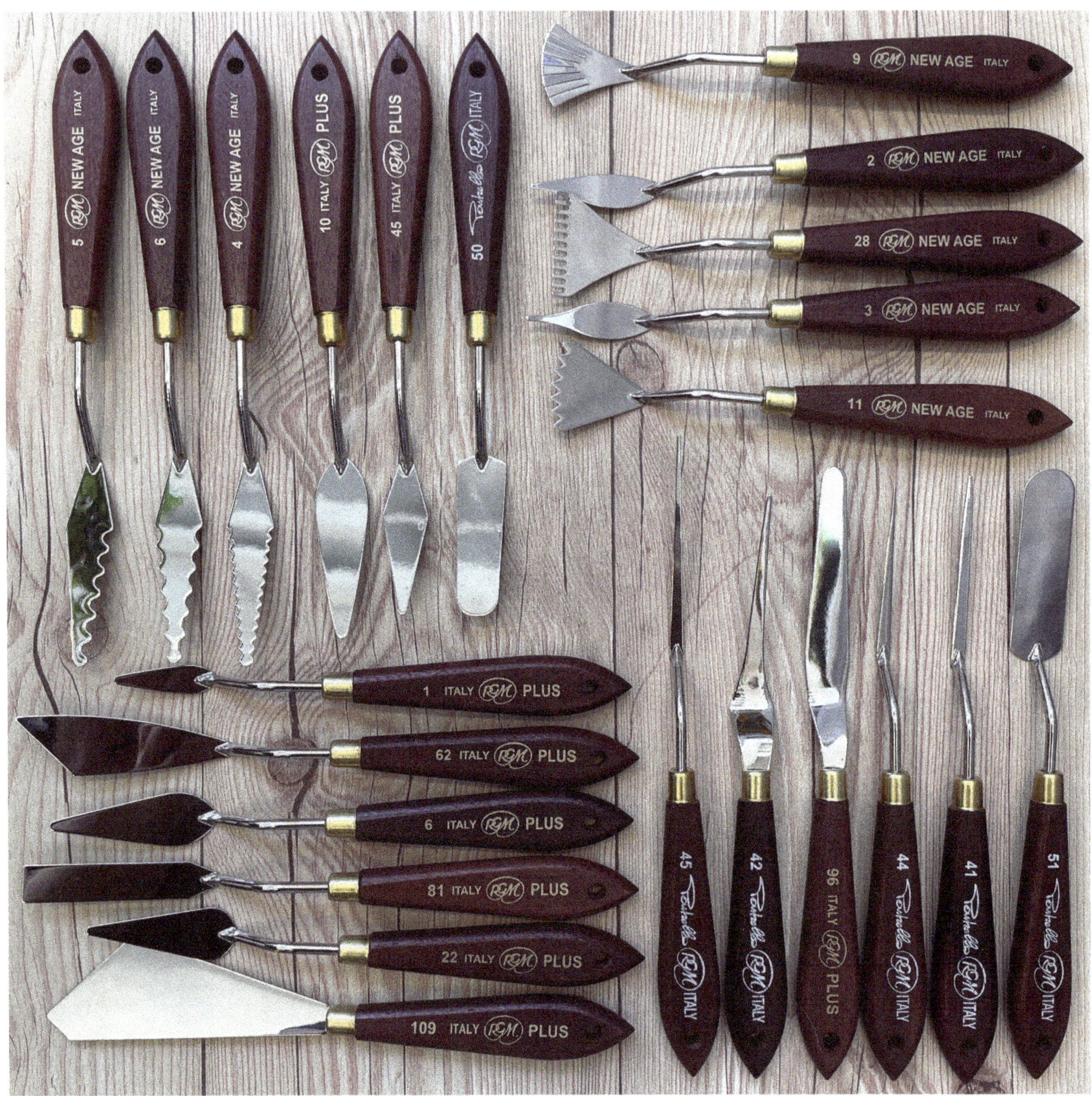


## PALETTE & PAINTING KNIVES

**Palette Knife or Painting Knife? Which One Do I Need?**

Let's start at the beginning and distinguish between a palette knife and a painting knife. A palette knife is more like a spatula, or a baker's knife, with a long, large blade that attaches to a handle. Palette knives are used mostly for spreading larger areas of paint.

A painting knife has a skinny, cranked neck where it attaches to the handle, to help keep paint off your fingers and to allow more maneuverability. It's also usually smaller than a palette knife. Painting knives are used for more detailed work and are my main tool. The better-known term *palette knife* is often used for both.

## TYPES & CARE

Purchase a knife with a flexible but sturdy metal blade. Do not use plastic knives. They are not flexible enough to paint with or to blend paint and do detailed work.

My favorite brand is RGM Italy, a family-owned company that focuses on quality. I've used hundreds of their knives, and they're strong, flexible, stylish, and last indefinitely. They are readily available at most art stores and online.

*Note:* The brands I have mentioned in this book are my authentic favorites and not sponsored.

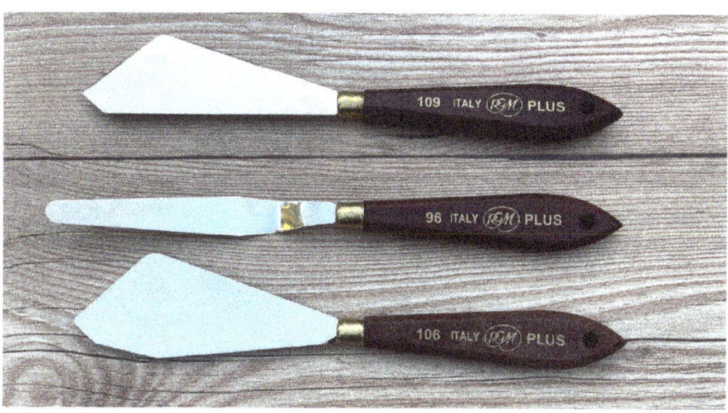


## MY FAVORITE TYPE

I've spent many years experimenting and using all sorts of palette and painting knives. I have a few that I gravitate toward regularly, including the ones used in the projects in this book.

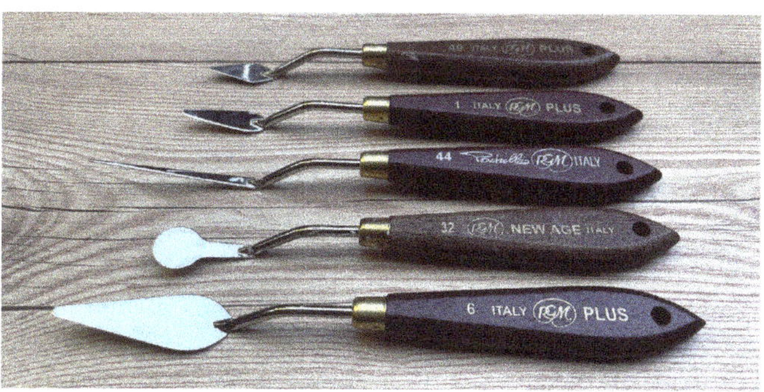


### Main Knife: Teardrop Shape

My main knife has a teardrop shape with a rounded point. The blade dimensions are ¾" × 2⅛". This is the RGM Plus #6. This is a standard shape and size, so you should be able to find an equivalent.

I have many of these and use several for each project. I like to keep the color I am using loaded on the knife and pick up a clean knife to start on another color. Knife painting requires a clean blade, so you will be wiping it a lot to avoid muddying your colors.

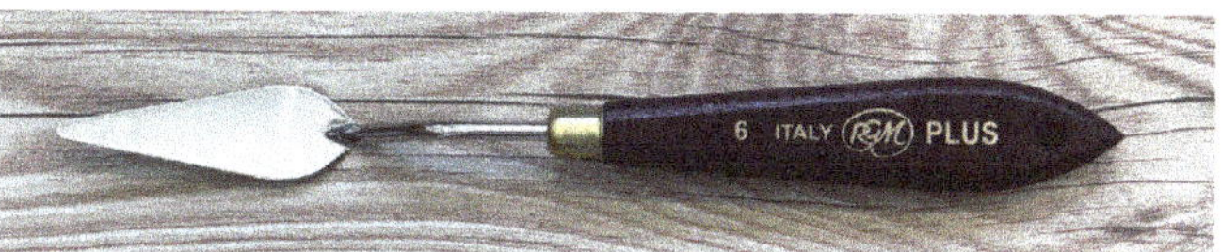


*Teardrop shape*

## OTHER FAVORITE TYPES

### Small Teardrop Shape

This is a smaller version of my main knife, the same shape but much smaller with around a 1-inch blade. It is great for creating smaller paintings and details.

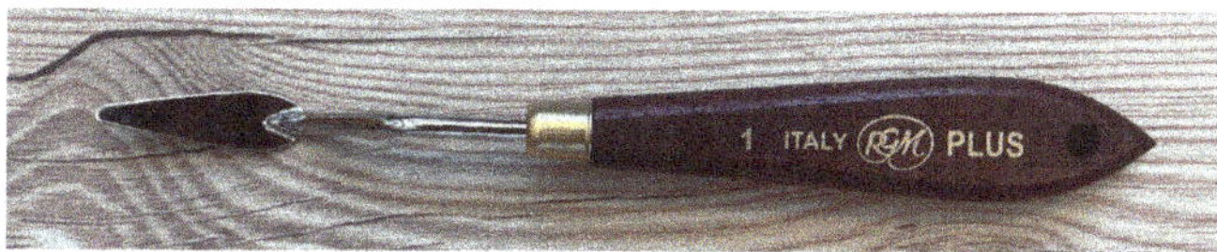


*Small teardrop shape*

### Small Diamond Shape

A small diamond-shaped knife with a 1-inch blade and a sharp tip for scratching out details, such as tree foliage, branches, grass, flower stems, and architectural elements. This knife is great for detailing small paintings.

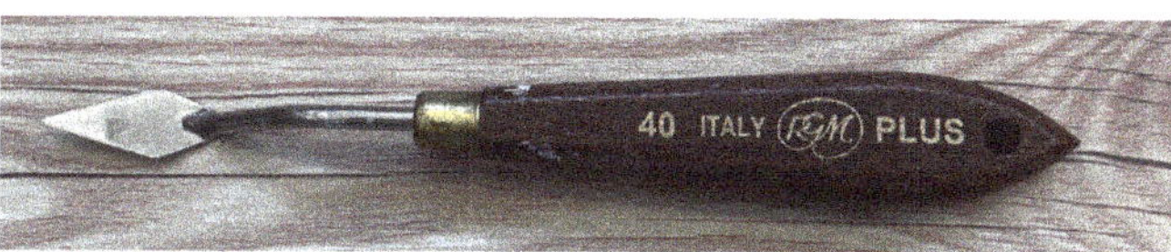


*Small diamond shape*

### Skinny Tip

The long, skinny blade is great for painting grass and foliage details, as well as curved lines on boat rigging, telephone wires, and clotheslines.

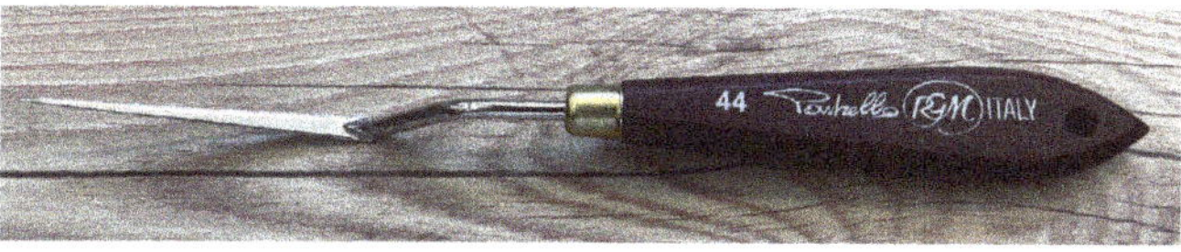


*Skinny tip*

### Round Tip

A round blade makes perfectly circular suns, moons, and flower petals.

I have many knives, large and small, and love reaching for my big ones when I'm painting large or when I'm experimenting with fun new shapes—the possibilities are endless!

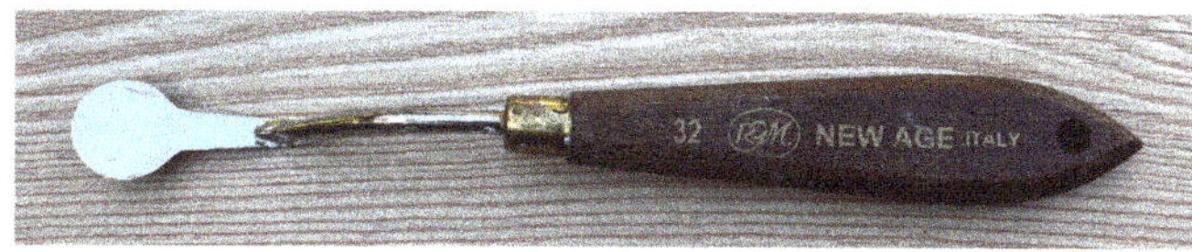


*Round tip*

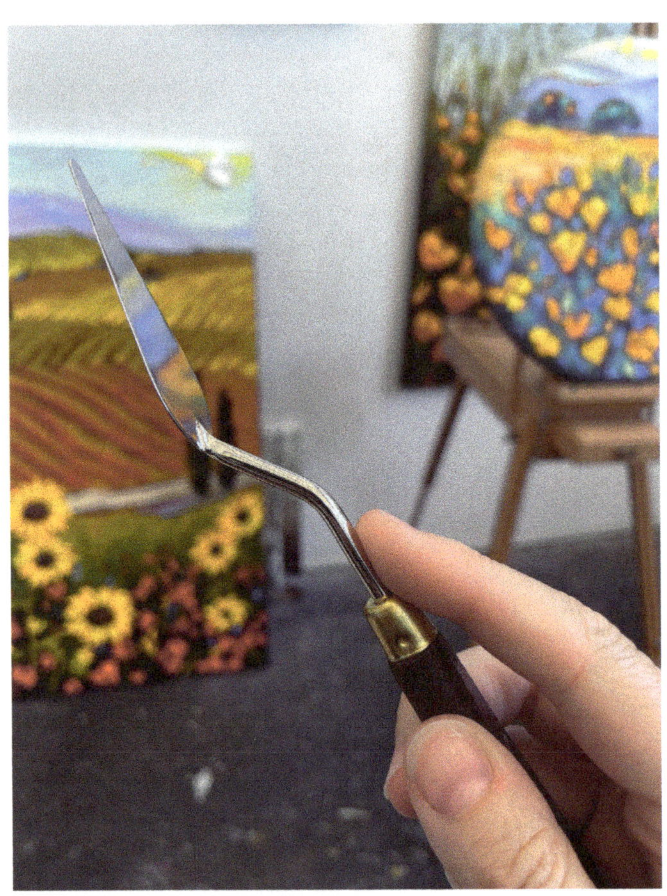

## HOW TO HOLD & HANDLE THE KNIFE

Hold your knife with your wrist loose, between your thumb and middle finger, toward the top of the wood handle, and with your index finger lightly touching the cranked neck. This is where you will apply pressure to blend and create sweeps and strokes.

By pushing down gently on the neck, you can move your knife in the direction of your stroke and control the texture, form, and shape of the paint. By rotating your wrist, you can create many different types of strokes and effects. This is my main motion with all my knives, large and small, and how I execute all my paintings.

Imagine an orchestral conductor holding a baton, a baker with a frosting knife, or even the motion of waving a magic wand. You really want to keep your grip flexible, fluid, and easy here, with your wrist doing the work. You'll need to practice, as it's quite different from holding a paintbrush or pencil.

### How to Load the Knife

Using the flat, straight bottom edge of the knife, scrape up a blob of paint from your palette and place it down on your canvas, almost with a wiping motion. It's easiest to flip your knife over and load up paint onto the underside of the knife, but you can also scoop it up onto the front side as well.

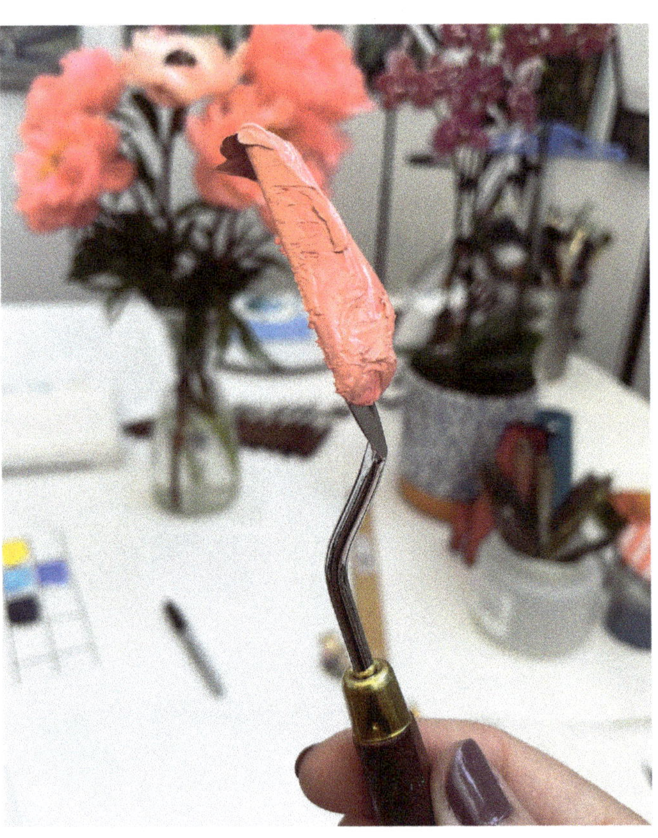

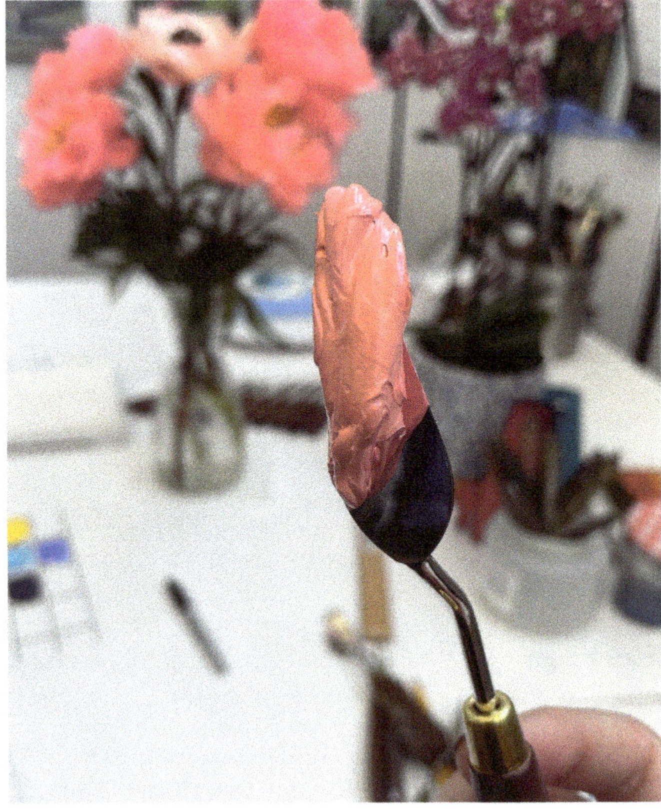

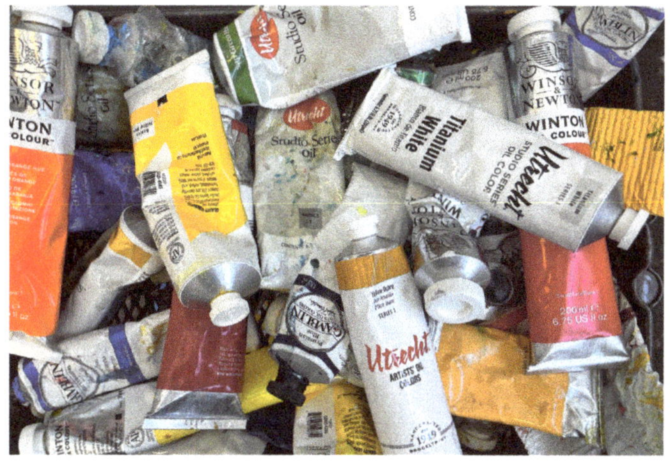


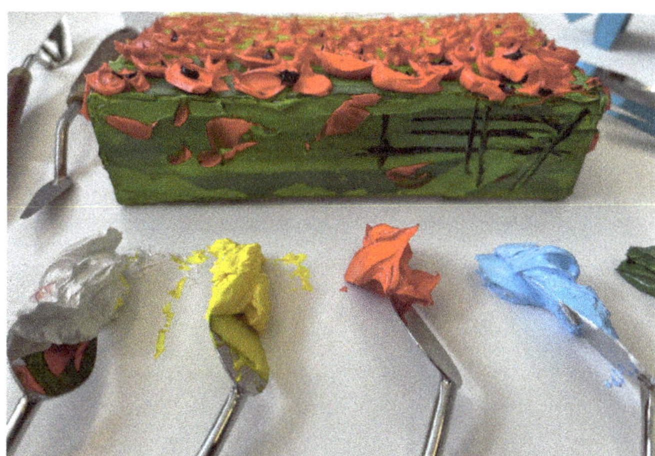

**Cleanup**

It's important to keep your knife clean and wipe it often during projects to avoid accidentally transferring and contaminating your colors. Clean paint off of the knife with a cloth or paper towel before changing colors. I prefer to keep small portions of paper towels stacked up on top of each other, on top of nonskid rubber that you purchase for cupboard drawers. This way the paper towel doesn't move around when you wipe it, and you only need one hand for the wiping motion. I fold over little portions of the used paper towel as I go, so as not to waste it. Clean the paint that accumulates around the neck, as it can also muddy your colors.

You can use a small amount of mineral spirits if you need to remove the oil paint—just try not to get it on the wood handle. Also, try not to get the wood handles wet with water. That will affect the beautiful grain of the wood. You may notice after time that there is dry paint buildup on the blade. To remove that, simply boil some water and submerge the blade for 10 minutes, then scrape off the softened paint.

**Where to Paint & Time for Projects**

I painted for many years at the kitchen table before finding my dedicated studio space. I started out small, using 6-, 10-, and 12-inch canvases, and a table easel that I bought for $2.50 at Big Lots.

I still have my IKEA cart to store my most-used paints, and my studio paint storage wall racks are from IKEA as well. You really don't need much space to start out, but it sure helps to have an area that you can dedicate to painting and that you don't have to clear away all the time. The less work you make for yourself when you get started, the better!

The projects in this book all take less than an hour, so set aside around 40 to 60 minutes for each tutorial.

## PAINT & MATERIALS

**Should I Use Oil or Acrylic Paint?**

Probably my most-asked question is whether you should use oil paint or acrylic paint. I use both! However, for my daily painting I prefer oil paint, and the projects in this book are all executed in oil.

If you would like to use acrylic paint to complete the projects in this book, you can go ahead and do so, as the technique with the actual painting process is the same.

Keep in mind that acrylic dries quickly, so you'll have to work very fast. You also will need to use some kind of thickening medium, such as molding paste or modeling paste, as well as at least medium- to heavy-body viscosity paint. You can't use fluid paint, as there is no way to build up texture and to retain the peaks. Acrylic also is harder to blend, relaxes a little as it dries, and changes color somewhat as it dries. The upside is the fact that your extremely textured painting is dry in a couple of days. When I have a time-sensitive commission, a piece needed for a show, or just feel like a change, I'll use acrylic. It really is very convenient.

Oil is slower drying, so there's less pressure to complete a piece quickly. It has a natural buttery feel, is easier to blend, and requires no medium. You can just use the paint straight from the tube without adding anything for bulk. If you want to add a medium to try to speed up the dry time or add stability and flexibility, you can add Winsor & Newton Liquin Impasto.

**How Long Does It Take to Dry?**

Oil paint cures rather than drying through evaporation like acrylic paint, and it takes a long time to harden. Once I've completed a piece, I hang it on the wall in my studio, which was what Van Gogh used to do. In fact, it is said that some of his pieces are actually still pliable—so in effect, still drying!

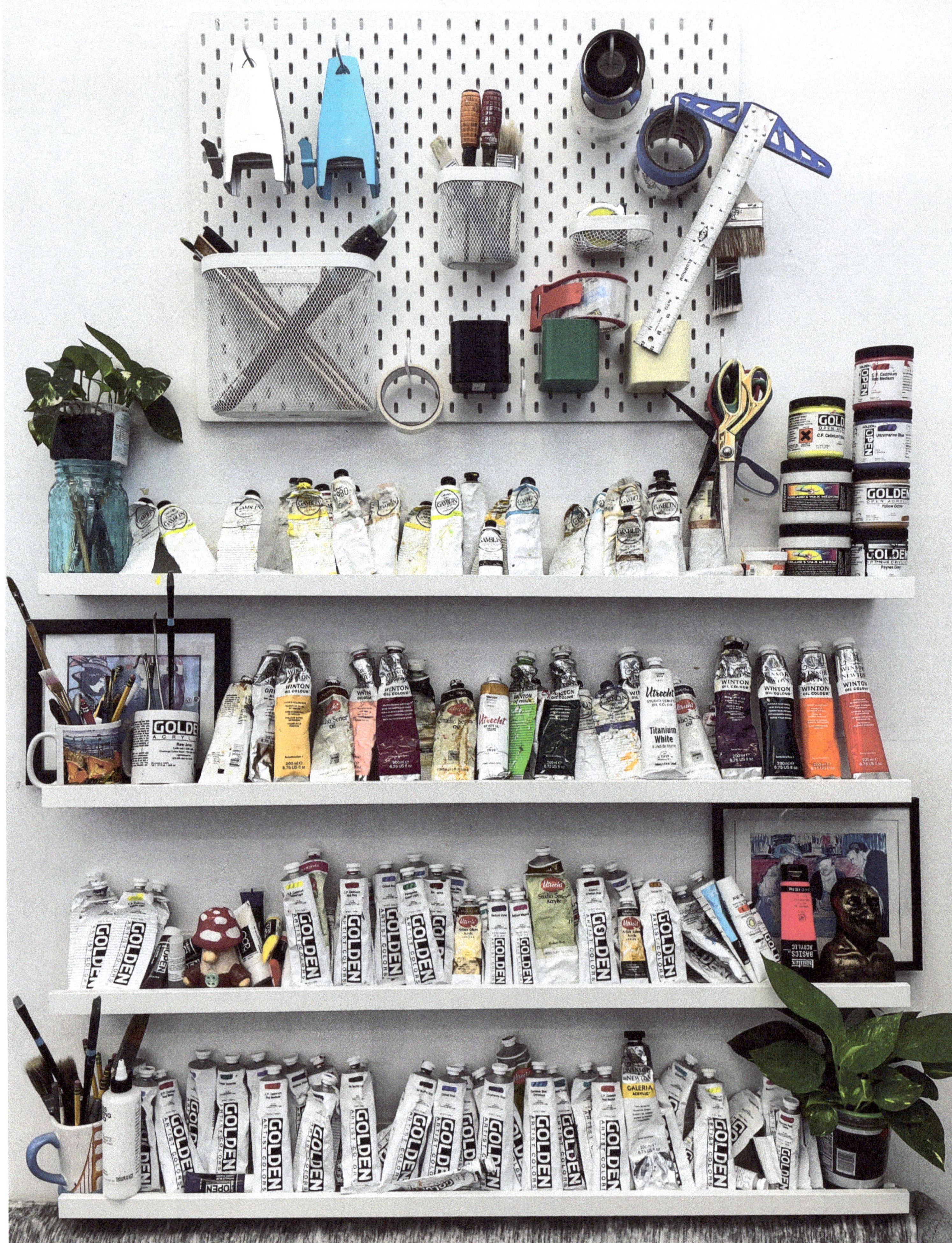
GOLDEN
WINTON OIL COLOUR
Utrecht
Titanium White
GOLDEN

A thick impasto painting in oil takes about two or three weeks to form a skin on the outer layers of paint, while the paint underneath stays wet and takes much longer, usually six months to a year or more to harden, depending on the thickness. Also, some colors dry faster than others, and paint will dry slower in winter. Oil paint is fairly temperamental, but most modern paint is excellent quality—just purchase what you can afford. (But do not buy cheap craft paint. It will degrade.)

## ESSENTIAL SUPPLY LIST

Your main paint colors that you should always have at hand and that we use in the projects in this book are the following:

- Titanium white
- Cadmium yellow
- Cadmium red
- Alizarin crimson
- Cerulean blue
- Ultramarine, or French ultramarine blue
- Prussian blue

Some lovely extras, and ones we also use in a few of the projects of this book are:

- Payne's gray
- Sap green
- Yellow ocher
- Viridian green
- Yellow green
- Turquoise
- Cadmium yellow deep
- Pale rose blush
- Magenta

You will also need:

- Quality canvas. I like stretched canvas with a 1½-inch depth, and the projects in this book use 6″ x 6″ to 10″ x 10″ canvases.
- Flat wood or plastic palette or palette paper. If you're using palette paper, try to purchase a 12″ x 16″ size. Just make sure your palette surface is flat, as plastic paint palettes with the little molded cups do not work for mixing or scooping up paint with a knife.
- Paper towel or rag
- Medium painting knife, standard-sized teardrop shape with rounded tip
- Small painting knife, small teardrop shape with rounded tip
- A table easel or lazy Susan

**What Paint Should I Buy?**

For larger areas and more used colors such as white and yellow, you can purchase good-quality academic oil or acrylic paint to save money. You can save the professional grade for details.

Some of my favorite brands are Winsor & Newton, Utrecht, and Golden. Both Winsor & Newton Winton and Professional lines have nice pigmentation and a firm consistency that retains the peaks. Utrecht is my favorite USA-made brand. I use both their acrylic and oil, Professional and Studio lines. It's great quality, nice and firm, and very reasonably priced. I also like Golden artist quality acrylic paints. If you're using acrylic, you'll need a molding paste to add body and to help the paint retain its peaks. For this, I prefer the Golden extra heavy duty molding paste. There are lots of options here, and experimenting is part of the fun, so don't be afraid to try new things. I usually buy a small jar of a new product to start, then purchase larger if I like it.

Most modern paints are great quality; we are so lucky! Don't get distracted by what brands to buy. Purchase what you can afford and do the art. Just don't buy cheap craft materials. They will break down and do not give the desired results with color, texture, or longevity.

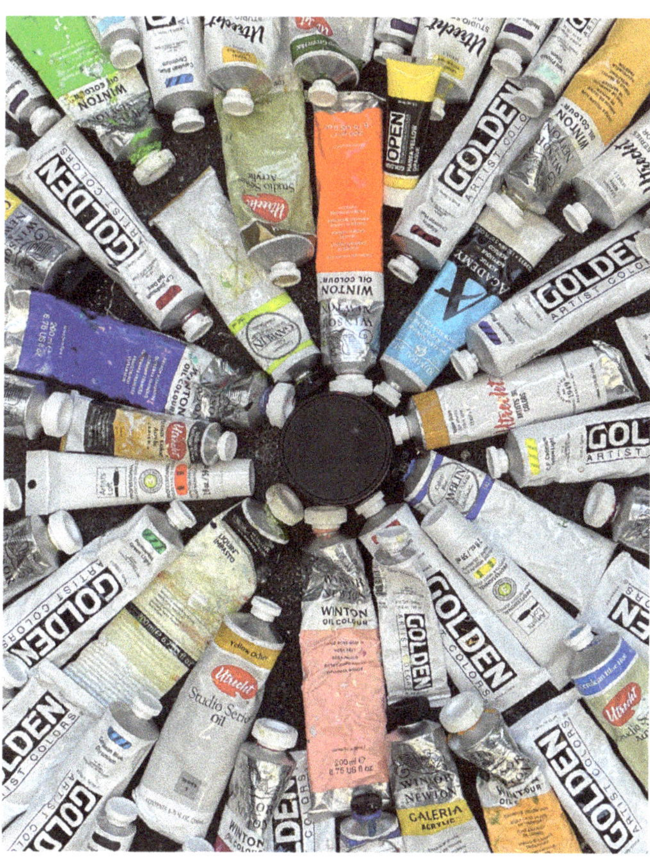

**What Canvas Should I Buy?**
Either board or stretched canvas will work well with palette knife painting. Some people prefer the stiffness of the boards, and it's very practical when holding the weight of heavy impasto paint. Heavy-duty stretched canvas will also hold the weight; however, just make sure you're purchasing a quality product and not cheap crafting canvas, as this will tear and fall apart very easily. I started out painting small, as the wet-into-wet technique requires that you finish your piece *alla prima*, which means in one sitting. This will also give you a daily burst of creativity that will keep you feeling super productive.

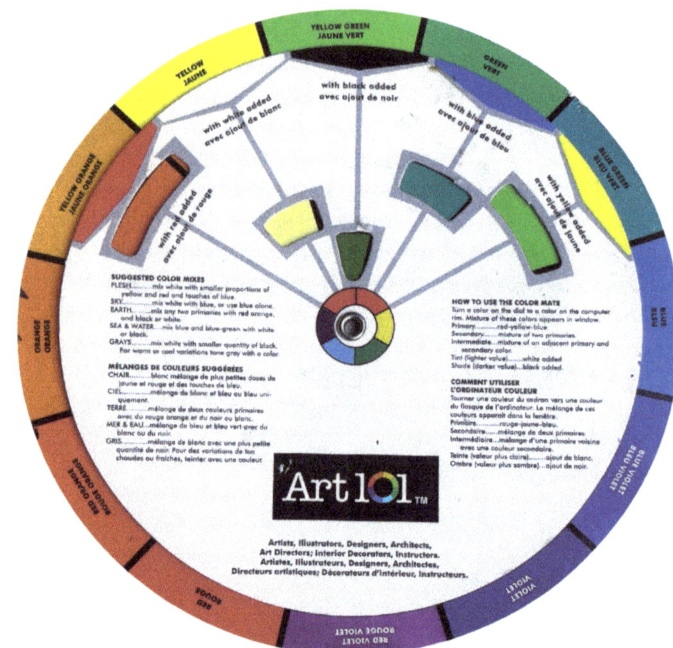


**Which Colors Should I Use & When?**
Palette knife painting is a color-blocking technique and works best with bright saturated colors, due to the layering and dramatic effect of the paint strokes.

Color theory is a long conversation, but the one basic rule I have always applied keeps my knife painting balanced, vibrant, and interesting, and that is simply paying attention to complementary colors. Here's what that means in a nutshell:

Your three primary colors are red, yellow, and blue. The complement of any of these primary colors can be made by combining the two other primary colors. For example, to achieve the complementary color of primary yellow, simply combine red and blue. The result would be purple, which is directly across from yellow on the color wheel.

By following this rule, I can tweak and ascertain any color palette. Colors don't look quite right, but you can't put your finger on it? Add the complementary color, and it will usually correct the disharmony.

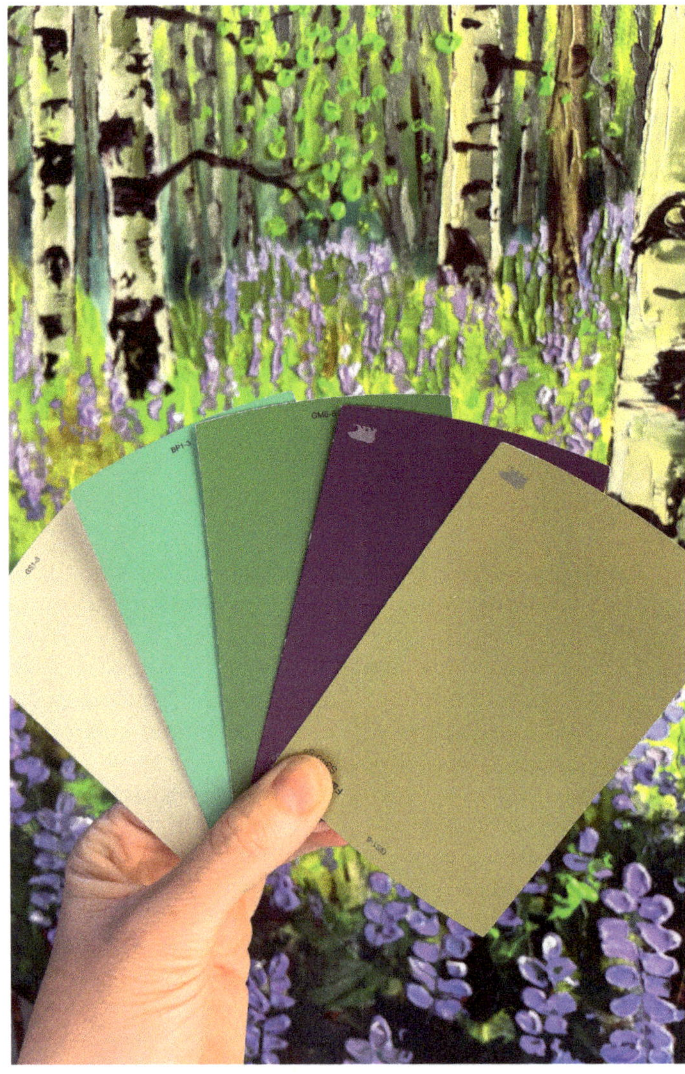

**Where Do I Start with Choosing Color Palettes?**
I use Pinterest a lot for choosing color palettes (find me there @paintersknife). Just type in "vineyard color palette" or "coastal color palette," and many variations will populate.

I also use the free paint swatches at Home Depot. Choose two complementary colors, such as red and green or purple and yellow, and then choose two more variations that are lighter or darker in value—plus one neutral. It's a great place to start, and there are a ton of colors to choose from. The store even curates collections and has free brochures with color ideas every season.

## ADDITIONAL SUPPLIES

Here are some additional supplies you will need before you start painting:

- Odorless mineral spirits for oil paint cleanup. Mineral spirits also are useful sometimes to thin oil paint that is too thick—for example when you're wanting to sketch thin lines.
- Tube squeezers to maximize paint (paint is the most expensive part). My tube squeezers are available on my site at www.lisaelley.com.
- Cotton swabs, good for cleaning up mistakes and detailing
- T square, good for architecture and angles
- Varnish, optional, but gives your piece a lovely shine and protects against dust and UV light damage. For thick oil paint, use a retouch varnish if it is not completely dry.
- A sturdy box cutter-type knife and a good pair of scissors
- A few brushes. Numbers 4, 6, 8, and 12 bright are my favorites (we won't be using any brushes in the projects in this book, but you may feel like you want to incorporate some brushwork).

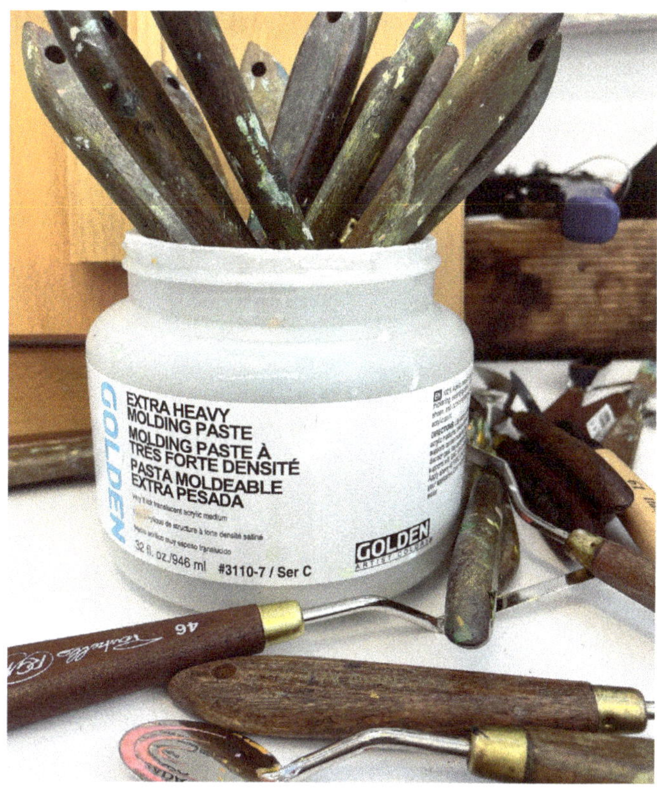

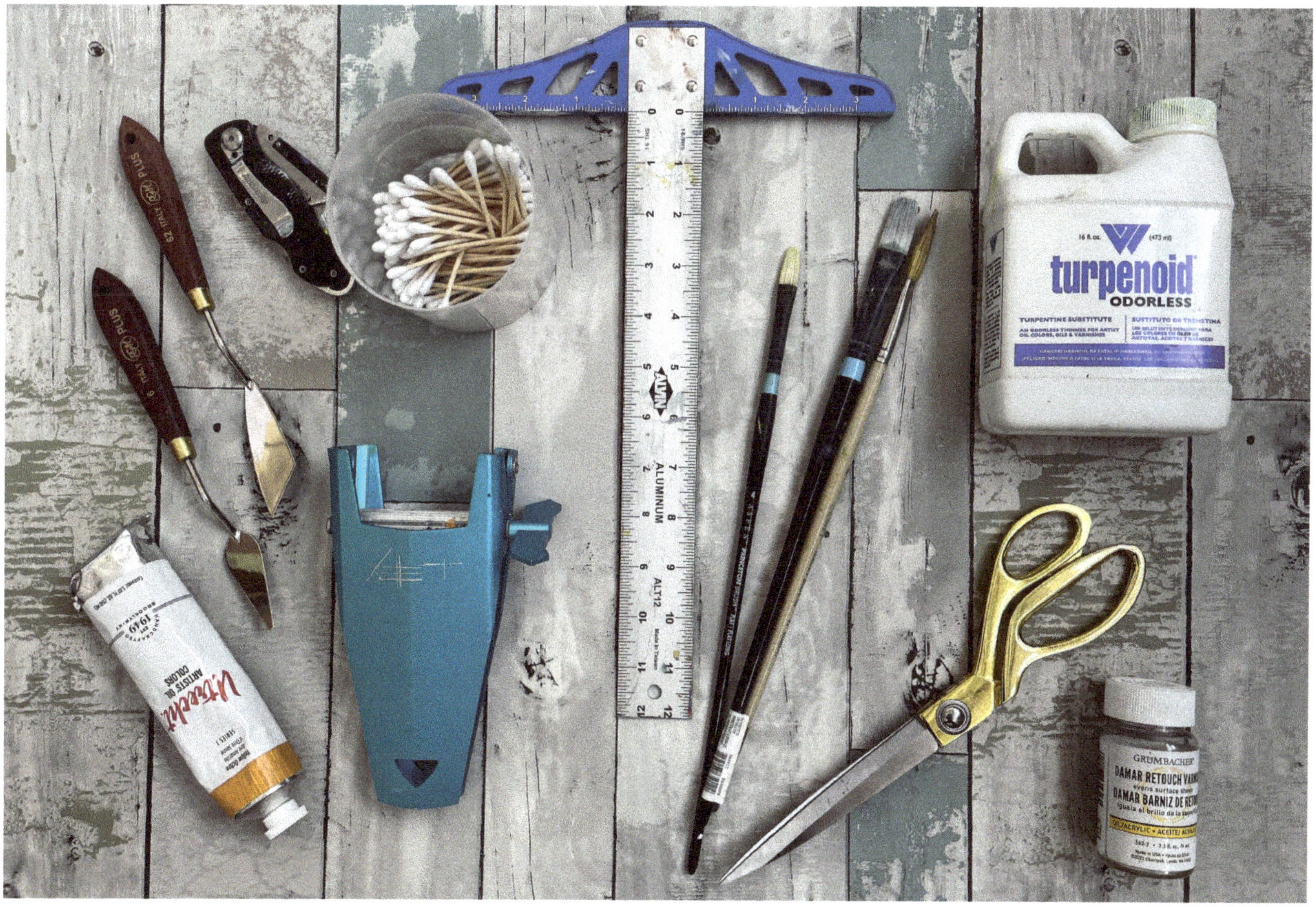

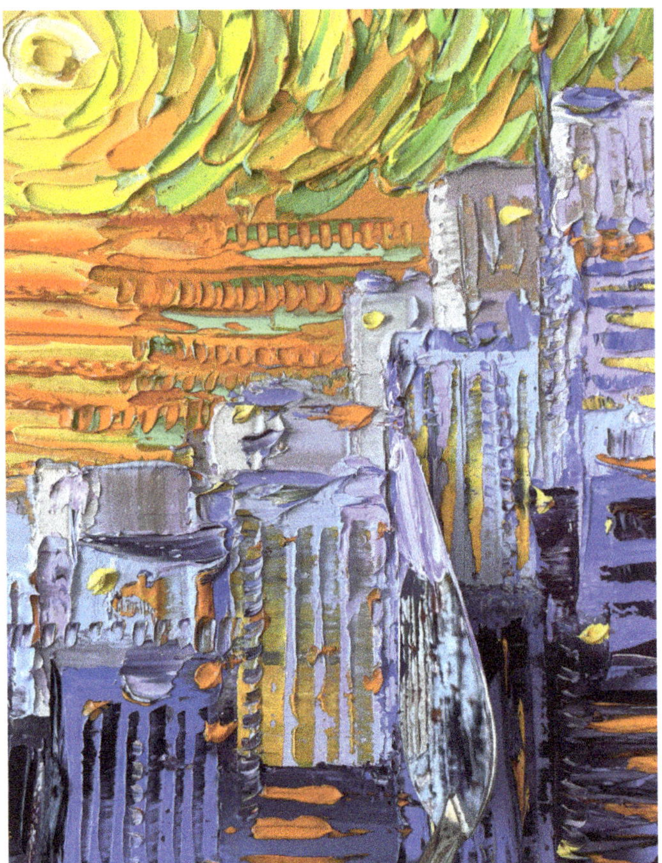

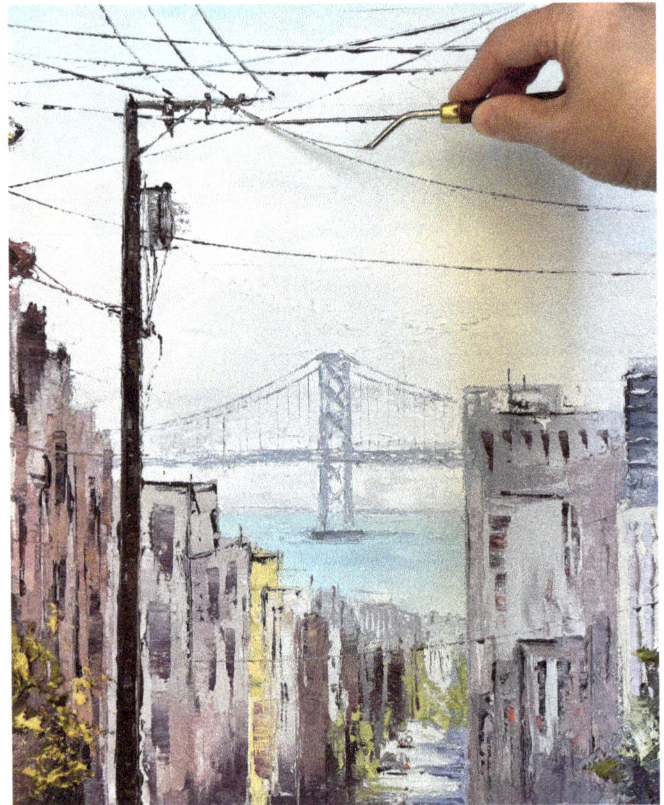

*Using the edge for curved lines*

## PALETTE KNIFE PAINTING TECHNIQUES

### Using the Blade for Straight Lines

Lines and edges can look very striking in a palette knife painting. All you need to do is load the edge of the palette knife with paint, and then place the edge on the canvas and pull it across and up fairly quickly. Make sure here that the paint is evenly spread across the edge of the knife.

For thin lines, load only the edge of the knife with a sliver of thinner paint, and place the knife edge down, or pull the knife in the direction of the line for longer lines. Note here that you will get one line per stroke, as you don't want to fuss and muddy your colors, so you will need to keep wiping and reloading your knife between strokes.

### Using the Tip for Blended Edges

To make great atmospheric tree lines in the distance, apply a little pressure to the tip and press in anti-clockwise circular motions (like when washing your car or waxing a surfboard).

### Using the Edge for Curved Lines

Sometimes you'll want to create a long, curved line—for example, if you're painting suspension bridges or boat sails. I paint a lot of San Francisco cityscapes, so I often need to create a sky full of cables and telephone wires right across the canvas that require a little slack in them. Using a larger knife, you can scrape out a long curve, applying pressure and pulling the knife all the way across the canvas, using the edge of the blade. This is tricky! Abstraction can be one way to approach this, keeping it loose and gestural. You can create suggestions of complete lines, rather than perfectly complete ones.

### Carving Out Details or *Sgraffito* (Italian for "scratch")

Apply an underlayer, then another layer in a bold color, and scratch out the details, sometimes even exposing the white canvas underneath. This technique is very effective when painting tree foliage, grass, and bushes, as well as vineyard vines.

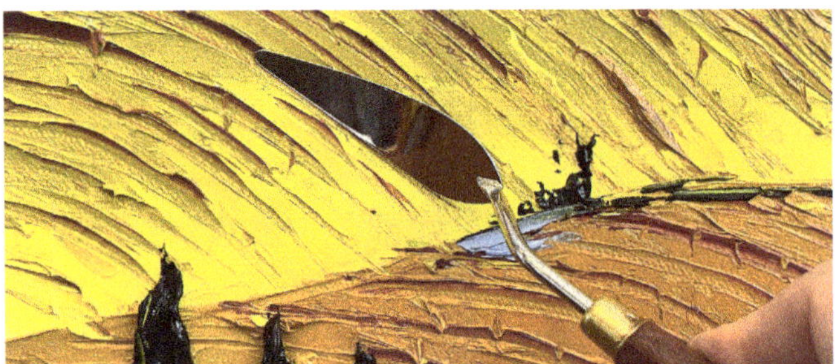

*Carving out details or* Sgraffito

**Extreme Texture and 3D Thickness**

There's no rule here. Just remember, the thicker you go, the longer it will take to dry! The example to the right in oil is around a ½-inch thick, and this 24″ x 48″ painting has been happily drying in my studio for the past six months. It may even take a year or more to harden. I don't mind waiting for them to cure, as I get to enjoy them in my studio for a while before they are listed for purchase.

**Pulling One Color over Another to Create a Broken Affect (or Scumbling)**

You can combine colors by dragging one color over the top of another. It helps to use bright and contrasting colors here, as muted colors may muddy and get lost more easily. One layer of paint glides over the top of another layer of paint in a contrasting color, creating a broken effect with the color underneath showing through. This results in a rustic and scattered edge with little holes peeking through, which is fantastic for effects such as snow, ocean spray, and tree leaves. On dry or coarse canvas, you can create larger holes, and a wet underneath layer creates smaller holes. I use this technique a lot for sky and water effects, by dragging white paint over blue to create white water or clouds.

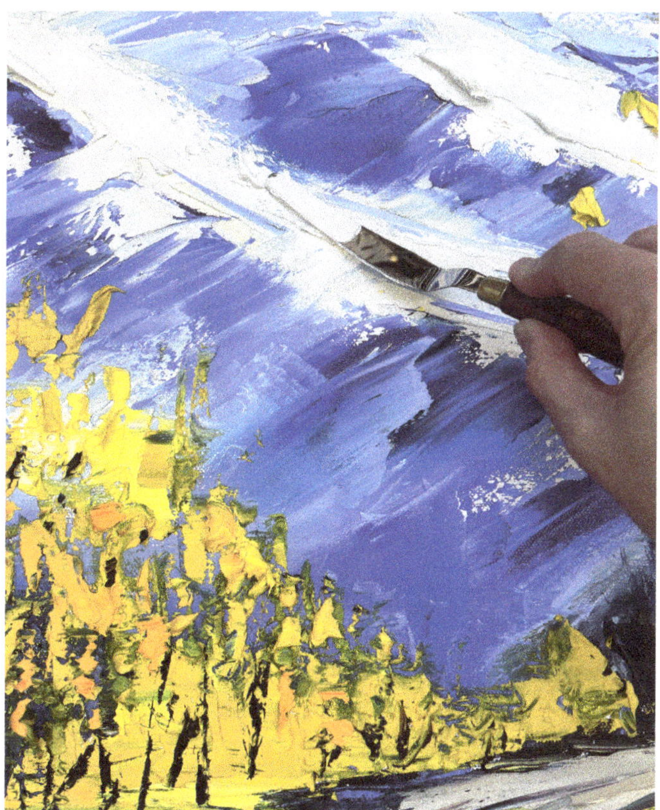

*Scumbling*

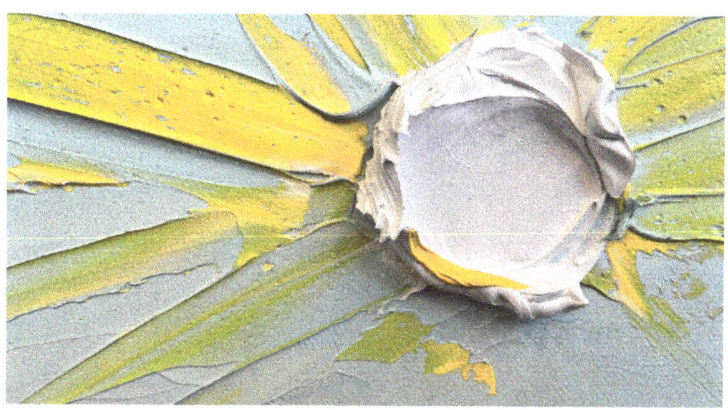

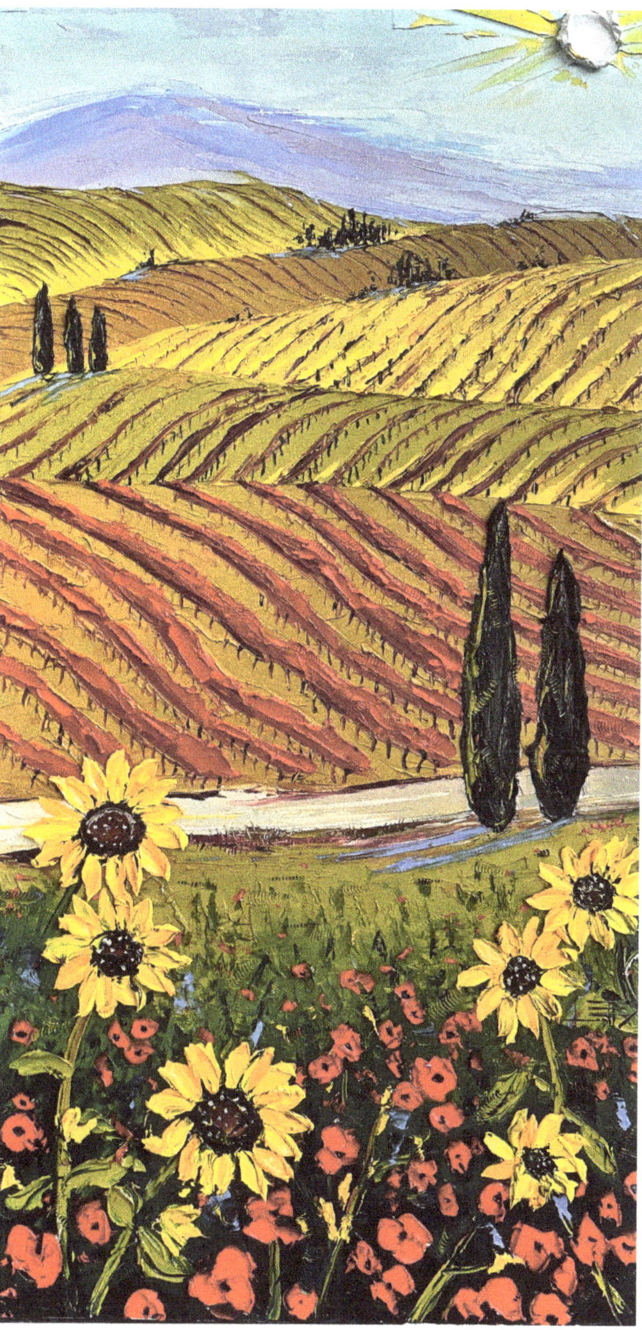

*Extreme texture and 3D thickness*

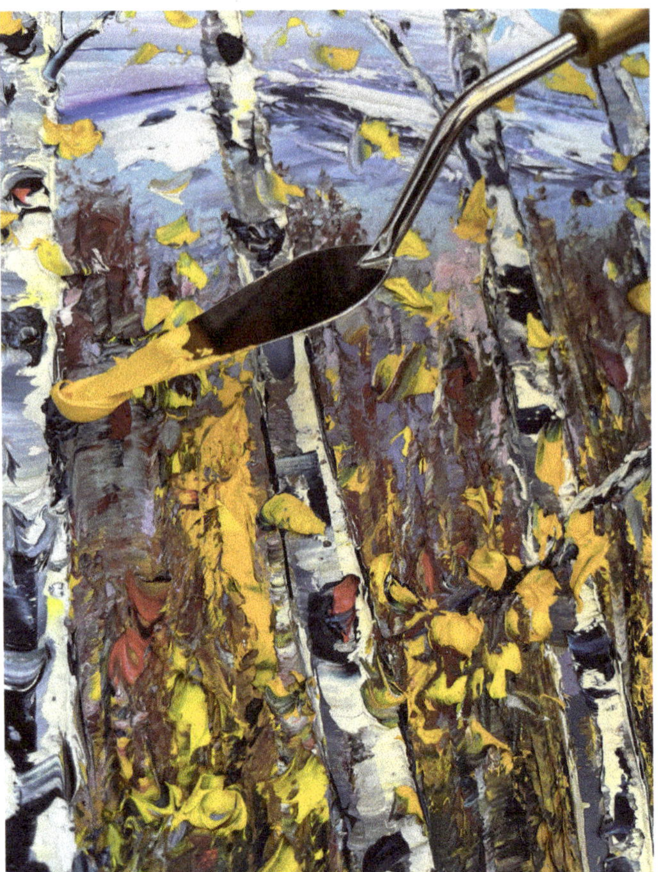

Sweeping, dotting, and dabbing

### Sweeping, Dotting & Dabbing to Build Up Texture & Create Movement

This technique is perfect for painting grass and tree foliage. Leaving the background less textured, you use the tip of the knife to place pops of color here and there, making sure to cluster them and use different directions to suggest movement. It's also good for highlights and flower petals.

### Two or More Color Sweep

Using two different colors such as blue and orange, load a blob of each of them both side by side on the edge of the knife, touching each other but not mixing. Then sweep the knife along the canvas to create a striking stripe. This technique is perfect for creating geometric and abstract effects and also for creating more delicate flowers with streaks of different colors in the petals, such as irises and daisies.

### Blending with the Edge & Middle Blade

You'll be doing this a lot, so make sure you practice until it feels good. Using the tip, middle portion, and rotating the knife blade slightly, leaning to the right edge of your knife, gently apply pressure with your index finger and swipe the knife left, lift it up, and repeat, almost like buttering a slice of bread. Think of the motion you'd use if you were scraping the burnt top off a piece of toast, but do this more gently.

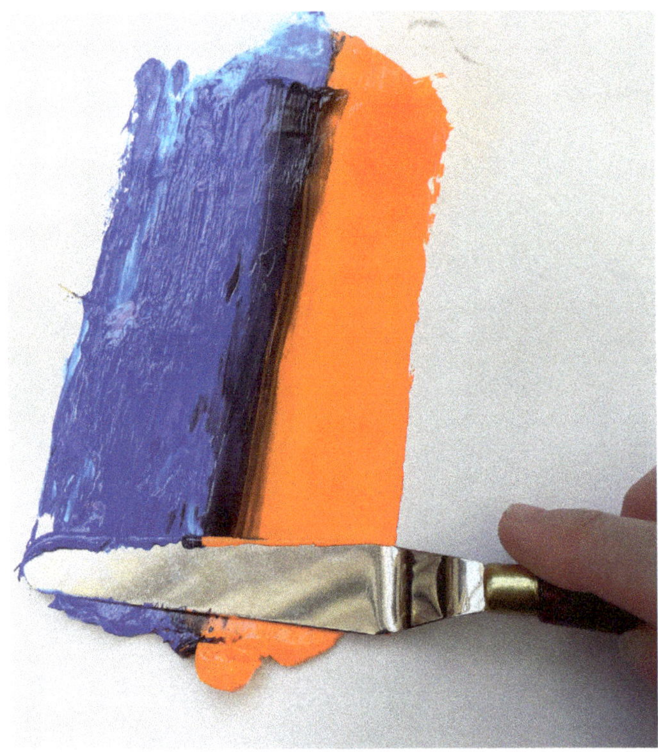

Two or more color sweep

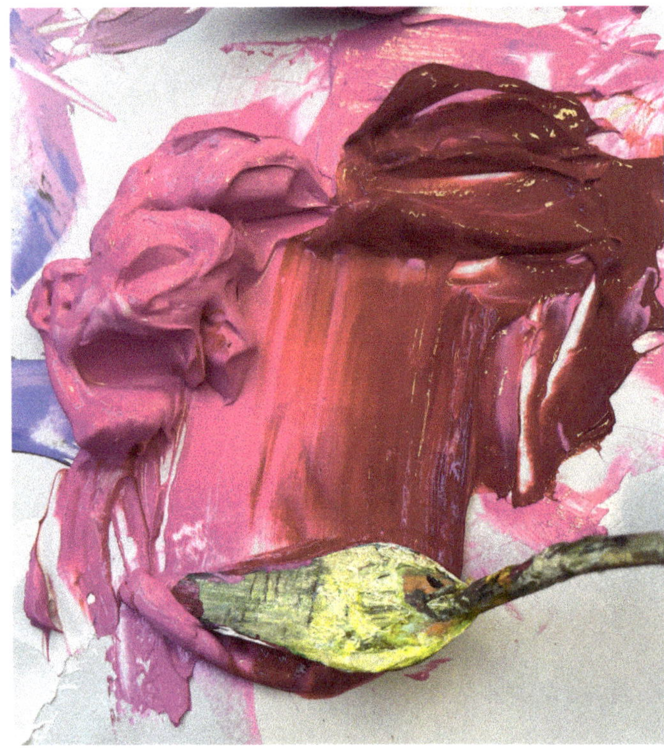

Blending with the edge and middle blade

**Streaks of Unblended Color**
Not completely blending the paint results in lovely streaks of color, perfect for flower petals, water, skies, and foliage.

**Using Fancy Tip Knives for Details**
Some great knife options are available for creating marks with extra lines, squiggles, zigzags, and patterns. I like to create variations in my grass and foliage, as well as fancy and different flower petals, which you can only achieve by scraping out with a particular knife. The tip below has cutouts that allow for more flexibility and a lovely carved-out series of lines that make beautiful iris petals.

**Scraping Off Mistakes**
One of the best benefits of using palette knives is being able to scrape off mistakes. You can really just scrape off anything and start over, without having to cover anything up, and it also doesn't affect or dilute the color notes underneath. I like to reuse the paint if I can, so keep it on your palette for future use.

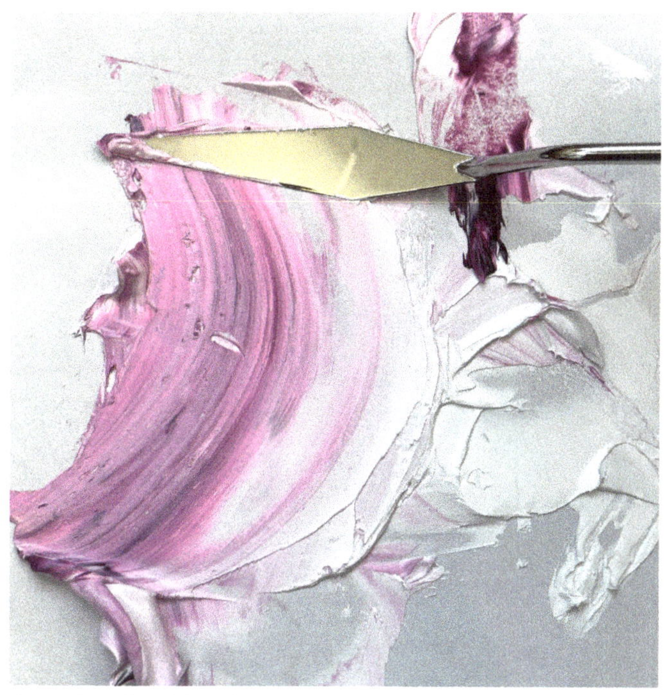

*Streaks of unblended color*

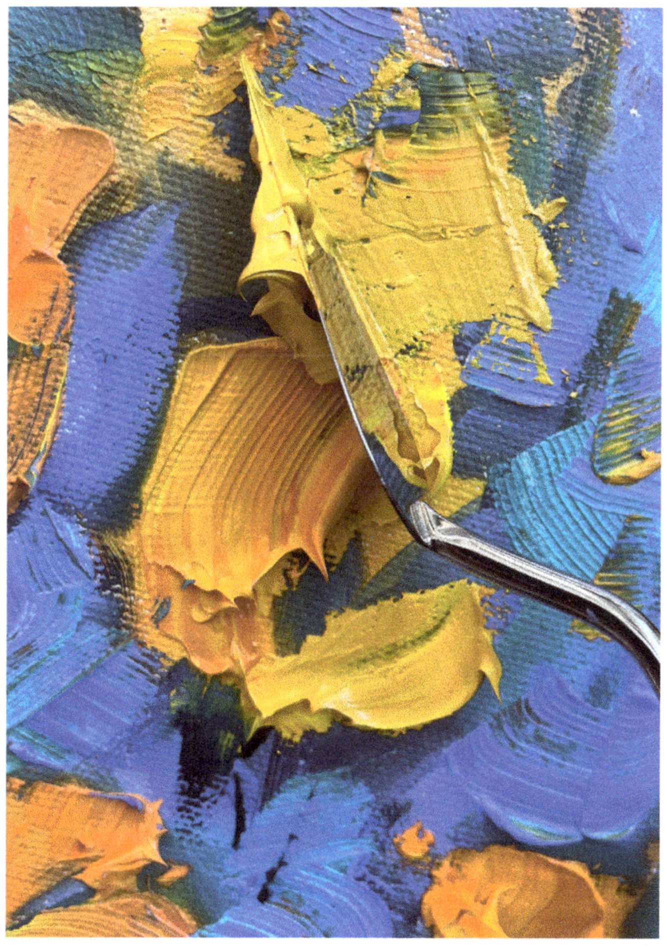

*Scraping off mistakes*

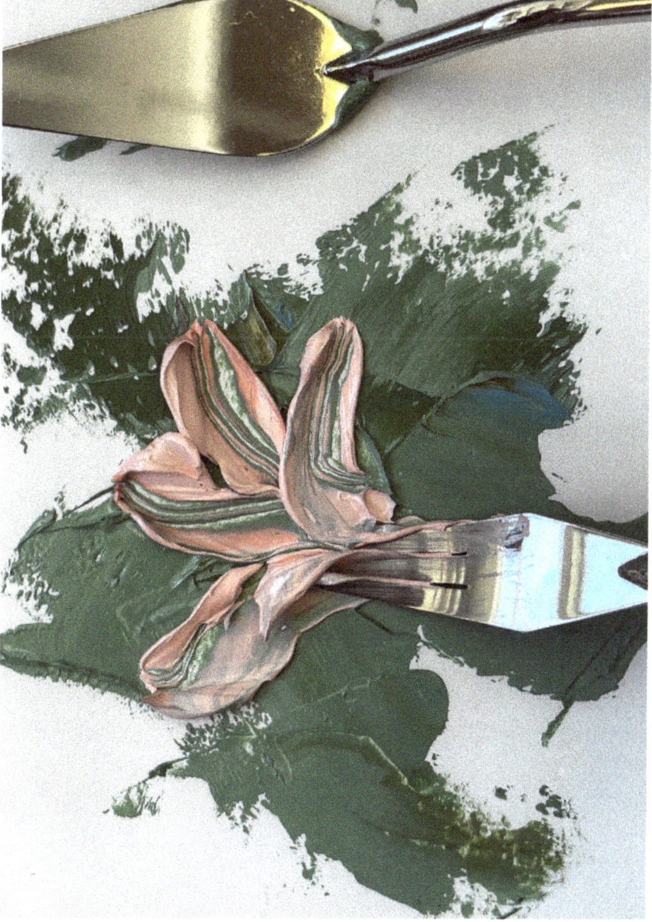

*Using fancy tip knives for details*

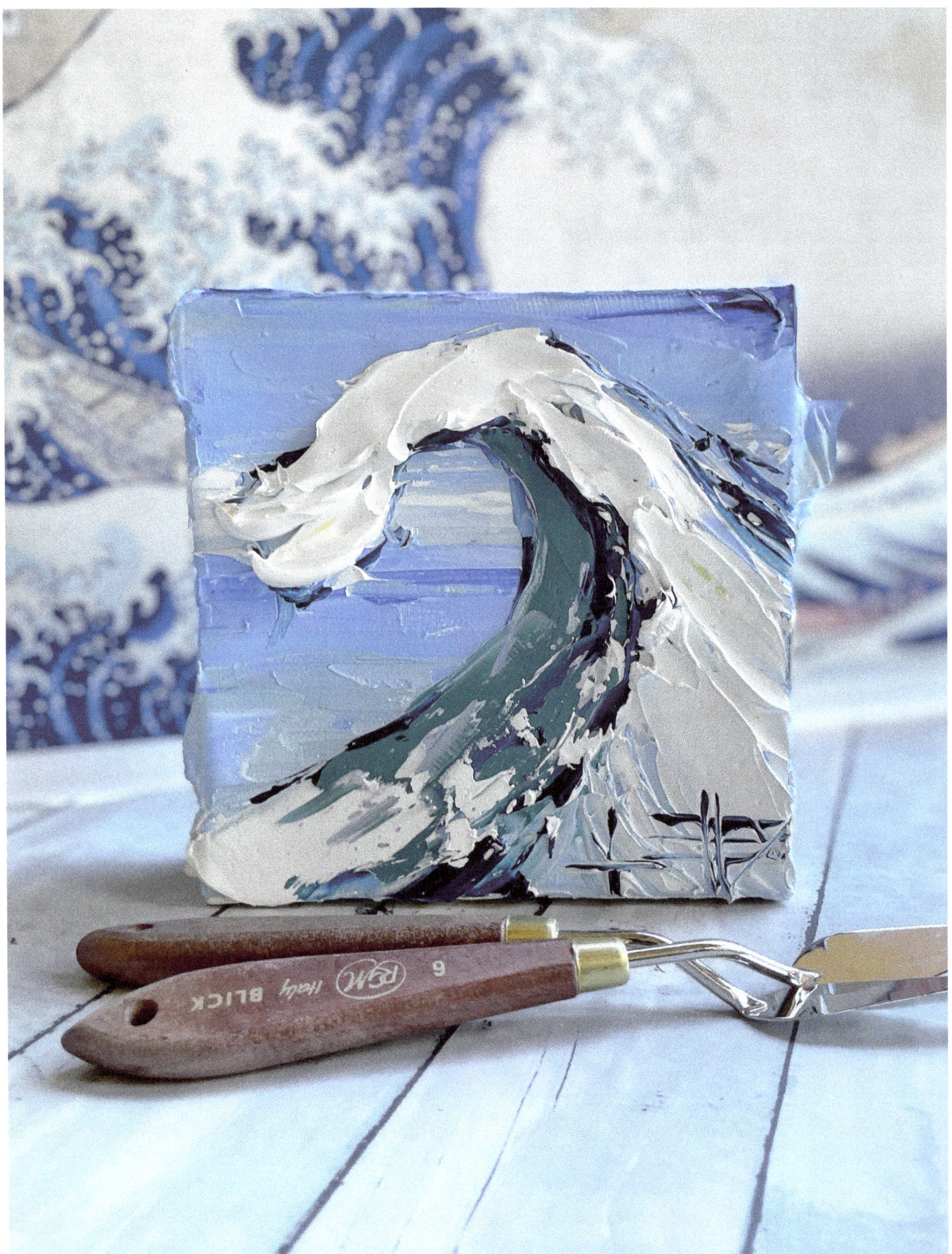
6
Italy
BLICK

# HOKUSAI-INSPIRED OCEAN WAVE

**Tools & Materials**

- Stretched canvas, size 6″ x 6″ with a 1½-inch depth
- Palette knife: medium size, teardrop shape with rounded tip
- Table easel or lazy Susan
- Palette paper
- Paper towel or rag for wiping your knife

**Color Palette**

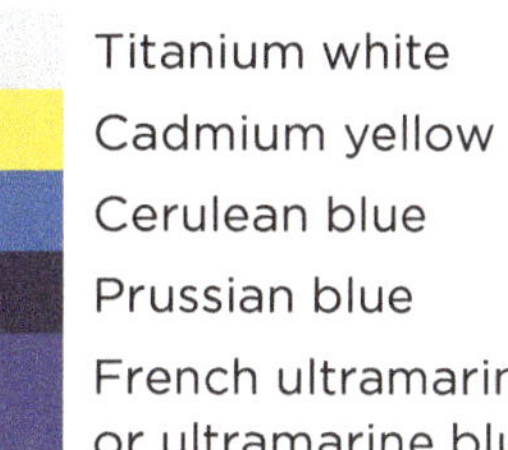

- Titanium white
- Cadmium yellow
- Cerulean blue
- Prussian blue
- French ultramarine or ultramarine blue

**Difficulty Level**

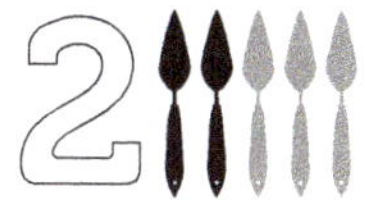

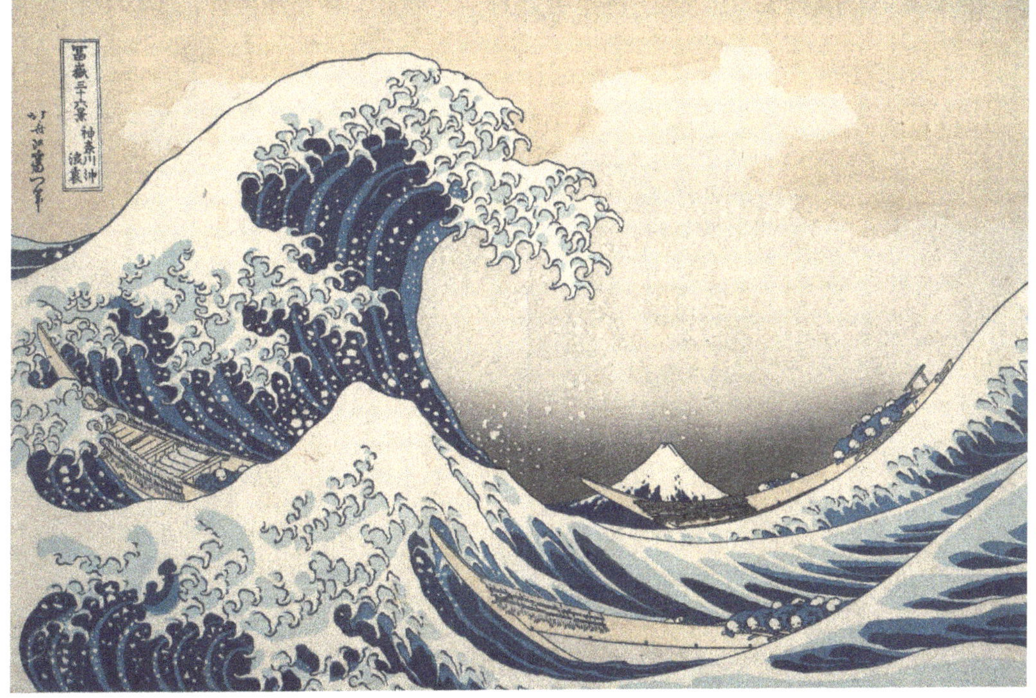

## *Inspiration*

If you are a beginning palette knife painter, I recommend starting with this ocean wave painting. It's an excellent project in which to practice the flow and movement of the palette knife, with a simple palette of blues and white. It is inspired by the famous painting *The Great Wave off Kanagawa* by Japanese artist Katsushika Hokusai.

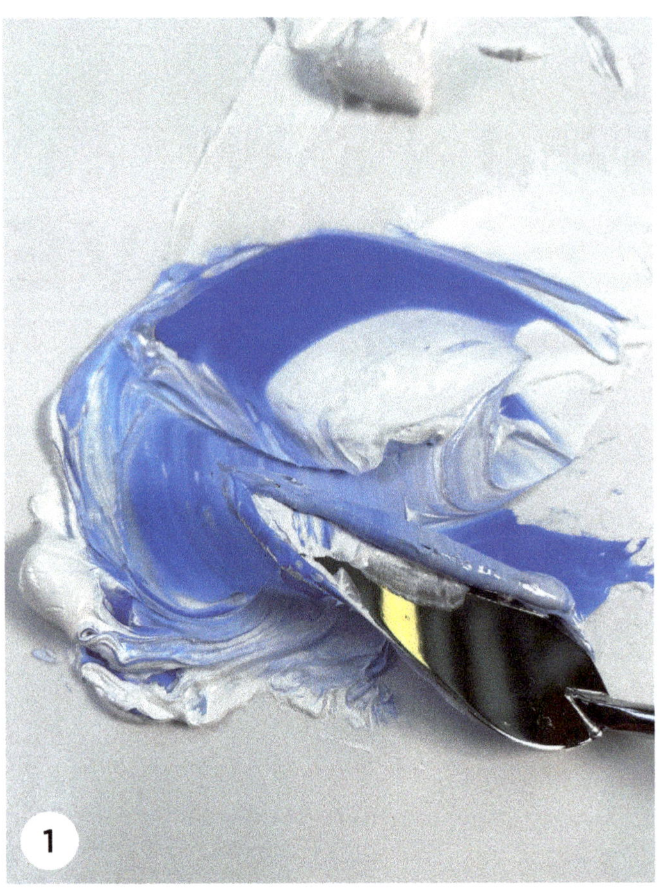

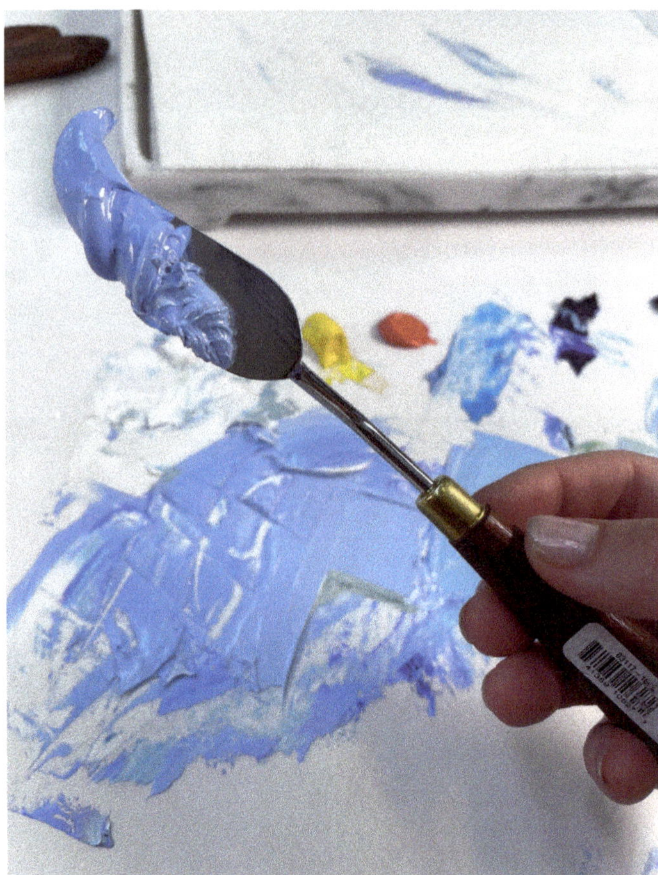

## Step-By-Step Instructions

**Step 1: Lay out your colors & mix your blue sky color**

- Squeeze out a large blob of white paint, about the size of 3 heaped tablespoons on the top left of your palette. We are going to use a lot of white in this project to build up the texture in the luscious, frothy wave. This extreme texture will also create movement and shadows, which will really give your wave a 3D look and feel to it. Squeeze out about 1 tablespoon each of cerulean blue and ultramarine blue, and about 1 teaspoon of yellow. Again, I like to put them in that order across the top of my palette from left to right so that I can drag the paint down to mix it with my palette knife, adding to it as I go.

- Drag down about 2 tablespoons of white and about 1 teaspoon size amount each of cerulean blue and ultramarine blue, and mix them all together with your knife. You can go ahead and leave some streaks in your paint here, just by not mixing it entirely. We want this painting to have a beautiful gestural quality and a looseness to the wave.

- So, make a couple of variations in value here, with a slightly darker blue, and drag some more white in to make a lighter blue.

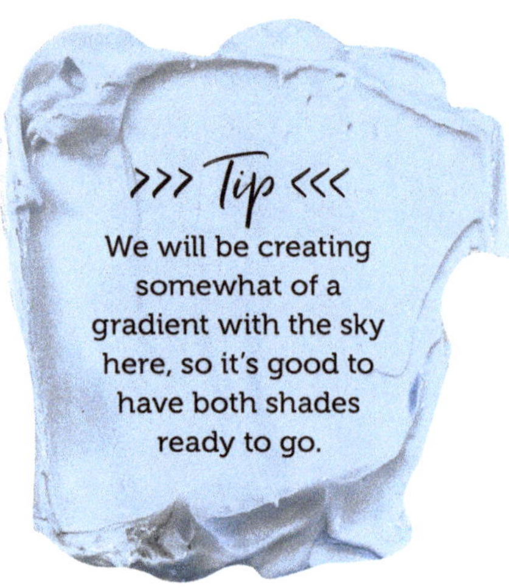

>>> Tip <<<

We will be creating somewhat of a gradient with the sky here, so it's good to have both shades ready to go.

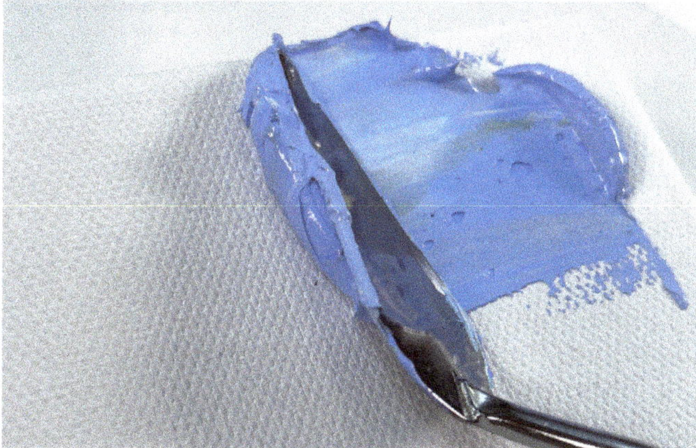

**Step 2: Lay in your blue sky**

- Once you've mixed your colors, load your knife with a large tablespoon of your darkest shade of blue, and swipe this right across the top of your canvas from right to left.
- We want to use big flowy sweeps here, like spreading frosting on a cake.
- Reload your knife and repeat this motion from left to right, slightly under your first sweep, blending the two sweeps together as you go. In this painting, we are not trying to blend the sky perfectly, but rather we want some variations and streaks to show through, giving it interest and movement, and an uncontrived look and feel.

**Step 3: Painting off the edges**

- One of my signature moves is to use thick paint protruding from the edges. This is a super fun technique that adds interest and a really dynamic flair, making your painting just leap off the canvas.
- Load your knife again with another tablespoon of slightly lighter blue this time. Start with your knife positioned slightly off the canvas, but with the paint touching the canvas lightly. Do not press too hard here. We are just gently placing and swiping the paint, leaving a smoothed-out blob protruding from the edge. If you press too hard, it will squish the paint over the edge, and then it will droop down the side. We want to leverage the natural firmness of the paint to create a 3D dynamic, but paint has its limits, so there is a sweet spot here with the texture. Too much and it becomes heavy and unpainterly.
- You also can go back and add a little more texture off the edges if you have not progressed too far into your painting. I decided this piece would look more interesting if I added some off-the-edge texture on the left. I usually put some on both sides for compositional balance.
- Using the darker blue with streaks that I had on my palette, I went back and added a swipe straight over the top of the original one. Starting

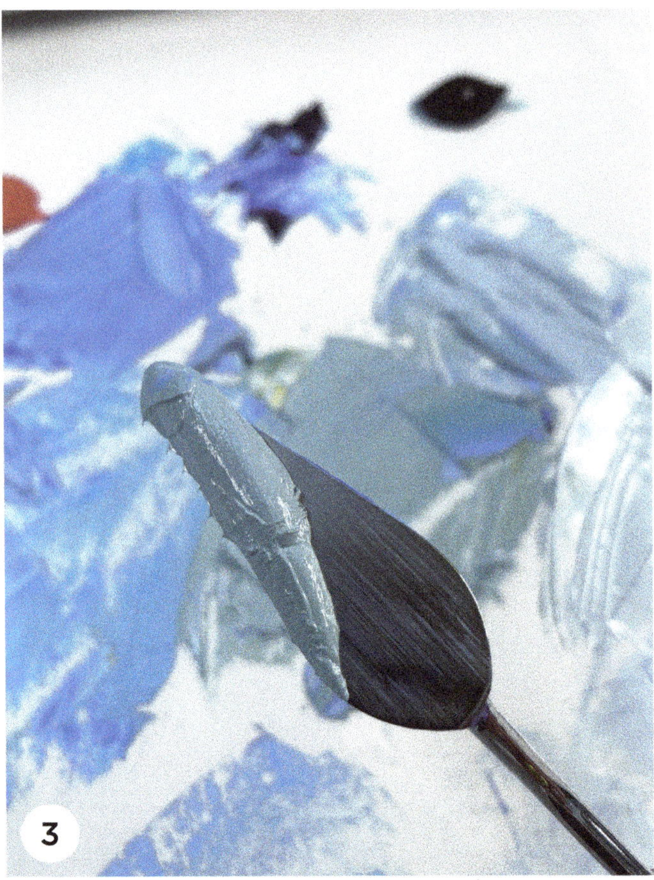


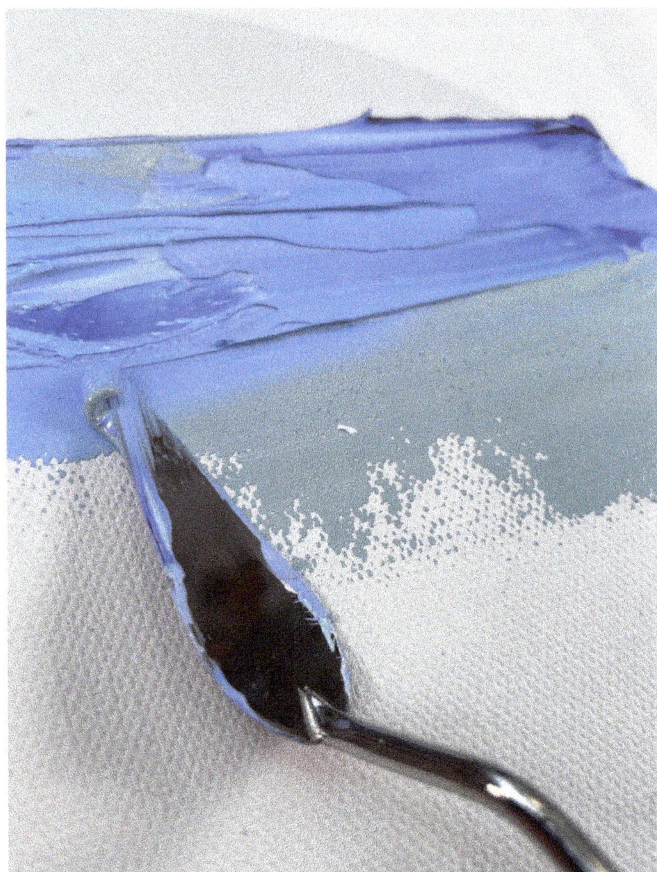

with a tablespoon-sized blob on the left, I gently pressed the blob down and across from left to right, leaving the texture protruding slightly. This gives it a nice, natural border too.

- With my paintings, I am always trying to marry good technique and painterly details with texture, interest, and movement. Finding your balance here is a personal journey, with many hours of practice leading you to your own sweet spot.

- Repeat the motion of laying it on from right to left, sweeping it right across the canvas. Load your knife again with lighter blue and sweep it across from left to right, slightly under your previous swipe. By now you should have most of the top of your blue sky filled in.

- Now we are going to lighten the sky up a little around the horizon line. This creates depth and recession. With a clean knife, go ahead and drag down around 1 teaspoon of white, and a half a pea-sized amount of yellow. We're going to add these to the blue you have already mixed to lighten it up a bit. Do not add too much yellow; start with just a dab and add to it if you need more. We're aiming for a lovely aquamarine or very light turquoise color here.

- Repeating the steps with the first sweeps of blue, slightly under your last sweep, go ahead and add a long, flowy sweep of your lighter blue from right to left, as far across the canvas as you can go, using all the paint. Repeat the action with a loaded knife from left to right to end up with a complete lighter blue swipe across the canvas.

### Step 4: Creating your horizon line & blending your sky

- Now we want to lighten up our horizon line a little more, which will also create a focal point for the portion of the wave interior curve that peeks through.

- Go ahead and drag down about 1 teaspoon of white to your lightest blue and mix so that you have a very light blue, but more white than blue. Load your knife with about 1 teaspoon of the white-blue by scooping with the right edge. Then sweep all the way across as far as you can go.

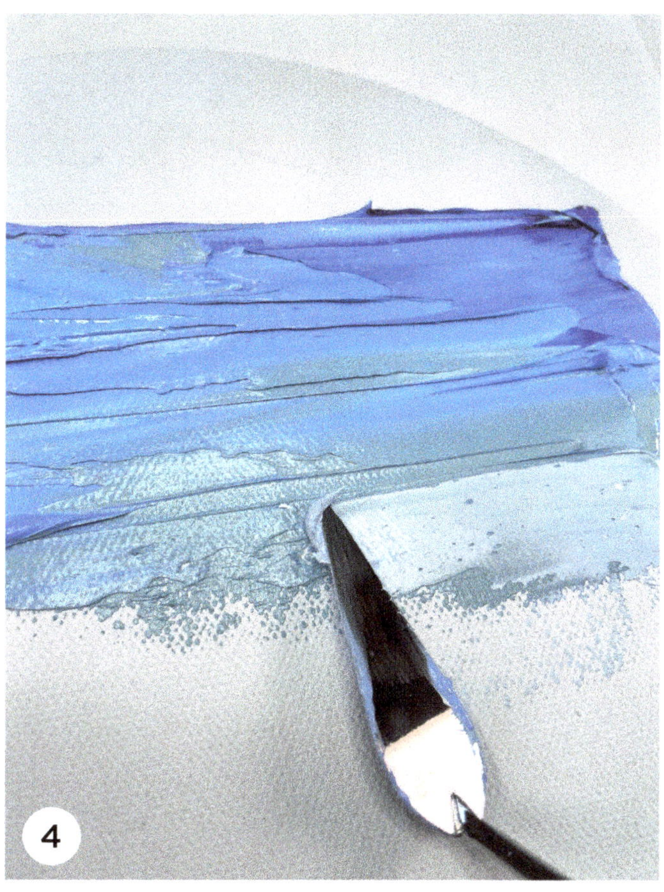

- I decided that the composition needed a more prominent white portion, so I went ahead and repeated this step using a clean knife, and about 1 teaspoon of pure white, more toward the tip of the knife (but not on the actual tip, remember no dabbing!).

- Now all the stripes in the sky need blending so that there are fewer visible lines. Go ahead and blend them by using side-to-side sweeping motions with the flat portion of your knife. Make sure you don't blend away your crisper white horizon line.

**Step 5: Laying in your water**

- Now we'll finish the rest of the underpainting before placing our delicious big wave on top. For this portion, we're mostly just laying in paint as the base portion of the wet-into-wet technique. If we go ahead and paint the wave in now, without the base paint underneath, it will be harder to carve out a natural flow.

- Mixing some of the darker blue you already have on your palette, load your knife with about a tablespoon of it, and repeat the side-to-side motion straight across the canvas from right to left. Line up the tip of the knife to where you want your horizon line to be. Remember not to put it directly in the halfway point of your painting. This is a compositional no-no.

- Also, be careful not to scrape off too much of your white right at the horizon line as you draw your knife across the canvas. Try to do this nice and steady and straight, and all the way across the canvas. It doesn't have to be perfect; straightish is fine. Do not go back in and fuss with it, as the dabbing will ruin the gestural look. Remember, if you need a do-over, you can just apply more white, and then do the horizon line again.

- So far it's looking good. We have a nice gradient in the sky, and the light blue and white has organically blended to look like clouds or fog, perfect for a coastal-inspired scene.

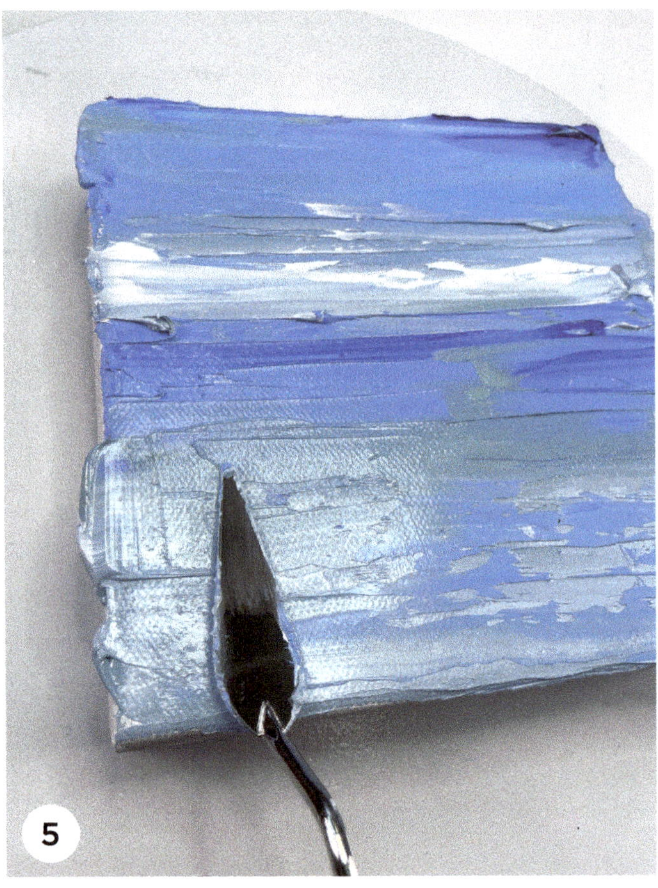

5

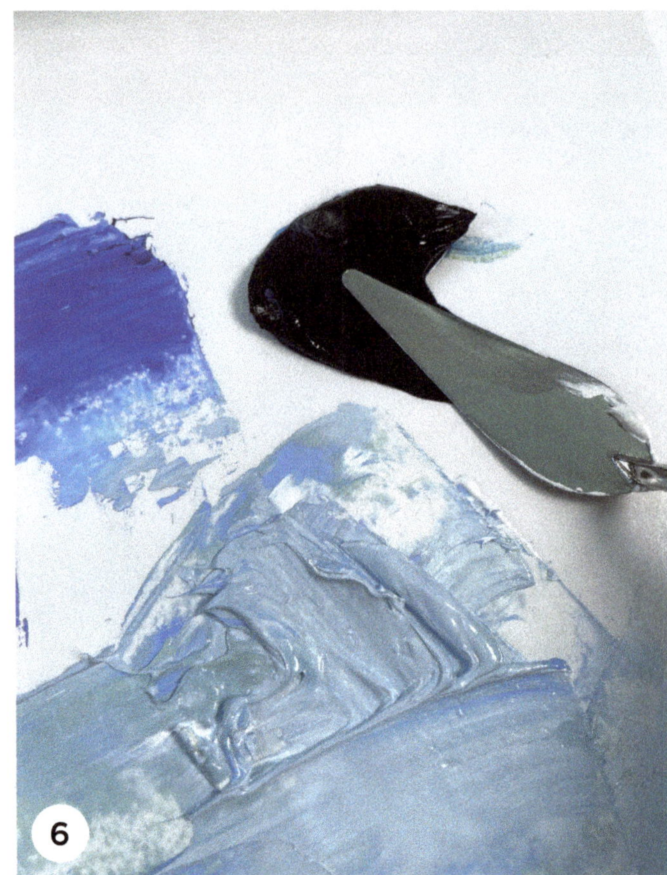

6

- Now we'll finish the underpainting by using up our blue and lightening things up as we bring the water forward. Drag down some white and a tiny dab of yellow to mix the light aqua blue. Load your knife and continue the side-to-side motion across the canvas. Add a little more white as you go to make it lightest at the front edge of the canvas. I decided to also paint off the edges again for interest.

**Step 6: Sketching in the wave**

- Now we're headed into the fun part! It's so much fun piling on the paint here to create an incredible, thick 3D wave, so let's dive on in!
- We're going to be sketching in the basic outline of where we want our wave to dance across our canvas.
- Drag down a small amount, about 1 teaspoon, of Prussian blue. Using a clean knife, mix the paint so that it is nice and pliable. With this portion of sketching, we are not building up texture, but dancing the tip of the knife along the surface of the paint underneath to "sketch."
- Load your knife with about a pea-sized amount of paint on the tip and on the bottom portion of the blade.
- Starting at the top left of the wave crest, start gently sketching with the tip, using long strokes. Create an arc shape, ending with your knife pulling off the canvas on the right. When you run out of paint, load more on your knife and repeat.
- Next, we'll create the underneath portion of the wave, including the little keyhole through which the ocean will peek through. It's OK to go slow here and take your time.
- Load your knife again with a pea-sized amount of Prussian blue, and sketch in the underneath line, starting on the left and moving up and over, then downward and back toward the bottom left of your painting, leaving enough space for the keyhole. Try to use long, loose strokes here,

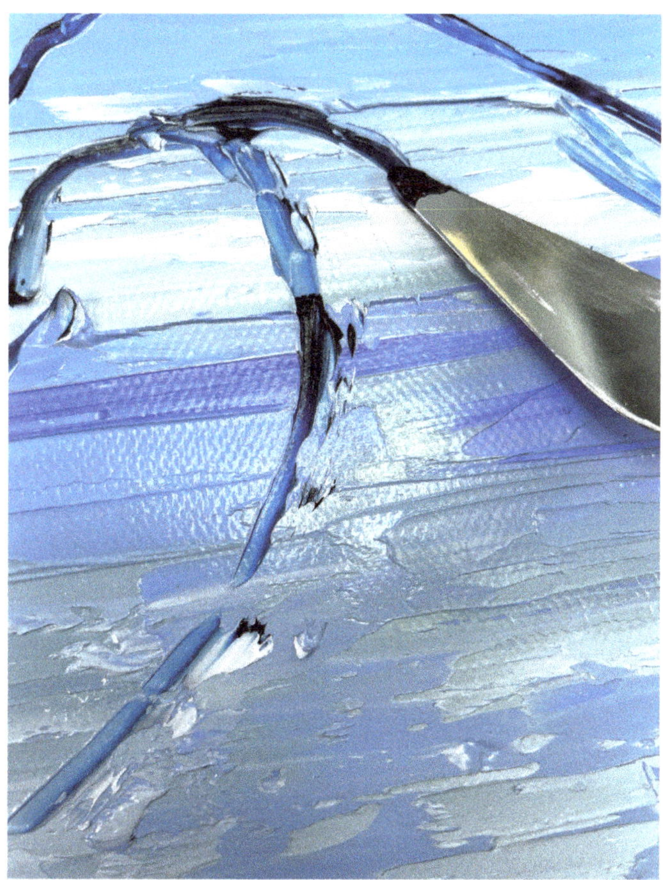

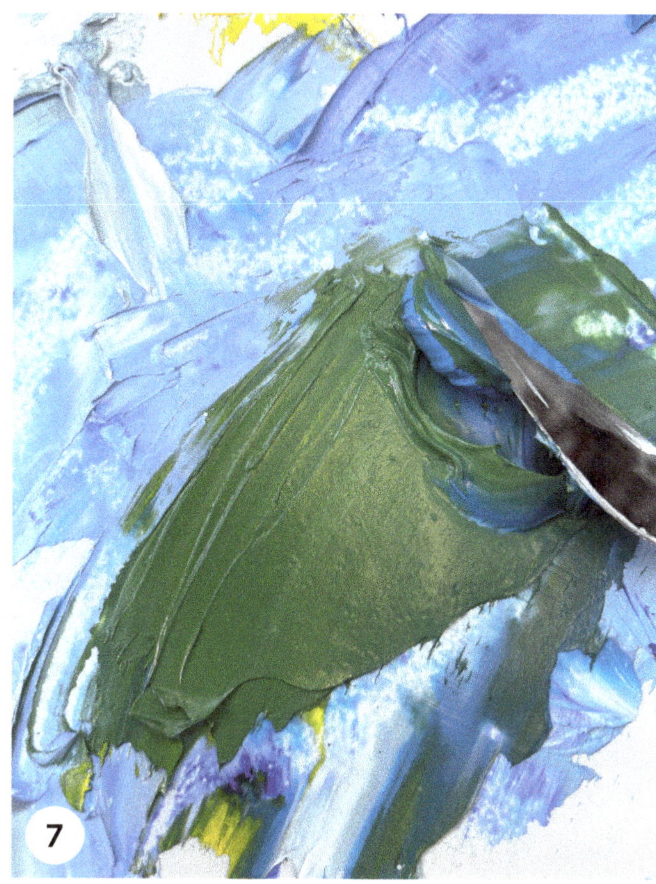

7

and remember, if you really don't like the shape of your wave, you can always scrape off the Prussian blue line with the clean tip of your knife, and then blend your underpainting, and then start over.

- Continuing on from the crest of the wave, we now want to create a line showing the underneath turquoise portion of the wave, and to separate the front from the back. Sketch a line all the way down to the bottom, following the curve and widening as you go down.

- Now fill in the tip of the wave, making it a little fluffy and voluminous. Waves are unpredictable and inconsistent, so we want to reflect that in our composition. The tighter and more perfect it is, the less gestural it will look, and it quickly loses its playful appeal. We don't want our wave to look contrived or fiddled with. I use several smaller strokes to fill in the tip of the wave.

### Step 7: Adding the turquoise underside of the wave

- Drag down around 2 teaspoons of cerulean blue and a pea-sized portion of yellow and mix them well until you get a rich, saturated turquoise color. Load your clean knife with about 1 tablespoon of this turquoise color, and starting at the underneath the crest portion, lay in a long swoop all the way off the edge of the canvas to the left. Try to keep it large, and do it all in one go. Remember, the less fussing, the better.

### Step 8: Adding the white foam

- This is my favorite part! It's so much fun adding huge swaths of paint to create the movement of a wave here.

- Squeeze out about 3 large tablespoons of white. Make sure you're using a clean area of your palette and that your knife is clean. Squeeze out about a pea-sized amount of yellow and mix it loosely into the white. We want a few streaks here and there, so don't mix it thoroughly.

- Load your knife with 1 large tablespoon of white, and starting at the tip of the wave, place your knife gently on the canvas, and then run your knife up and toward the right in a long, flowy swoop,

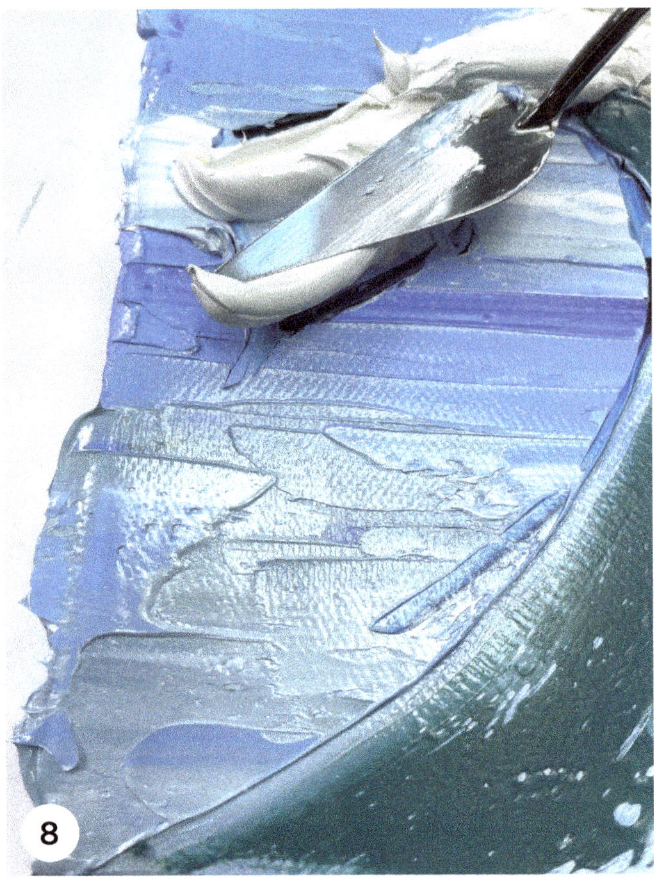


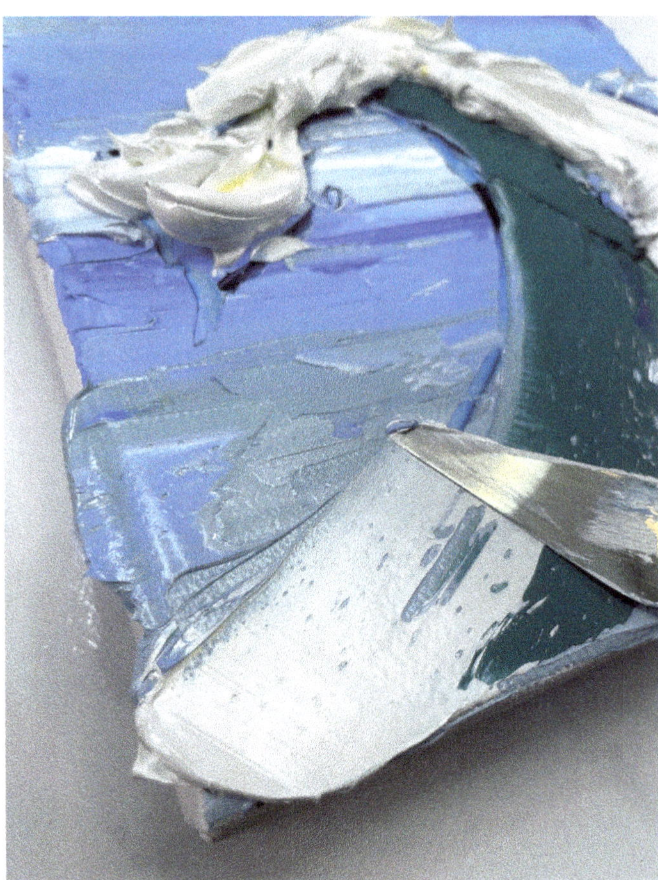

applying pressure, but not smooshing the paint into the canvas. Follow the dark blue outline as you go, gently swiveling the knife to create the curve. Continue all the way, curving down until you run the tip of the knife off the edge of the canvas.

* It's a good idea to practice this first on your palette with pure white paint. That way you're getting comfortable with the movement, and you're not wasting any paint.

- Wipe your knife and reload with another large tablespoon. Repeat the sweep starting slightly below the tip of the wave and under your first sweep and slightly touching. Follow the curve of the dark blue, being careful to taper and not go over your keyhole. The keyhole is important. It's a focal point of your painting, and the eye is naturally drawn there, so make sure you don't accidentally cover it up. Pull your knife up after you've put in the sweep on the tip of the wave.

- Now reload your clean knife with another large tablespoon of white, and continue with a large sweep down the right side of the wave, following the movement toward the right. We want the bottom portion to have specks of blue showing through to suggest foam and movement, and the palette knife has organically achieved this. One of the reasons why I love knife painting so much is the way you can achieve these striking effects quickly, and without a ton of work.

- Now we're going to finish off the front of the wave with some foam. With a clean knife, load 1 tablespoon of white, and starting at the bottom left and protruding slightly off the edge of the canvas, run a sweep from left to right, up the front of the wave but not all the way up.

**Step 9: Touch-ups**

- To complete this project, we're going to add some subtle highlights and details.

- Breaking up the large area of white foam on the bottom left, I add a sweep of turquoise very lightly over the top so that the blue is peeking through the white.

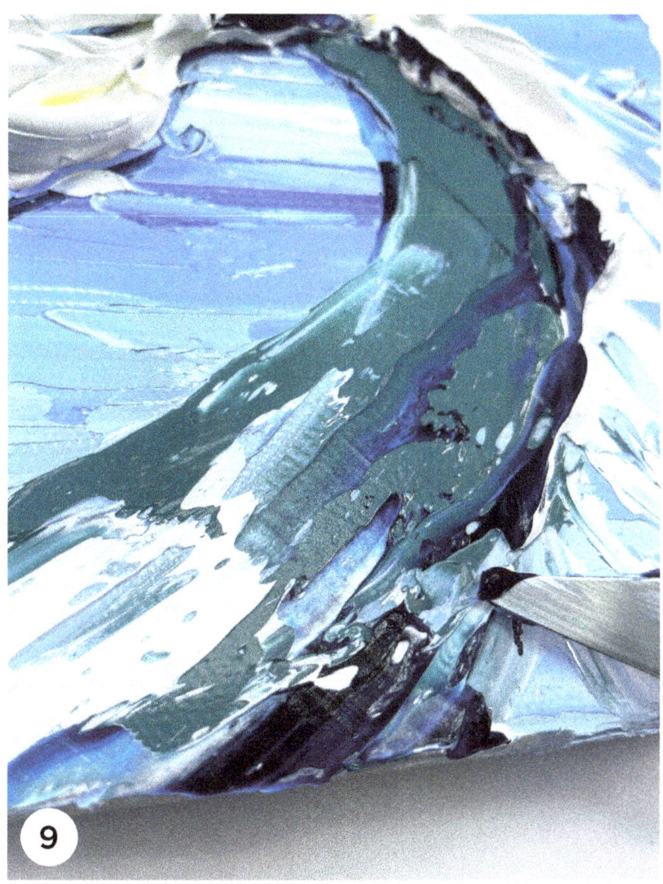
9

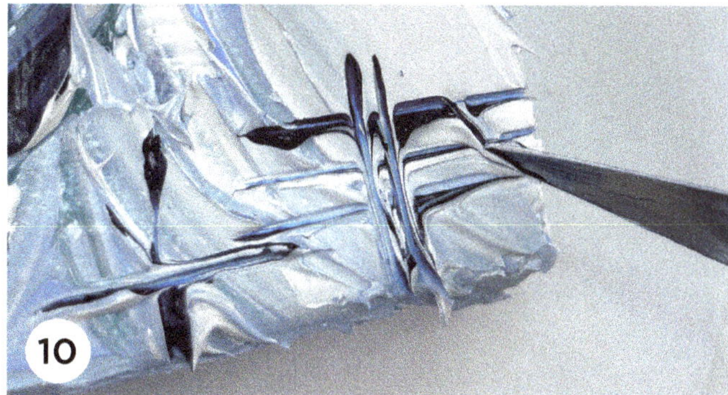
10

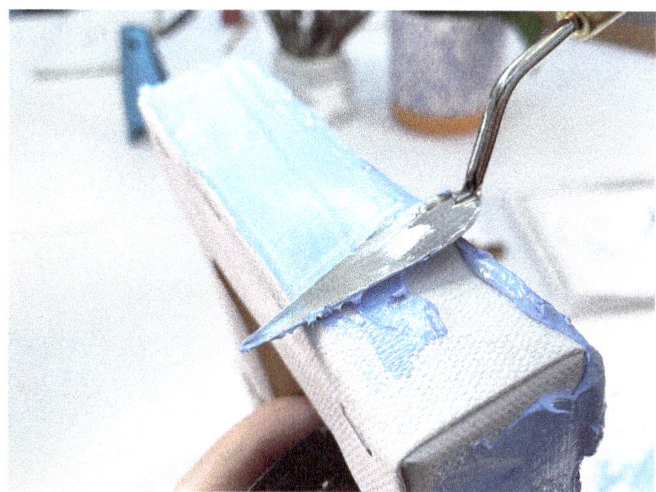

- Using some of the lighter blue left on my palette, I sweep my knife gently over the white paint on the bottom right portion to break up the large expanse of white. I add small highlights by skimming my knife right over the top.
- Next, load your clean knife with a pea-sized amount of Prussian blue, and sketch it carefully and subtly right on the edge of the white to create a dark ridge on the edge of the white. Run your knife using the tip and the top portion of the blade, all the way down the edge of the wave, keeping it inconsistent and natural, and without pressing too hard.
- Also create some rivulets and specks on the bottom portion by gently running the knife tip over the top of the white paint, being careful not to press too hard.

**Step 10: Sign your painting & paint the edges (optional)**

- Go ahead and sign your painting, either on the front or on the painted edge if you've run out of space, or if you feel more comfortable with it. I signed mine on the front, as I decided I had space.
- Again, with these little canvases, it's sometimes easier to just pick them up to paint the sides, swiveling them around on your fingers as you go. You don't have to be particular here, with no need to exactly match up the pattern. It's more of just a continuation of the colors, and getting rid of the white canvas. When you've filled in every portion with the blue paint that was left on your palette, you can go ahead and set it down to dry on a shelf, away from dust and other objects.

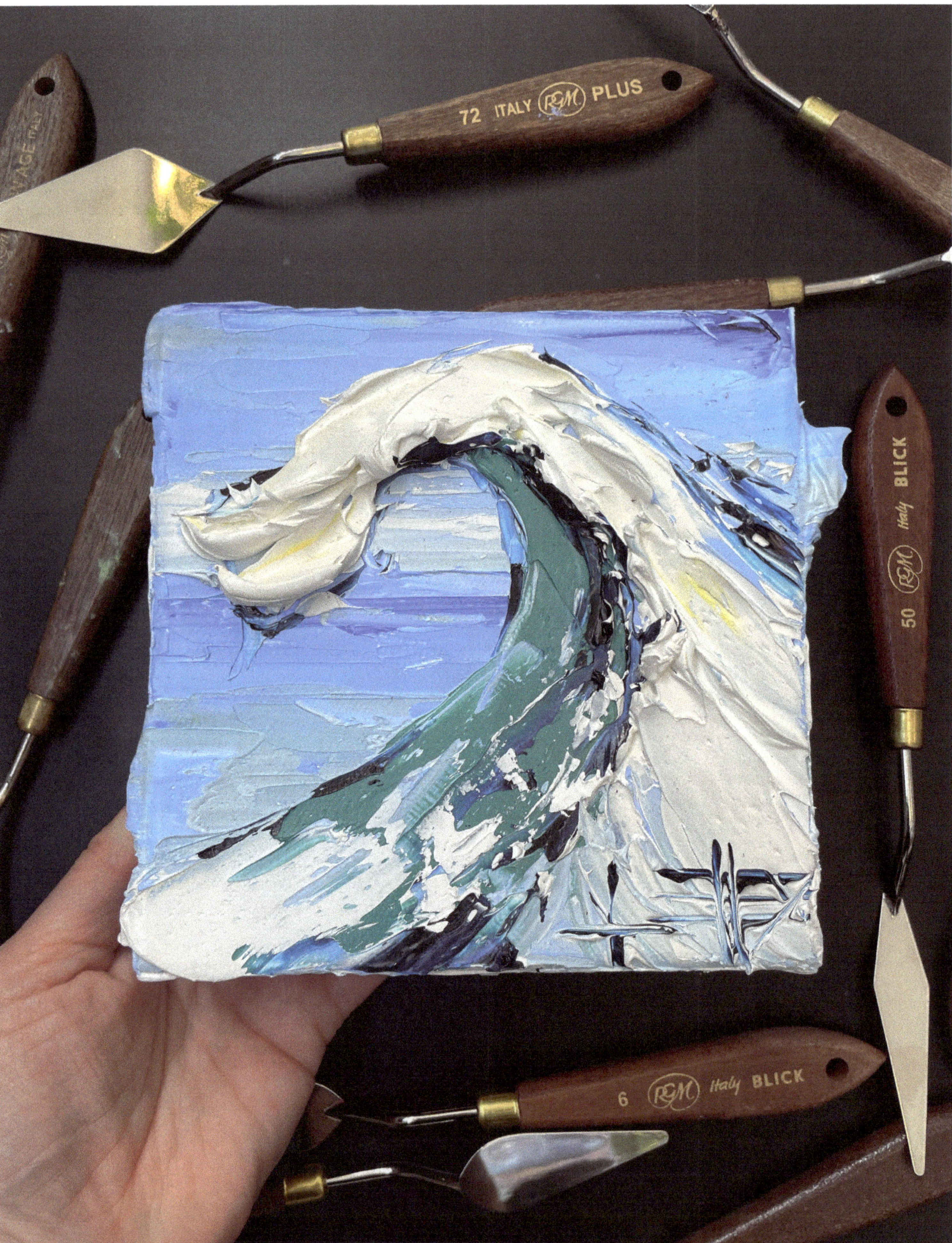
72 ITALY RGM PLUS
BLICK Italy RGM 50
6 RGM Italy BLICK

## SUMMARY:
## Are You Getting the Flow of It?

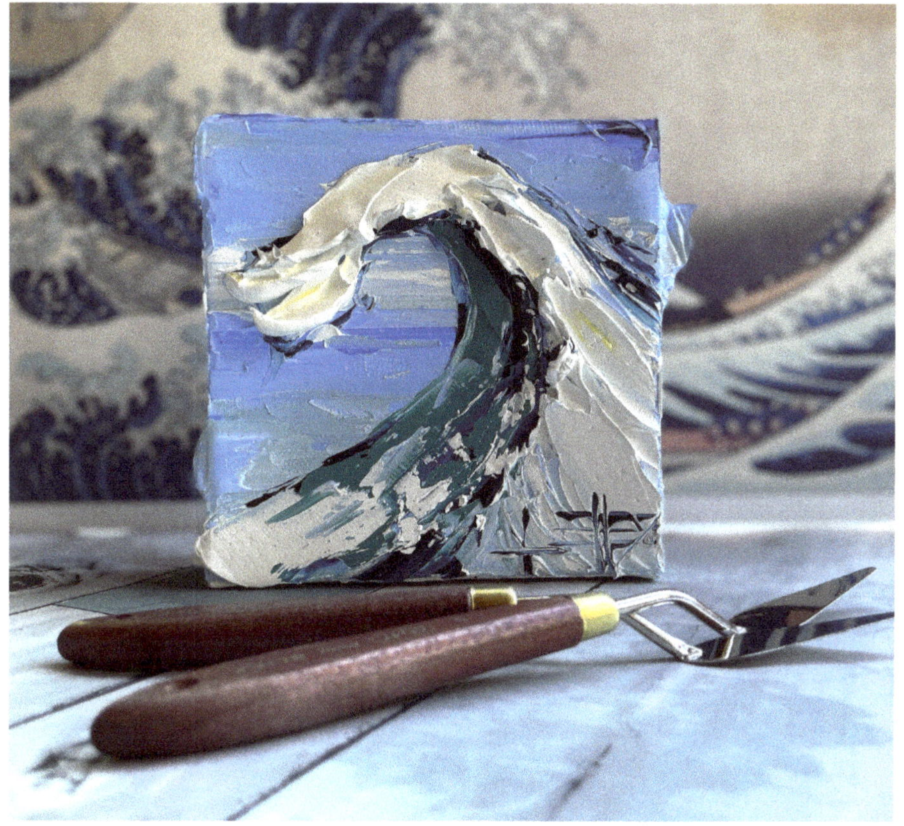

This painting is harder than it looks! The swoop of wave with huge movement behind it is best executed with large, flowing, and curved strokes of the knife. Easier said than done, I know.

It's a good idea to practice a little with pure titanium white on your palette before you attempt this, and remember, if you have to scrape it off, you can always mix blue into it and use it to paint your sides later. I like to use up all the paint when possible, so always keep the leftovers.

Striking a balance between good technique and the natural abandon that makes your knife painting visually exciting is a never-ending journey. I am always aiming for that sweet spot myself, and sometimes it works out and becomes a great, awesome, fabulous painting, and other times it's less exciting. Nonetheless, the practice will enhance your skill set and make you a better painter, so it's a win-win. By the way, when you finish your painting, always take a moment to pause, look at all the colors and shapes, and the emotion you conveyed in the piece, and really enjoy the feeling of productivity and creation. Creating is hard. Kudos to you!

"If heaven had granted me five more years, I could have become a real painter."

—KATSUSHIKA HOKUSAI

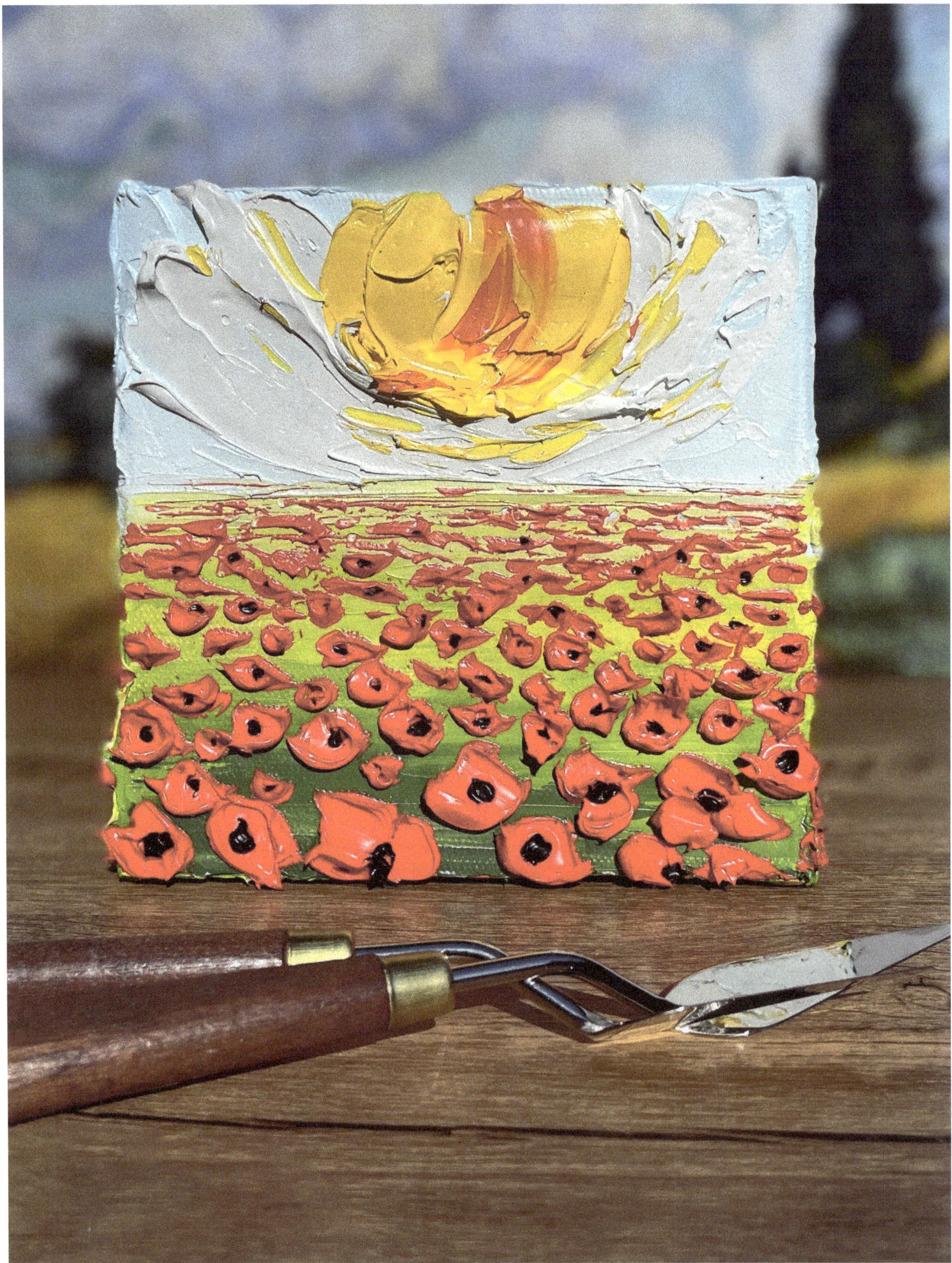

# VAN GOGH-INSPIRED POPPY FIELD

**Tools & Materials**

- Stretched canvas: 6" x 6" with 1½-inch depth
- Palette knives: medium size, teardrop shape with rounded tip; and small size, teardrop shape with rounded tip
- Table easel or lazy Susan
- Palette paper or palette
- Paper towel or rag for wiping your knives

**Color Palette**

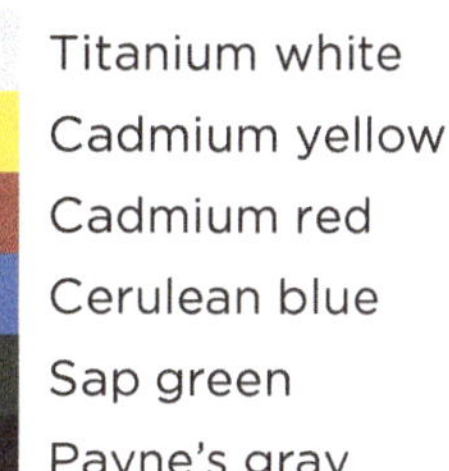

- Titanium white
- Cadmium yellow
- Cadmium red
- Cerulean blue
- Sap green
- Payne's gray

**Difficulty Level**

**LET'S CREATE** an eye-catching landscape, inspired by the great master Vincent van Gogh. This piece features a chunky field of flowers receding into the background and leading the eye to a mesmerizing, textured sun. It's important to follow the steps here. This painting uses the wet-into-wet technique, so stylistically you need to get the composition right and follow the correct sequence as you complete the piece. It's difficult to go back and make big changes.

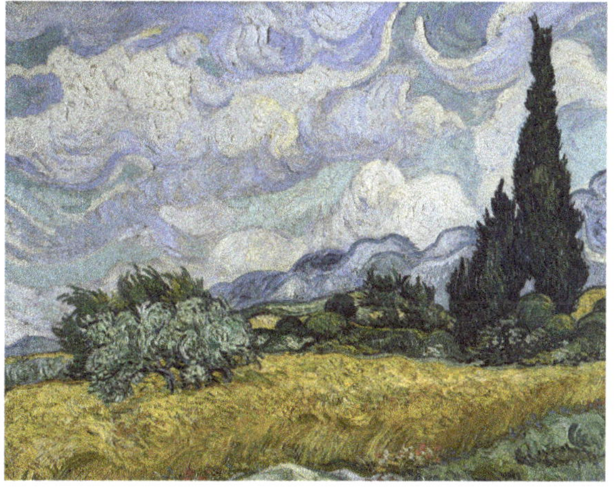

This project will probably take around 40 minutes, but don't worry if it takes longer—the key here is to enjoy yourself! Set aside the appropriate amount of time, when you know you won't be rushed, tired, or multitasking. This helps a lot! Painting is meditative and satisfying, and it's a great idea to make it a regular part of your self-care routine. Plus, you get to create unique and stunning original art! If you feel nervous about starting a new technique that may be out of your wheelhouse, remember that I started this technique as an adult in my mid-30s, carving out little pockets of time while I was raising my young children. You can do this too!

## *Before We Begin*

Let's start by talking about some best practices with palette knife painting. Knife painting is a color-blocking technique that uses bold color and texture and features less blending than brush painting. To achieve effective, striking color transitions, it's important to wipe your knife between every color—and even every stroke at times.

Also, remember that you are not painting with the tip of the knife. You mostly use the middle portion of the blade and rotate it slightly left and right as you pull it up and back and forth across your canvas (not unlike spreading cream cheese on a bagel). Painting with the tip may be tempting, but it leads to dabbing, which can look fussy and overworked. Aim for big, playful strokes that look natural and easy. (It's not easy, but that's why I'm here to teach you!)

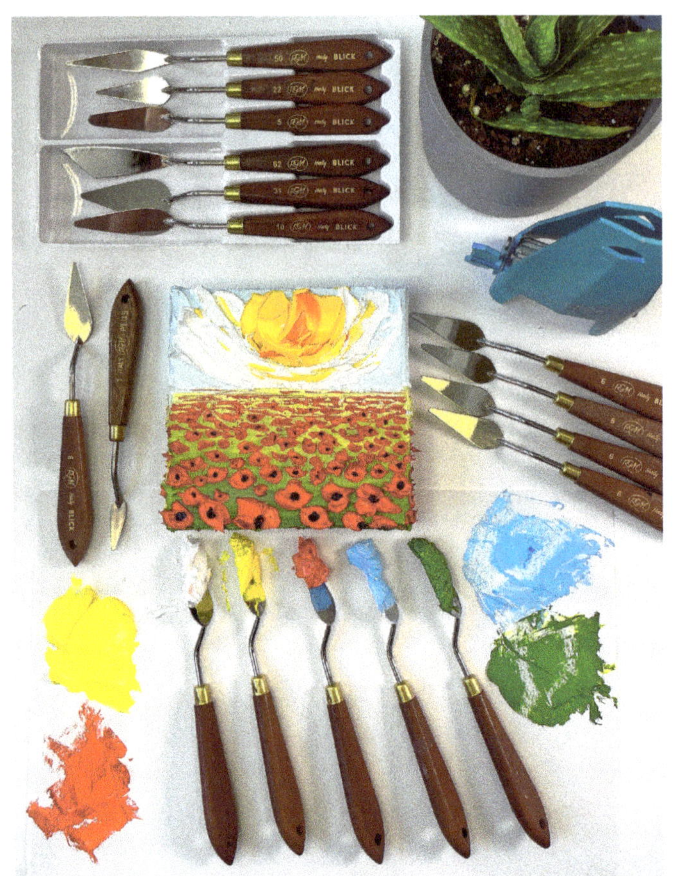

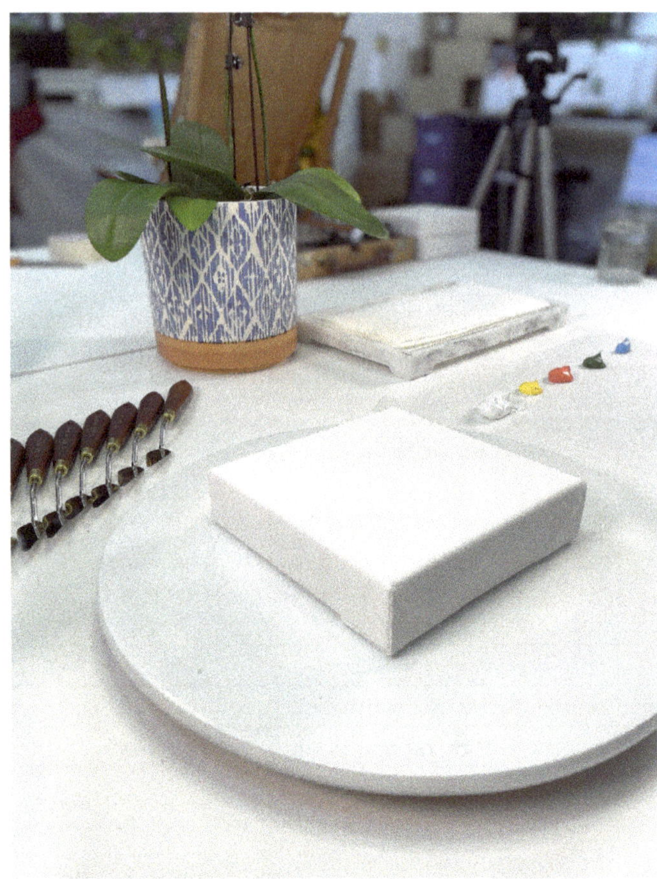

## Get Ready to Paint

1. It's a good idea to have all your materials laid out before starting. When using the wet-into-wet technique, you need to complete the project in one sitting. But don't worry—it's fast!

2. Place your easel or lazy Susan in a comfortable position and height, for either standing or sitting. Make sure that you have room to lift your elbows and maneuver the knife. Work in a well-lit area if possible—preferably with natural light—but artificial lighting is OK too.

3. Lay your palette or palette paper on your right side if you are right-handed (reverse if left-handed). Make sure your knives are clean and within reach. Have at least five to 10 half portions of paper towel ready and in a flat pile, next to your other supplies.

4. Now you're ready to lay out your paint colors and start your piece. Let's go!

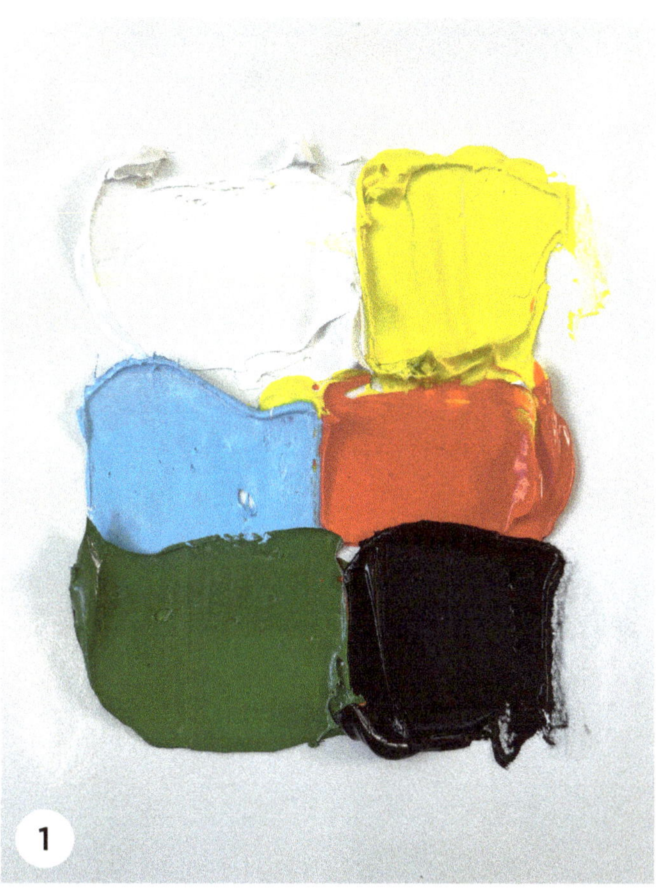


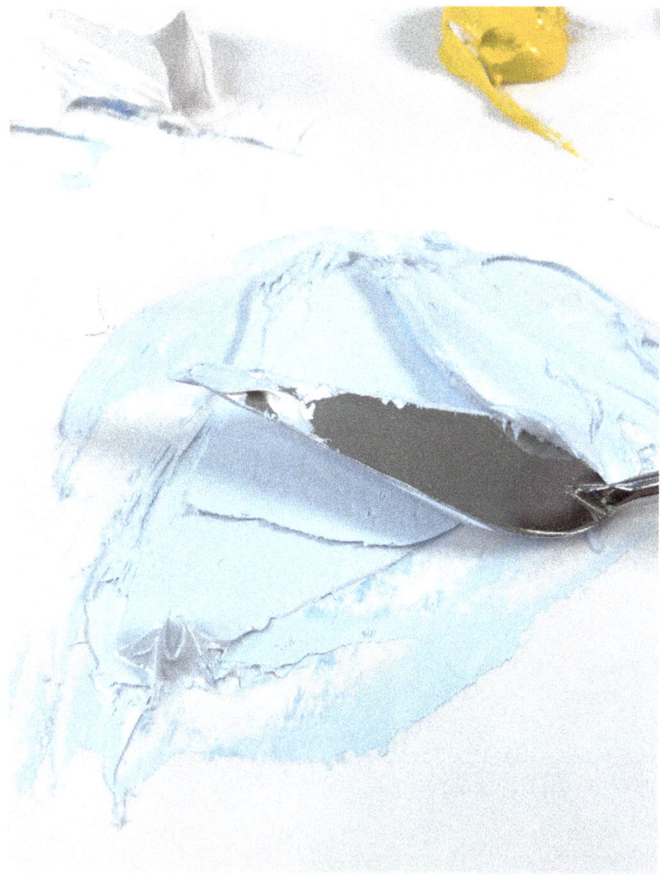

## Step-By-Step Instructions

**Step 1: Lay out your colors & mix your blue sky color**

- Squeeze out a large blob (about 2 tablespoons) of white paint on the top left of your palette. Squeeze out around 1 teaspoon each of cerulean blue, cadmium yellow, cadmium red, sap green, and Payne's gray. I like to put them in that order across the top of my palette from left to right so that I can drag the paint down to mix it with my palette knife. I don't like to waste paint—it's expensive!
- Drag down 1 tablespoon of white and about a pea-sized amount of cerulean blue, and mix thoroughly with your knife. Make a couple of variations in value here with a slightly darker blue, and drag some more white in to make a lighter blue. You will create somewhat of a gradient with the sky here, so it's good to have both shades ready to go.

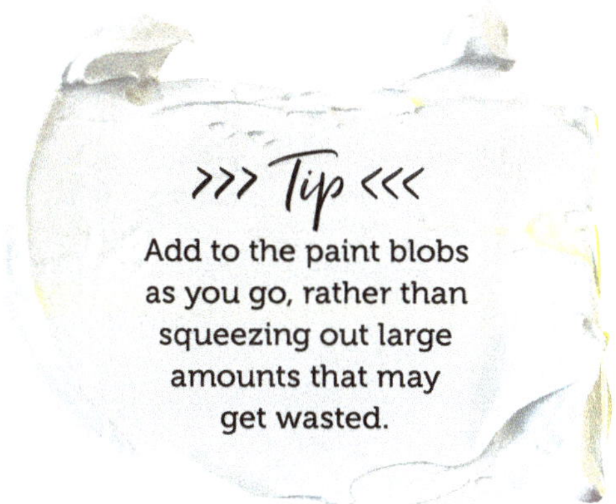

>>> Tip <<<

Add to the paint blobs as you go, rather than squeezing out large amounts that may get wasted.

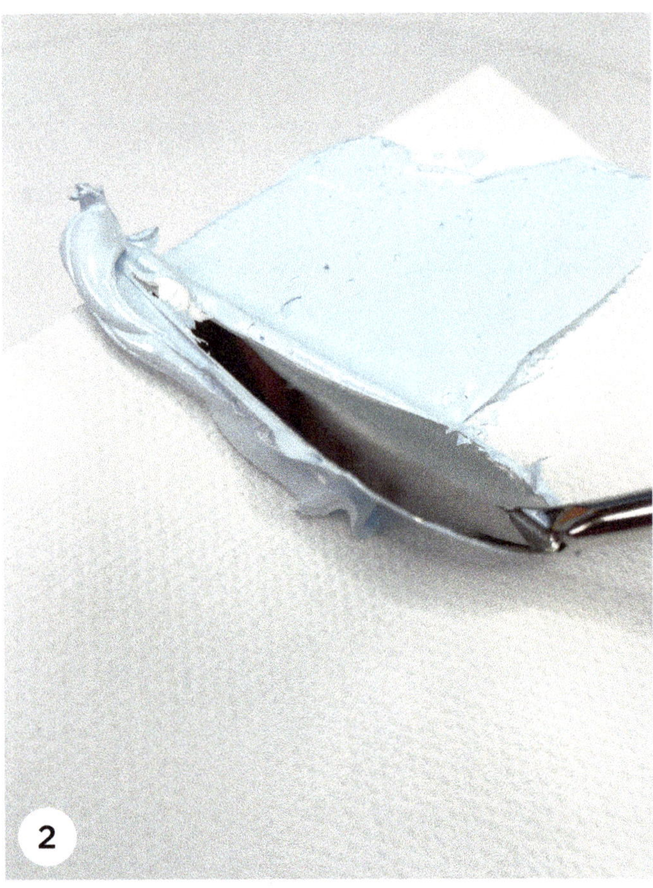

**Step 2: Lay in your blue sky**

- Load your knife with the darker blue and start laying in your sky with the knife. Use sideways, sweeping motions, beginning at the top right to left, and then left to right. Once you have a blue stripe across the top, load the knife again with your slightly lighter blue and repeat the sideways motion, ending with your lightest blue (almost white) on the horizon line, slightly above the halfway point on your painting. Never put your horizon line exactly in the middle. Blend the stripes until they are faded, and you should have a nice gradient.

**Step 3: Lay in the clouds**

- Load your knife with 1 large tablespoon of white, and sweep it down the canvas straight over the blue. Start at the top, slightly off-center on the right, and move in a curved shape ending on the horizon line. Repeat this on the other side. Reload your clean knife with another tablespoon of white, and starting off-center on the left, sweep down in a curve to end on the horizon line with a U shape. Leave a round portion of blue sky at the top-middle so you have a spot for the sun in the next step.
- Add sweeps of white if you need more texture. This motion is very gestural and should feel flowy and fun! It's important to know when to stop, as fussing with your knife will result in an overworked piece, which loses the playful abandon. The bigger the sweep, the better it looks, and as soon as you fuss with little dabs, it quickly loses the gestural look. If you really don't like what you've done, remember that one of the best perks of palette knife painting is having the ability to scrape it off and start over!

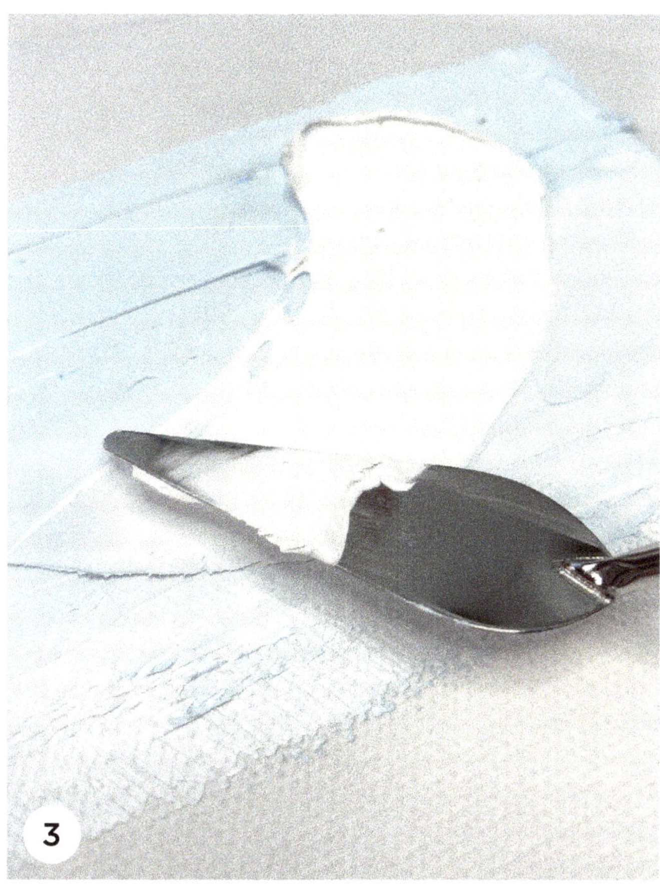

3

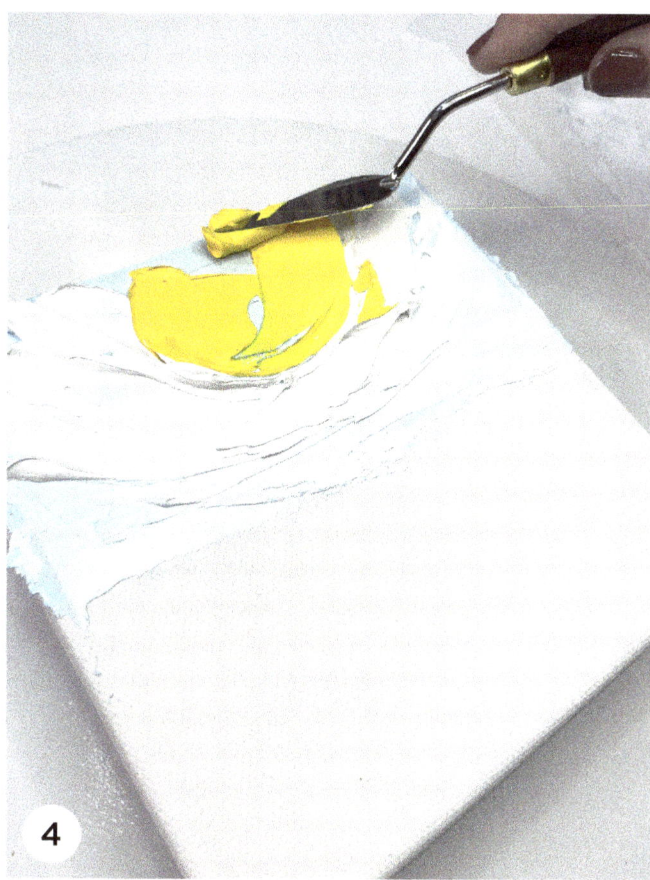

4

**Step 4: Lay in the sun**

- With a clean knife, load about 1 tablespoon of yellow on your knife, and using a similar sweeping motion, start at the top, slightly off-center to the left, and lay in a circular sweep. You're aiming for a round sun here. Repeat this step on the other side, starting at the top and slightly off-center on the right, ending with a nice, round shape. This part can be challenging, but remember that you're not aiming for perfection with knife painting, so if your sun is not perfectly round, it's OK. You can correct any blobs of paint that are preventing roundness by just scraping them off with the tip of your knife.
- Don't use the tip of your knife to overwork your sun; it won't look better. I like to add some streaks of yellow to the clouds as well, so the yellow and white transition isn't quite so stark. Using a clean knife, apply a dab of yellow to the tip of your knife and add some little streaks and highlights to the edges of your cloud sweeps, following the upward and outward movement of the clouds.

### Try a Lazy Susan

This is where the lazy Susan really comes in handy. Palette knife painting requires a lot of elbow room, so the ability to swivel your painting around to maneuver the knife and make more difficult and complex shapes is a bonus here.

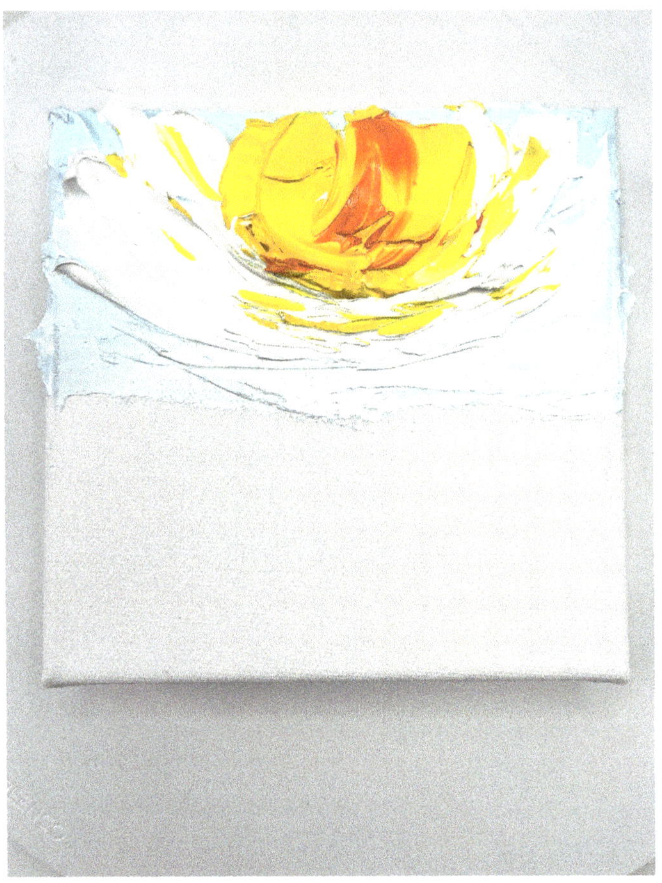

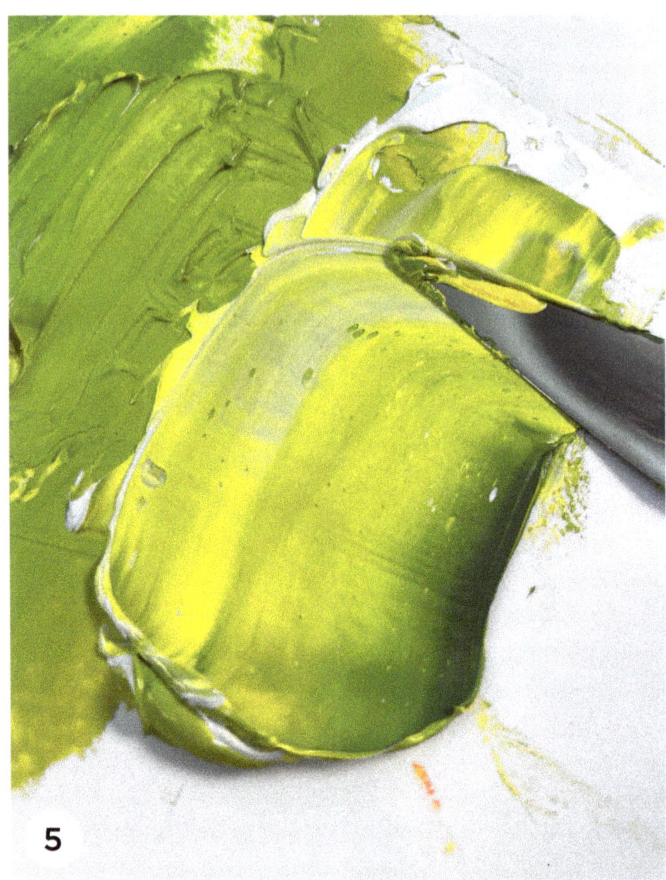

5

- Mix a little orange to give the sun more pizzazz and break up the big blob of yellow. Using a clean knife, mix about a pea-sized amount of cadmium red with 1 teaspoon of yellow to create a nice, vibrant orange color.

- Loading your clean knife with about a pea-sized amount of orange on the tip, create a sweep in a circular motion, effectively "sketching" with the tip of your knife. This sweep should be slightly off-center to create a compositional balance; you don't want everything exactly in the center.

- If you feel your orange stripe is too dark or too much, use a clean knife to go straight over the top and skim off some of the paint with the right side of the blade edge, using the same motion you used to lay in the stripe.

**Step 5: Horizon & grass gradient**

- Now, let's work on completing the rest of the background before tackling the final steps. This painting pops so beautifully in part because red and green are on opposite sides of the color wheel, which means they're complementary colors.

- Using about a pea-sized amount of green, mix it with 1 tablespoon of yellow paint. As you did with the blue sky, make sure you mix variations of green, with a very light shade for your horizon line and a darker shade for the foreground. This gradient will create a lot of depth in your painting.

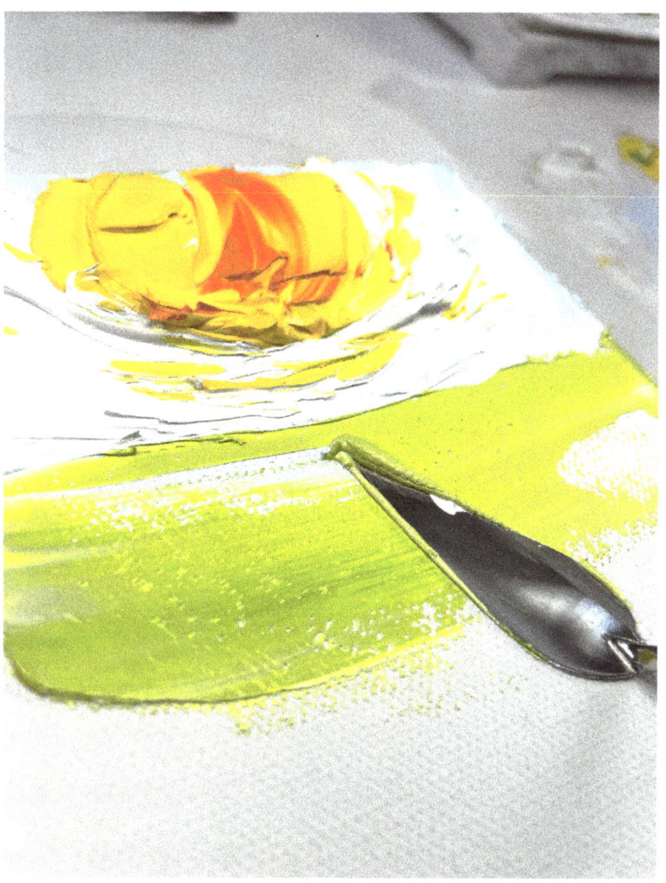

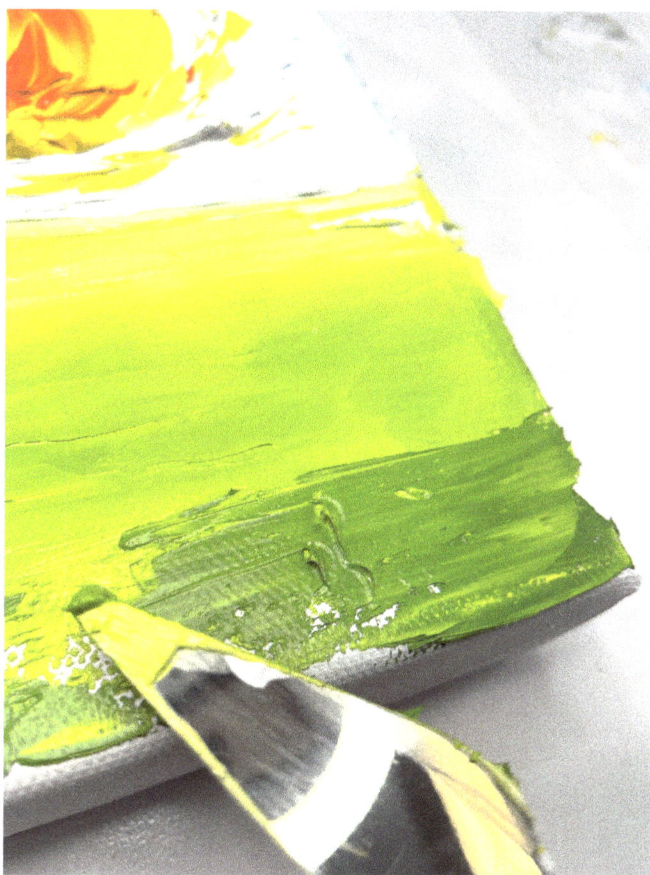

- Load your knife on the right edge with about 1 tablespoon of your lightest yellow-green, making sure you line up the tip of the knife with the bottom of the sky. Do not scrape off your sky or sun! Ideally only doing this once, make a big, flowy swipe from right to left, filling the canvas to create your horizon line. The knife's straight edge is great for natural lines.

- Now you can fill in the rest of your gradient. Load the knife with 1 tablespoon or less of slightly darker green, and repeat the swipe to make another stripe under the first one, matching up the edges.

- Wipe your knife and load it again with the darker shade of green. Make a final swipe across the bottom to finish. Now you can go ahead and blend your stripes with side-to-side strokes and the upper portion of your knife (not the tip).

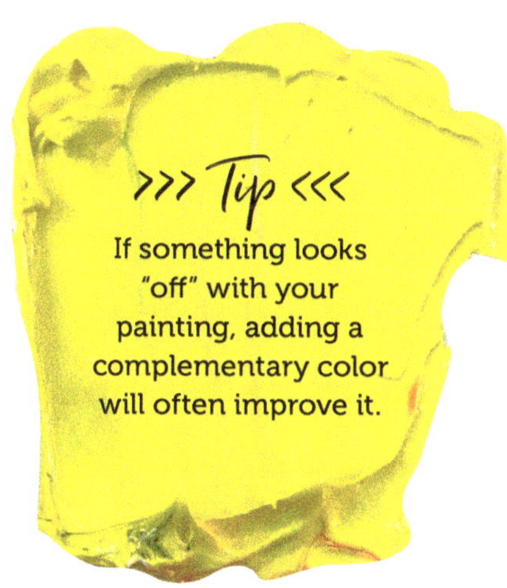

>>> Tip <<<

**If something looks "off" with your painting, adding a complementary color will often improve it.**

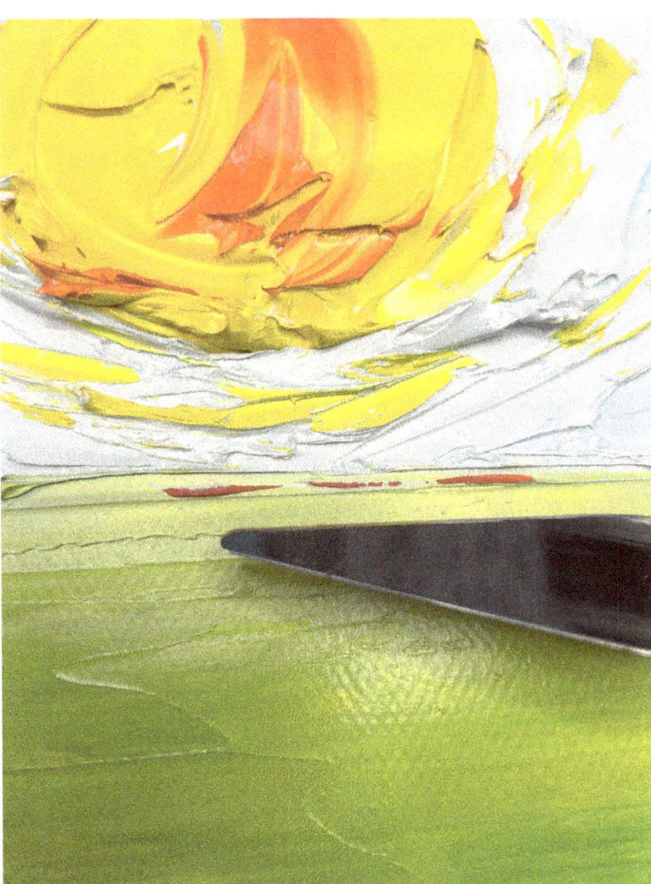

**Step 6: Mixing red & laying in the red poppies**

- Now comes the really fun part! Using the cadmium red on your palette, finish the piece with gorgeous, vibrant, and super-textured flowers. Starting with the horizon line, work your way forward to the large poppies in the foreground.
- You will use the right edge of the knife (not the tip). Mix a little of your red so that you have a thinner portion that is slightly more fluid and less textured. At this point we are not going for texture, as this is a smaller detail. Leave the extreme texture for the larger elements, such as the sun and the poppies in the mid- and foregrounds. To create depth and movement, leave some portions flatter, so that the texture on top can really pop and move forward.
- Loading a very thin sliver of red onto the right edge of your knife, use that edge to dot in some horizontal lines under your horizon line. Take care not to go all the way across and stagger them slightly so that they look uneven. These are the poppies in the very far distance, and they must be tiny to create depth.
- Wipe your knife and load it again, this time using a little bit more paint with texture. Repeat the inconsistent lines, making sure you leave little blobs behind. Make sure you leave plenty of gaps where the green peeks through.

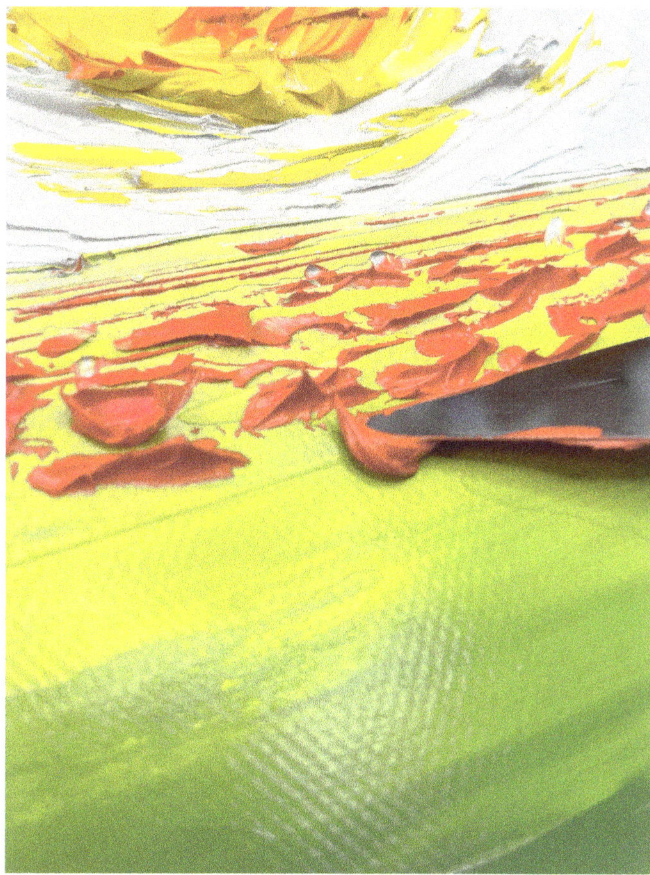

- Now it's time to start on the individual poppies. Load the tip of a clean knife with about a pea-sized amount of paint and dot it down quickly and firmly, without squishing it into the green paint layer below. Pull up your knife up as you go.
- Repeat this using different angles, and for some poppies, do several petals with the same motion, using the tip of the knife to join the blobs to create different variations of blooms. Flowers are haphazard, and the more we can capture this, the better the painting will be. This contributes a sense of movement and incredible light reflection. Along with the shadows created by the texture, it will really make your painting shine.
- As you move forward in the foreground, use more and more paint (wiping your knife each time) and make bigger and bigger flowers, ending with your thickest at the bottom. By now, you should use about 1 teaspoon or more of paint for each petal or bloom.

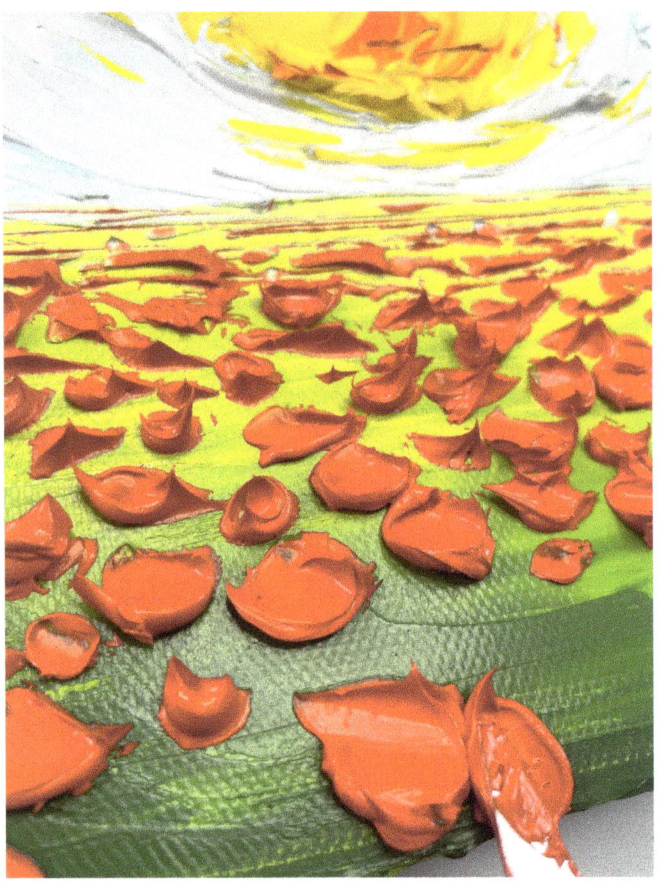

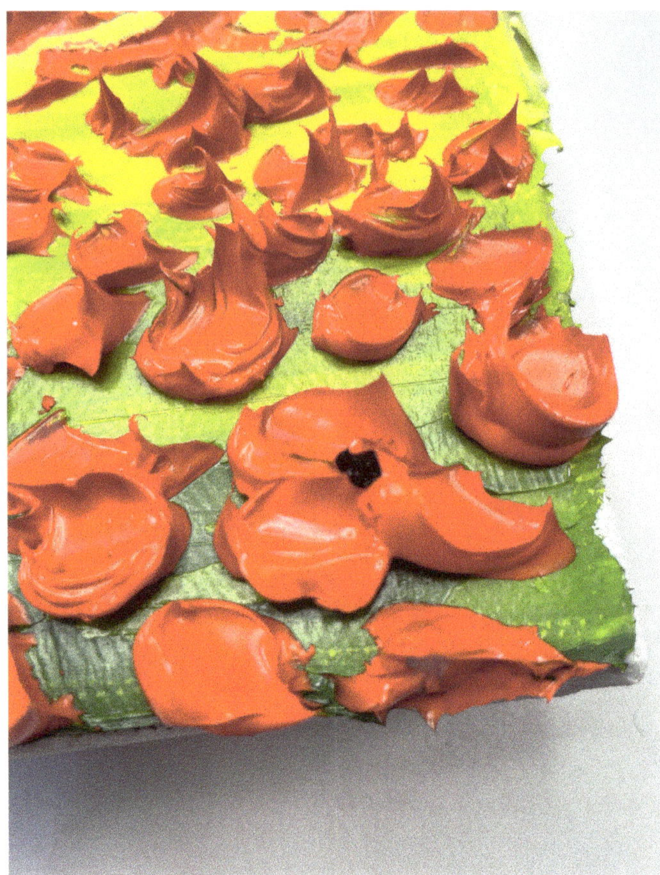

- Now it's time to finish the piece with some black highlights in the centers of the flowers to create definition and tie it all together.

- Using Payne's gray and your smaller knife if you have one, scoop a tiny dab onto the tip of your knife and dot it in the center of each poppy. Do this for all of them, using smaller amounts for the poppies in the background. Don't put any Payne's gray in the rows in the background without distinct poppy shapes.

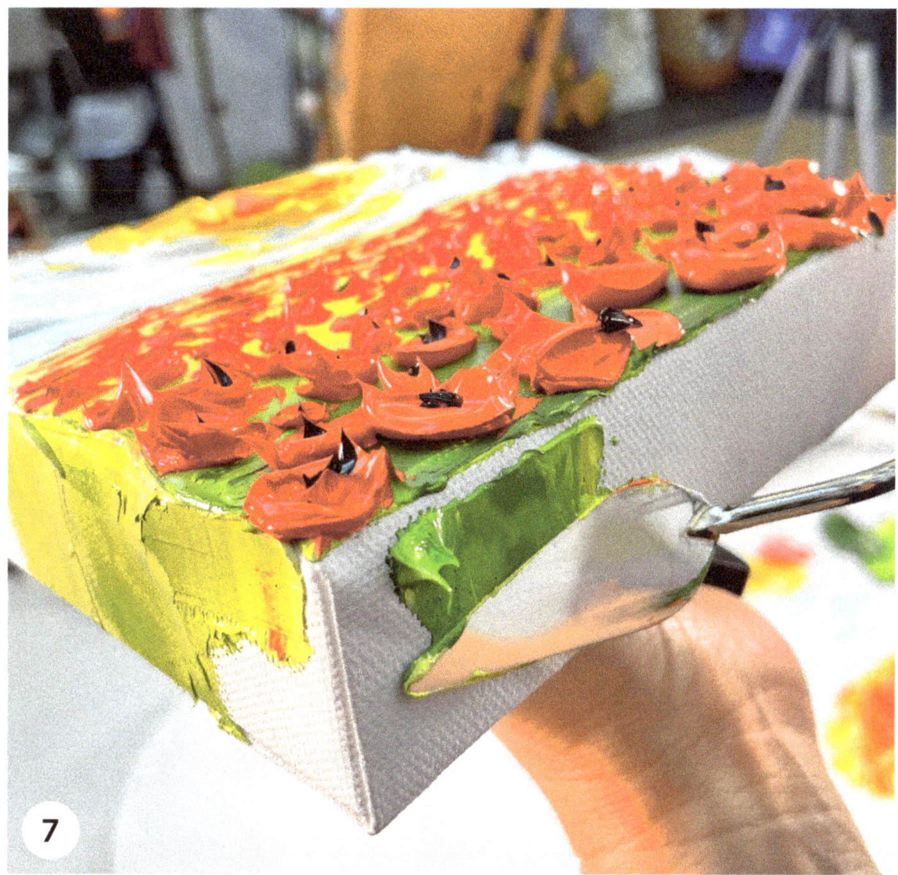

**Step 7: Finishing the piece**

- Congratulations—you've finished your piece! You can go ahead and sign it. With smaller pieces, I like to sign on the right-side edge. I also like to paint all the sides of my paintings with the same colors and patterns, but slightly less textured than the top. The edges are part of the painting and really add to the 3D textural effect.
- There's not really an easy way to do this. On an easel you can get to three sides, but I like to just pick it up and hold it while I finish the edges. Then I lay it flat on palette paper on a shelf to dry. Just make sure it's not in an area with dust; a bookshelf or closet shelf works well here.
- When it's dry to the touch, you can go ahead and hang it on the wall to dry, just like Van Gogh used to do!

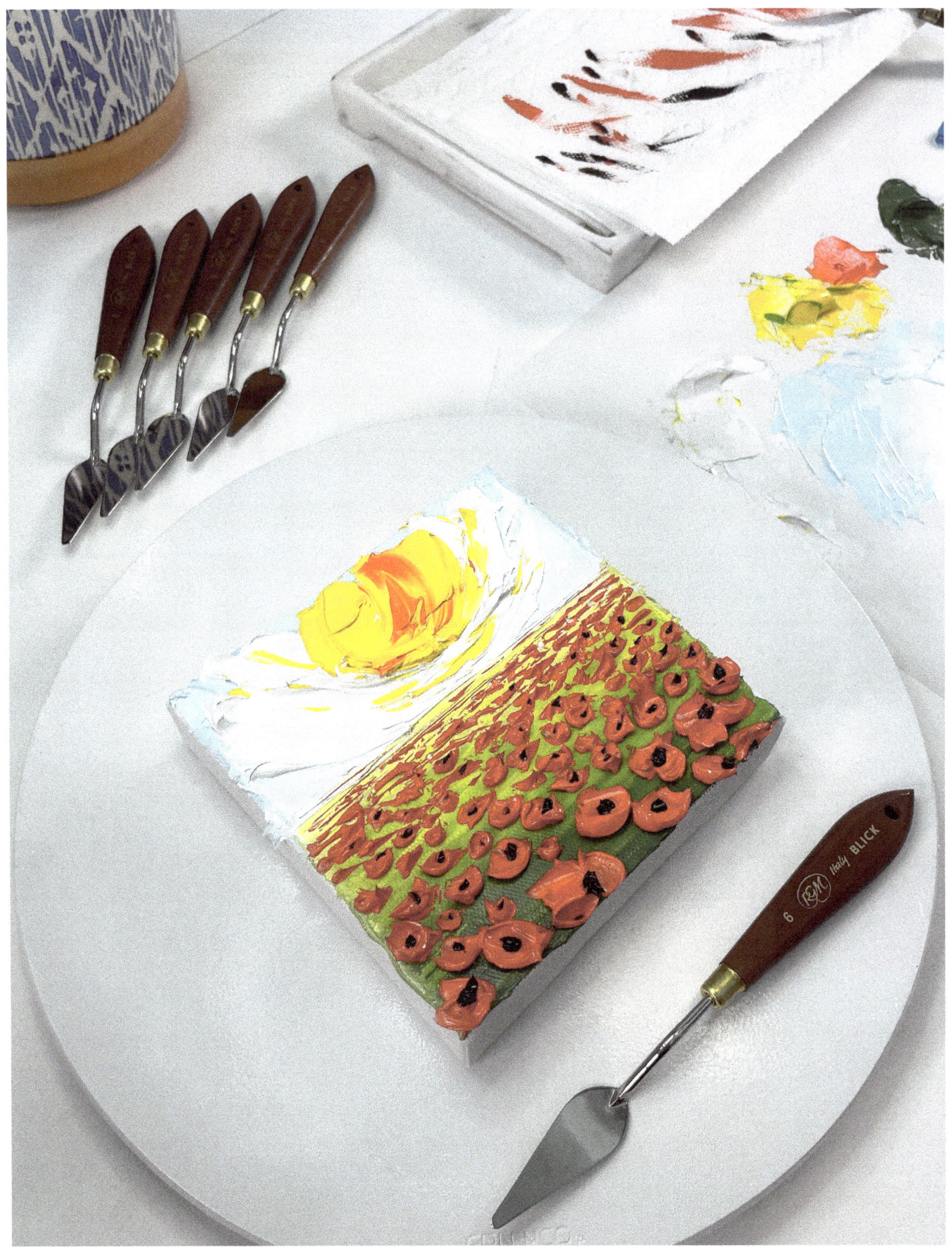
6
RGM
Italy BLICK

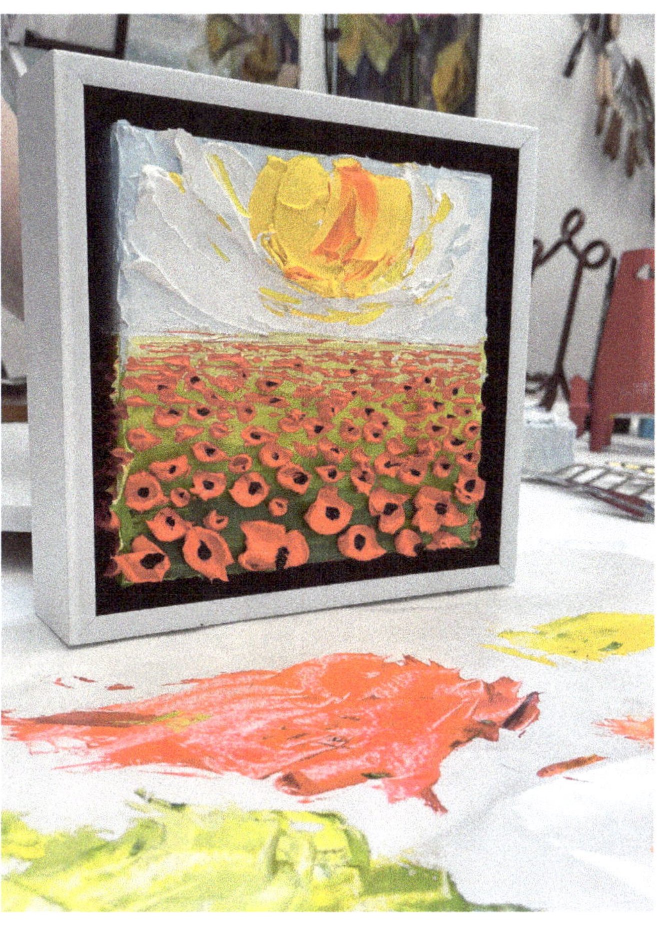

## SUMMARY: *How Did You Do?*

While painting, did you loosen up and let the knife flow? This technique is not easy and requires practice, so regardless of whether you liked your results or not, feel good that you got a painting under your belt!

I love the productive feeling of finishing a painting, especially these quick little ones. In a busy world full of commitments and responsibilities, it's my burst of creativity and spark of joy for the day. It just really fills my cup, which is why I have persevered with it and practiced long enough to hone my skill. As every artist knows, some paintings turn out better than others, and palette knife painting is very spontaneous. You just have to keep trying and enjoying the happy accidents!

If you stay open to improvisation, flexibility, and adjusting, and you know when to stop, you're off to a really great start. Remember that if something looks good and has flair, stop! Don't overthink it, fuss with it, or change it; just leave it and appreciate the beauty of these moments.

Are you also getting the hang of the color-blocking technique? Using limited, bright, and complementary colors will really bring the elements of your painting to life. Aim for smooth and decisive sweeps and strokes. Overworking, hesitating, and dabbing leads to muddied colors and a loss of the gestural look and feel you want for your piece.

*"What would life be if we had no courage to attempt anything?"*

—VINCENT VAN GOGH

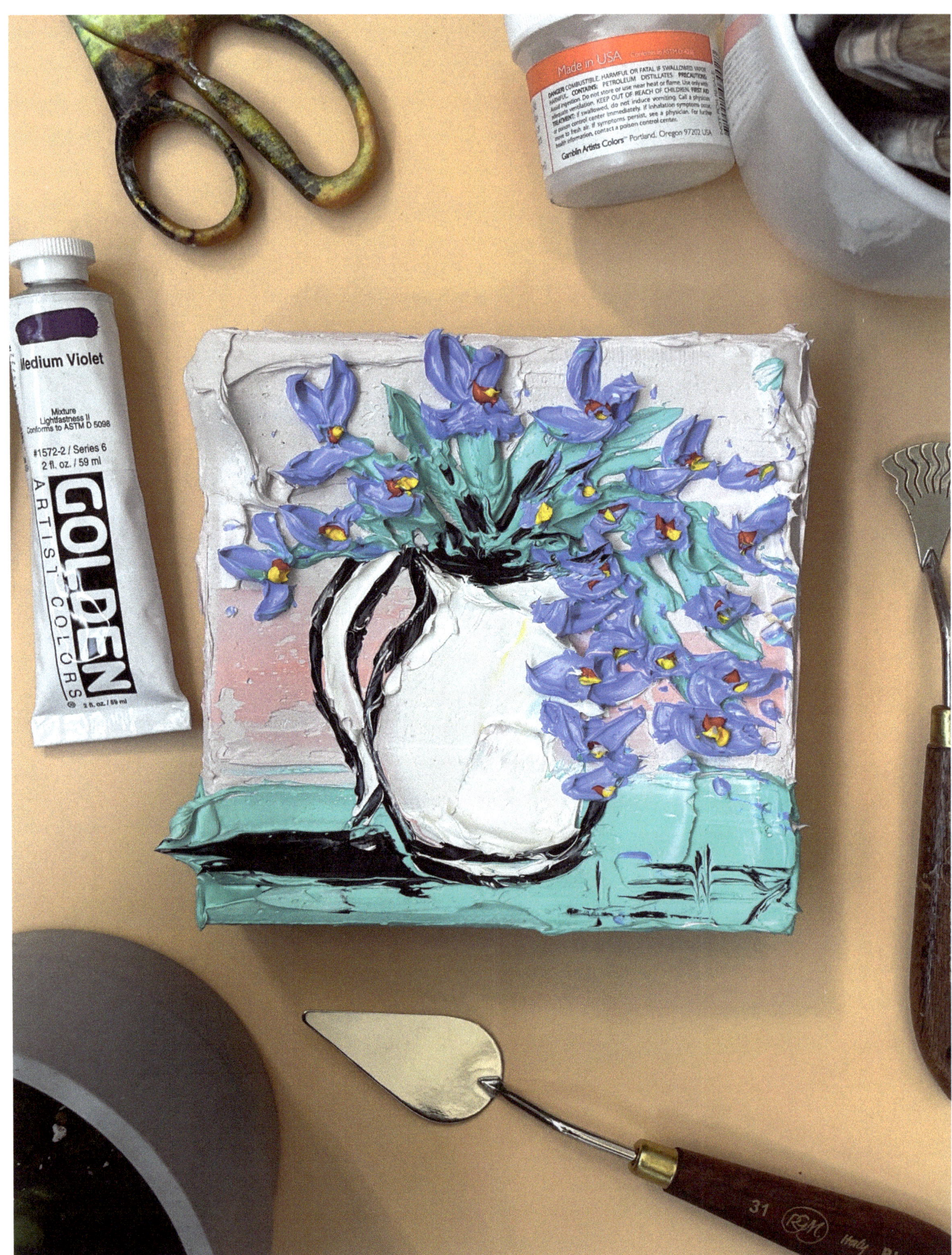
Made in USA
Gamblin Artists Colors™ Portland, Oregon 97202 USA
Medium Violet
Mixture
Lightfastness II
Conforms to ASTM D 5098
#1572-2 / Series 6
2 fl. oz. / 59 ml
GOLDEN
ARTIST COLORS
31
Italy

# VAN GOGH-INSPIRED IRISES

| Tools & Materials |
| --- |
| • Stretched canvas, size 6″ x 6″ with a 1½-inch depth |
| • Palette knife: medium size, teardrop shape with rounded tip |
| • Palette knife: small size, teardrop shape with rounded tip (optional) |
| • Palette knife: fancy tip with medium-length thin blade (optional) |
| • Palette knife: angled top (optional) |
| • Table easel or lazy Susan |
| • Palette paper |
| • Paper towel or rag for wiping your knife |

**Color Palette**

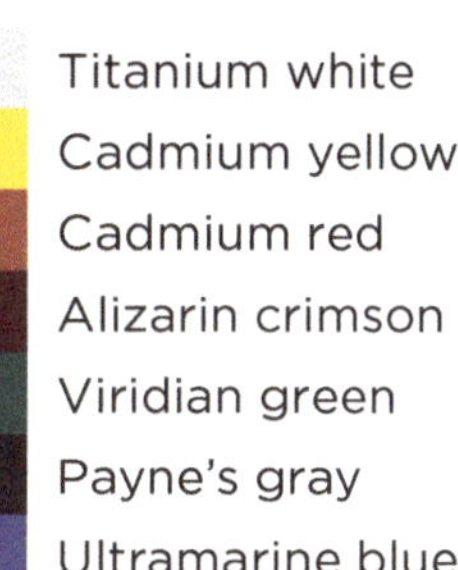

- Titanium white
- Cadmium yellow
- Cadmium red
- Alizarin crimson
- Viridian green
- Payne's gray
- Ultramarine blue

**Difficulty Level**

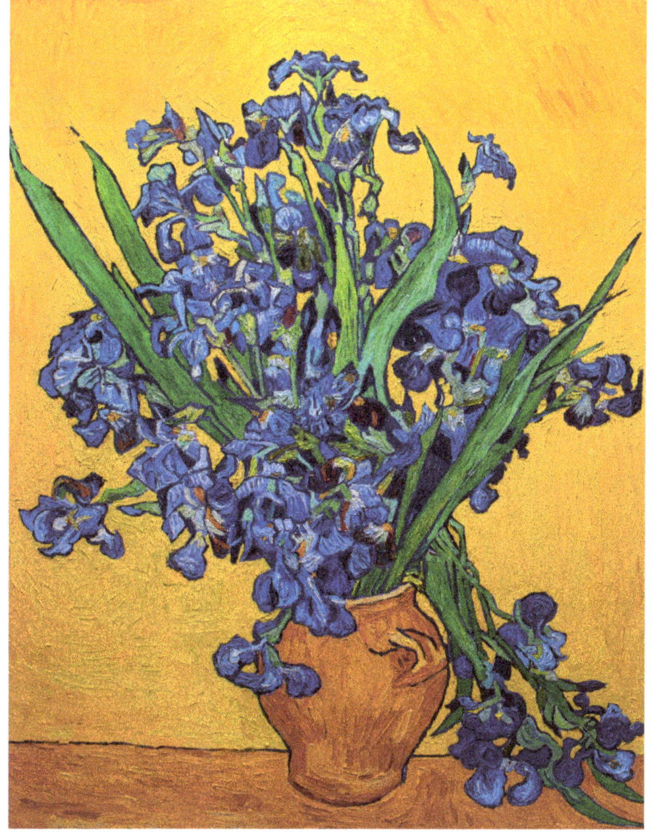

## *Inspiration*

In the summer of 2021, I was excited to have been approached by the Metropolitan Museum of Art and PBS to collaborate on a project for Instagram. I chose to paint a version of Vincent van Gogh's Irises, which is housed in the Met's permanent collection in New York City. It's a gorgeous, ethereal still-life piece, with a palette of muted pink, ultramarine blue, and viridian green. I really wanted to put a contemporary spin on the more traditional piece. The original was painted by Van Gogh in May 1890, just before he checked himself out of the asylum at Saint-Rémy, France. In *Irises*, he sought a harmonious and soft effect by placing the violet flowers against a pink background. The red background has since faded, owing to his use of fugitive red pigments. In my version, the colors are more saturated and vibrant, but still charming and harmonious. Luckily for us, with our incredible modern art materials, we have all the tools at our disposal, so let's *Gogh*!

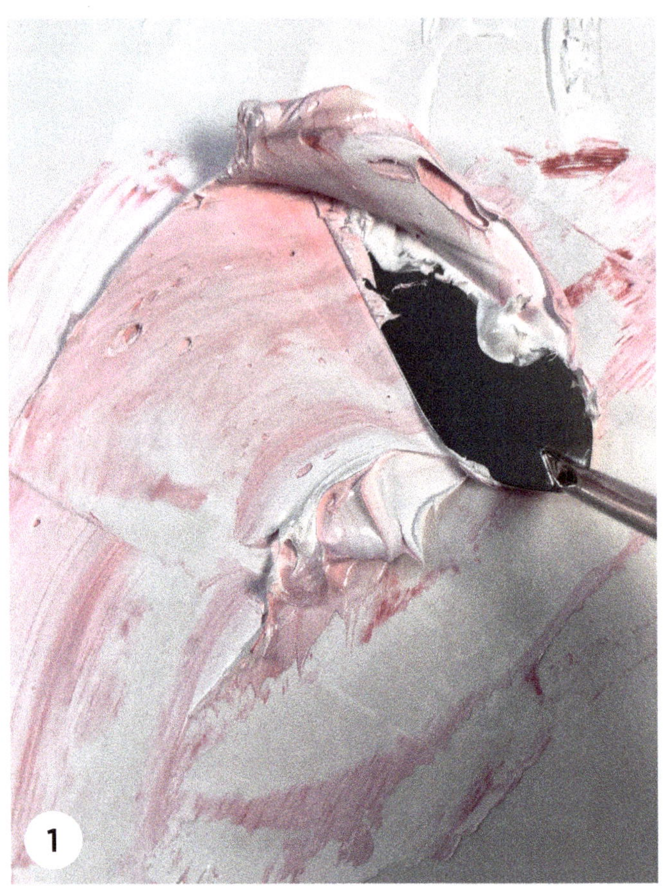
1

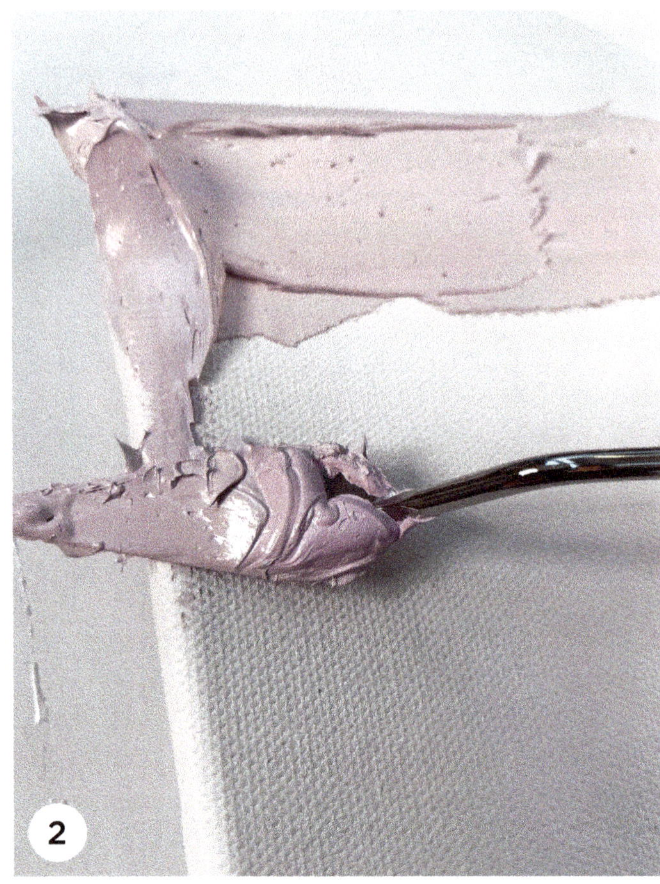
2

## Step-By-Step Instructions

**Step 1: Lay out your colors & mix your basic background color**

- Squeeze out a large blob of white paint, about the size of 3 heaped tablespoons on the top left of your palette. We are going to be blocking in the background color before filling in the vase on this piece, so we want to mix various shades of very light pink with some variations in colors to accentuate the textured wall behind the flowers.
- Squeeze out around 1 teaspoon each of cadmium yellow, cadmium red, alizarin crimson, ultramarine blue, Payne's gray, and viridian green.
- Start by dragging down 1 tablespoon of white and a ½ teaspoon of crimson. Mix them together until light pink. Then add a dot of viridian green to dull it down a little. We want this to be a fairly toned-down pink, but brighter than the original painting.
- Again, we want variations of this color, so leave some lighter and leave some streaks as well.
- Now we want to warm it up a little, so add just a tiny dot each of cadmium yellow and cadmium red.
- You should now have a nice pile of very soft mauve pink, with a few variations in hue.

**Step 2: Lay in your background**

- Load your knife with 1 tablespoon of pink, and starting at the top right of your canvas, start blocking in your background with a large sweep right across your canvas. Repeat this by reloading your knife with another tablespoon of pink and laying in a sweep from left to right. I decided to go right off the edge of the canvas here, which makes it much more modern and interesting.

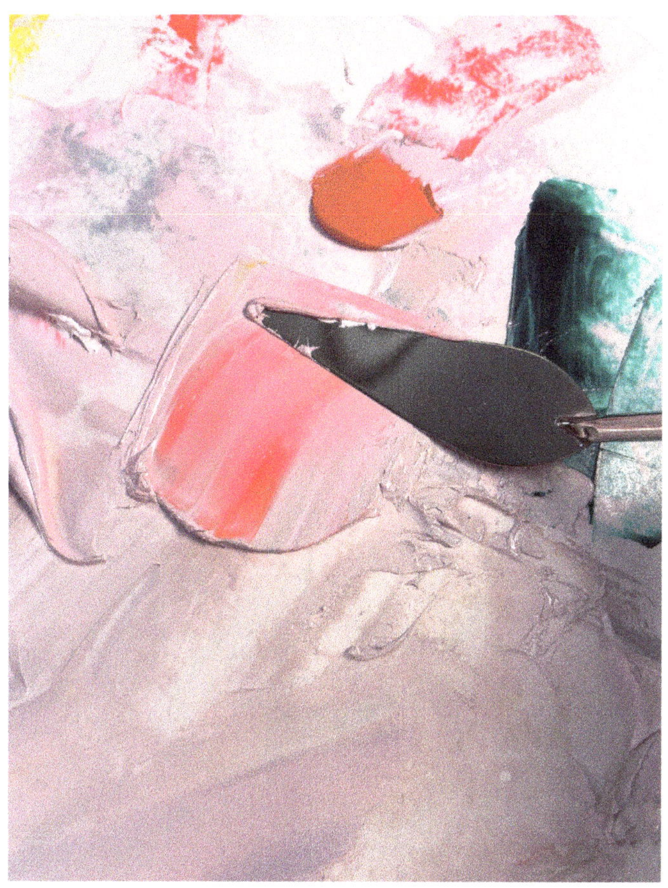

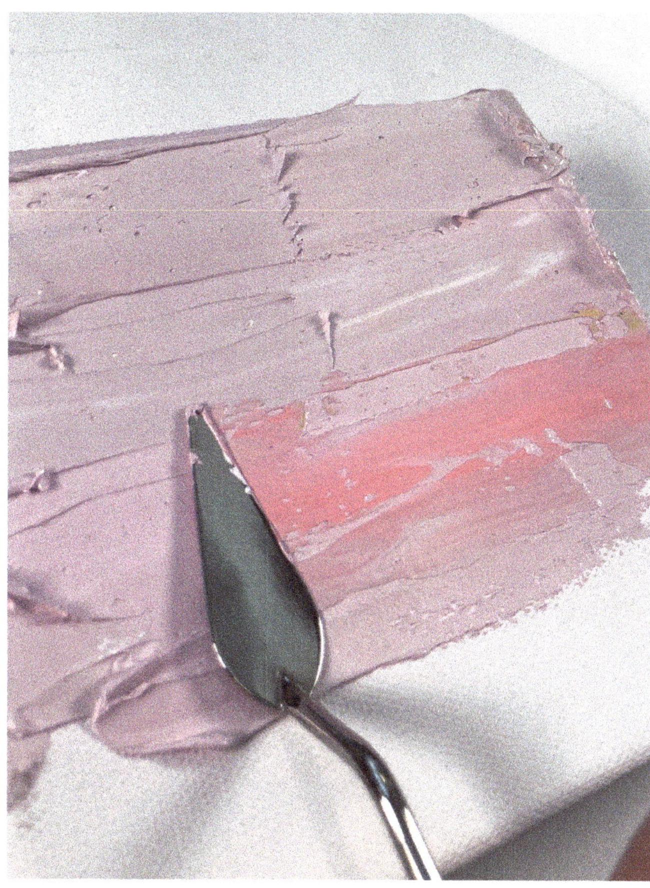

- I felt like the huge blob on the left was a little over the top, so I went ahead and tapered it off a little with a sweep downward on the edge. This is really just personal taste. Some people don't like the "off the edge" look, so just go ahead with what feels right for you.

- Continue on with your background, filling in the canvas from side to side with more paint with the same large and gestural sweeps. Stop when you get about three-quarters of the way down the canvas.

- This is where the wall joins the flat area where our vase is sitting, and we want to create some contrast here.

- Drag down a small dot of cadmium red, and mix it with about 1 teaspoon of your light pink until you have a nice, saturated coral color. We're going to skim it across the existing paint to create interest.

- Load your knife with a small tablespoon on the edge, and starting on the right, lightly glaze it across your pink paint layer while applying gentle pressure, but without blending the two layers together.

**Step 3: Lay in your green ground background**

- Now we are going to fill in our green background, and then start on the really fun part—the vase of super-textured flowers.

- Drag down 1 tablespoon of your white, and about 1 teaspoon of viridian green. Mix it so that you have a nice Van Gogh–inspired light minty green color. Then add just a dot of alizarin crimson to dull it down somewhat. Colors straight out of the tube are usually too bright, so adding the complementary color usually makes them look more realistic. Red and green are opposite on the color wheel, therefore complementary, and work well together. We also want to mix and have different

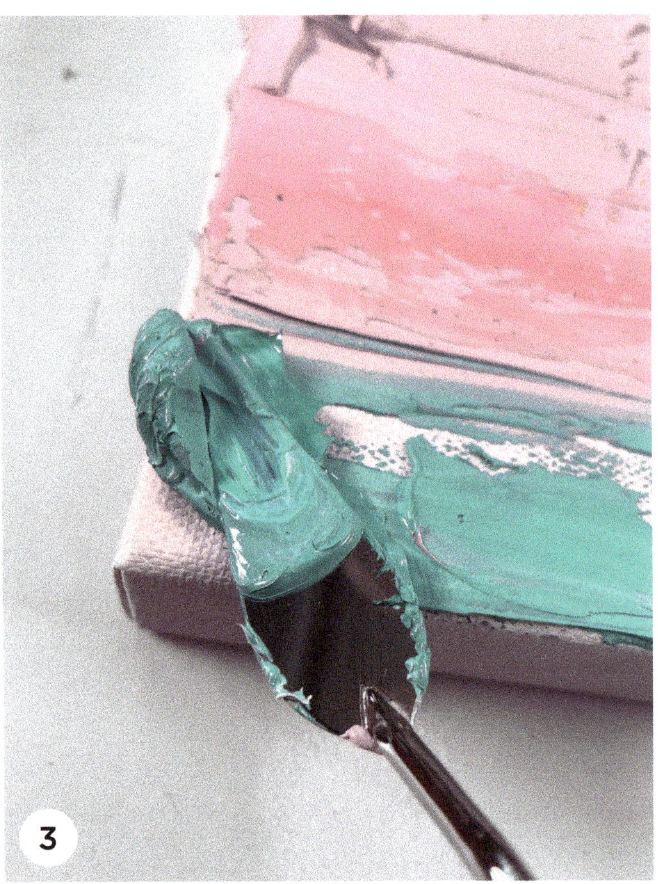


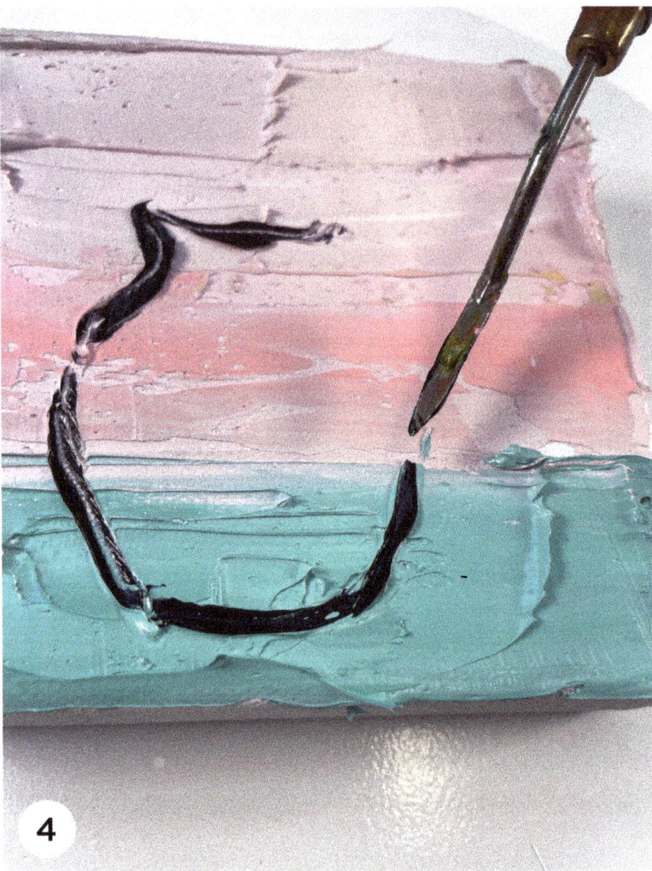


shades ready here, for both the background and the leaves in the vase, so keep some darker using more viridian green and lighten some up with white. Keep them all together on your palette ready to go.

- Start laying in your mint green background. Load about 1 tablespoon of the green on your knife, and sweep across the canvas from right to left, positioning it so that the tip of the knife drags through the bottom of the pink paint layer in a straight line, blending slightly, and creating a natural straight line. Wipe your knife and load another tablespoon of green. Start on the left and sweep your knife right, filling in the white canvas. I went off the edge again here just for fun.

**Step 4: Sketching in the vase**

- Now we're going to sketch the outline of our vase using a detailing palette knife. If you don't have this knife, you can use a regular or medium one instead. Drag down around 1 teaspoon of Payne's gray and mix it so that it is nice and pliable. No texture here, we're just sketching the dark outline over the top of the pink and green background.

- Load the tip and middle portion of your knife with a small amount of the Payne's gray, and begin sketching in your vase, starting in the top middle and lightly to the left, in a small arc.

- Wipe your knife and reload, and then start sketching in the left side of the vase in a curved shape, matching up the edges. This does not have to be perfect by any means, but it really helps to keep the knife very clean and not to use too much or too thick an amount of the dark color. You can easily scrape the dark paint out, smooth the pink over, and try again if necessary.

- We also don't want to try to do the entire side of the vase here. It's too hard and too great a distance to cover without reloading the knife. We'll run out of paint and lose the dark outline as well, so it's better to sketch in the lines in small increments.

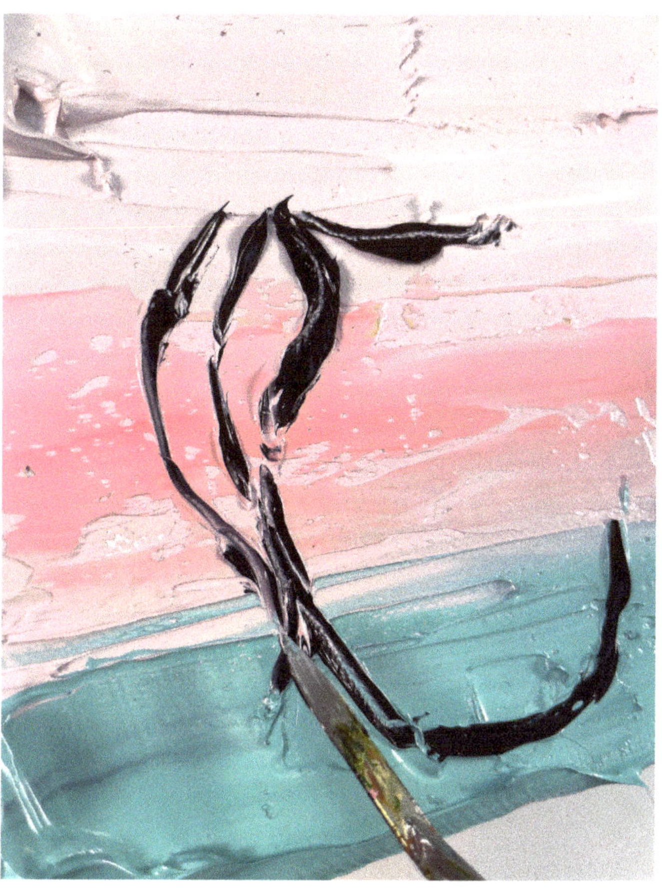

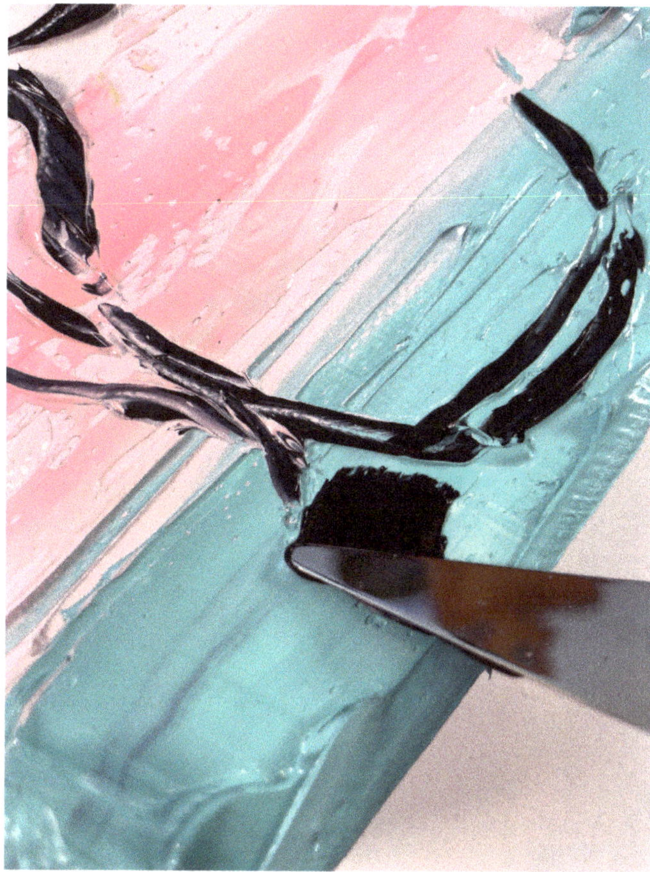

- Wipe and reload your knife, and start sketching in the bottom of the vase where it sits on the green, in a small arc, but making sure it's bigger than the top arc. Then wipe and reload, and continue sketching in the left side of the vase, following the natural curve of where the edge would sit. Now repeat this on the right side, ending just under halfway up. We don't need to fill in this portion, as the flowers spill out of the vase and cover this portion, so if we place the dark color here, it will interfere with the flowers and muddy the colors.

- Now we'll continue on to the handle. Wipe and reload your knife, and sketch in the dark handle using the same technique, making a curve, tapering off at the thickest portion of the vase, but then continuing to create another curved portion that protrudes further down, which is the end of the handle.

- Now finish the handle by wiping and reloading your knife, and then sketching in the top portion, following the curve of the previous edge.

- Wipe again and reload; then sketch in another line following the arc on the bottom.

- The last portion with our Payne's gray is to sketch in the shadow of the vase. Using your regular knife, go ahead and load the flat tip portion, and sweep it across the green on the left side of the vase, keeping it straight and moving it toward the left, barely touching the base of the vase. This portion looks best when the line is horizontal, so if you've accidentally made it too large or blobby, go ahead and scrape off the dark paint moving sideways from right to left, using either the tip of the knife, or the sharp edge, twisted on its side.

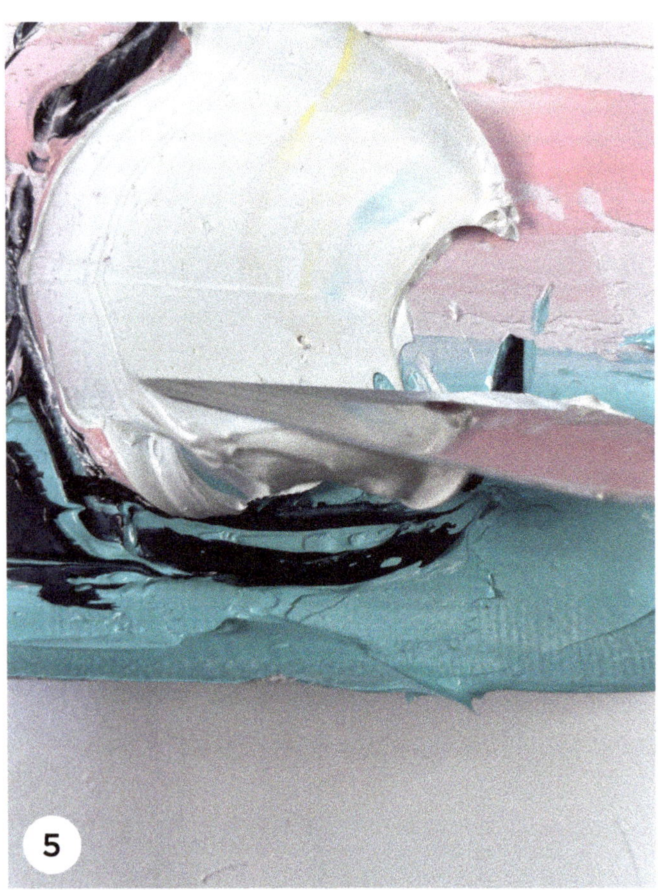


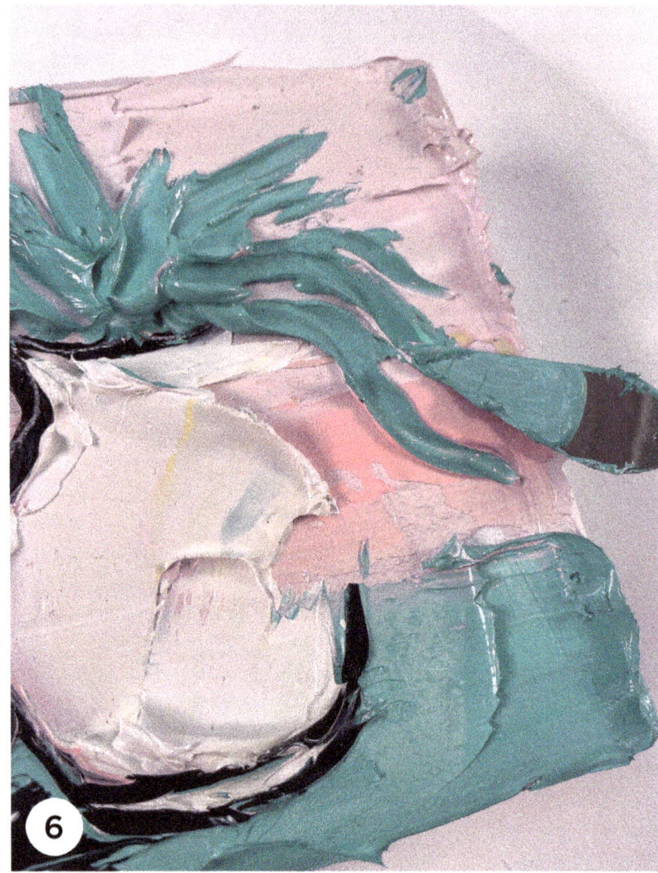


**Step 5: Adding the white to the vase**

- Now we're really going to start building up the texture on the vase. Drag down a couple of tablespoons of white and a dot of yellow and mix. Load your knife with 1 tablespoon and start at the top of the vase, but be careful not to cover the dark edges that you have sketched in. Place a sweep moving downward toward the center of the vase, filling up as much of the interior vase shape as you can.

- There are some nice, organic yellow streaks if you look closely, as a result of not mixing entirely. These always add more interest. Plus in this case, they dull down the stark white just a fraction.

- Wipe and reload your knife, and continue with another highly textured portion, starting this time at the bottom and drawing the knife upward.

- Next, we'll fill in the handle. Draw your knife through the paint sideways and downwards, which scoops up a ridge of thicker paint. We want a thinner, textured portion here to color in the handle between the two dark lines.

- Place the tip of the knife at the top of the canvas, and gently pull your knife down, letting the textured paint slide off onto your handle, trying not to go over your black lines. We also want a little portion of white at the bottom that curves outward, to give the handle that classic curved shape. If you're using a lazy Susan, it's easier to swivel your painting upside down to capture this detail. I also needed to touch up the dark color a little, so using my thin palette knife, I reloaded with Payne's gray and sketched in the dark lines around the end of my handle, just to tidy it up a little.

**Step 6: Adding the green stems**

- Drag down 1 teaspoon of viridian green and 1 tablespoon of white and mix. Load your knife with a tablespoon of this mix on the edge, and with the tip pointing outward toward the edge of the canvas, start laying in your stems by placing the paint on the canvas in strips, applying gentle

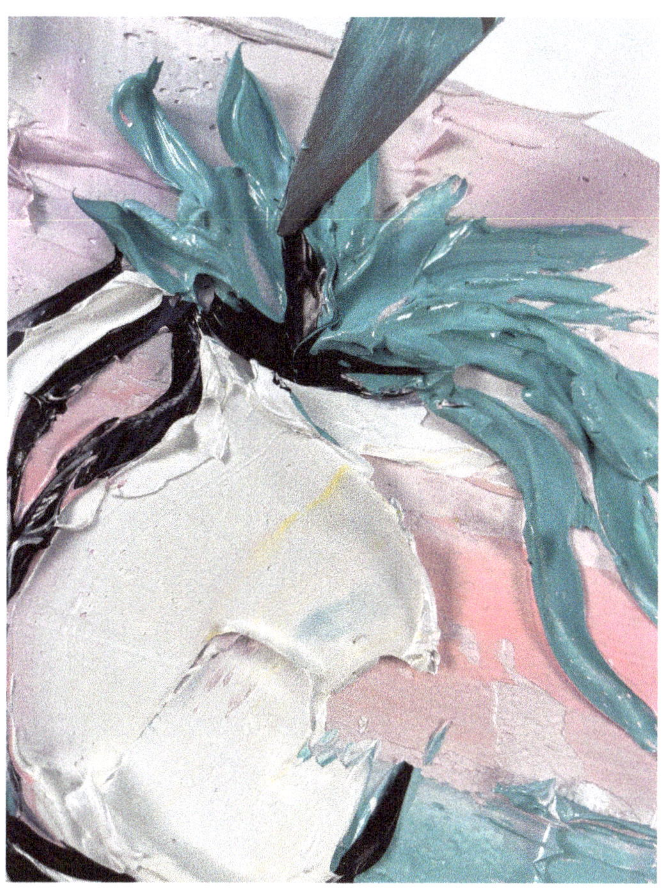

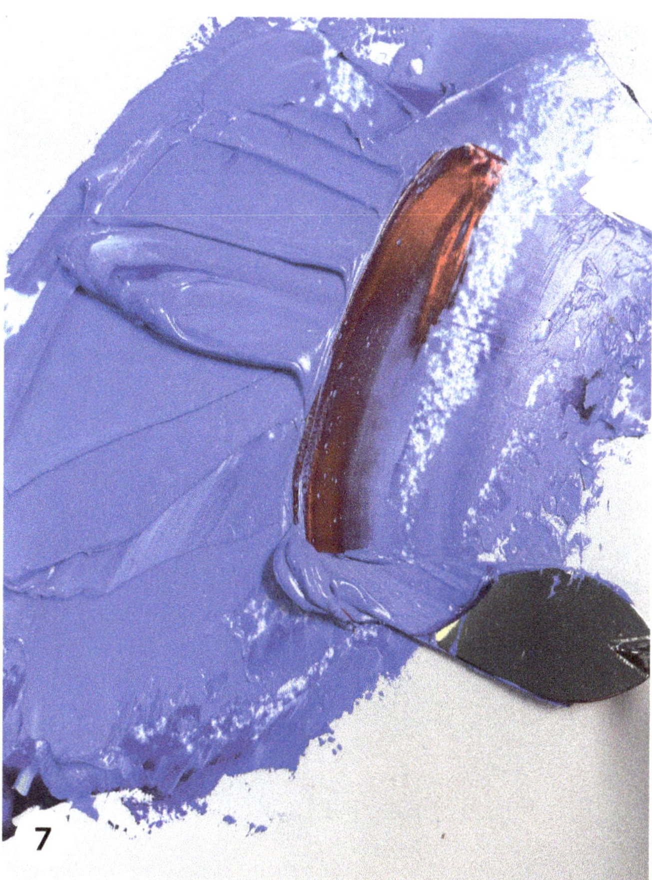
7

pressure and pulling the knife up before you go over the dark edge of the vase.

- Wipe and reload your knife, and repeat this again, making sure you are placing in strips in a fan shape, connecting to the opening of the vase.

- If you're using a lazy Susan, you can swivel your painting upside down and place in some strips starting at the vase opening, ending before the edge of the canvas. This will add a little more diversity to the shape of your stems.

- Keep these strips a fairly uniform height. Toward the right of our canvas, we're going to add some longer stems and leaves that fall over to accentuate the flowers cascading out of the vase. Add several longer strips on the right, gently flowing downward, until you have covered all the space moving upwards at the opening of the vase. Be careful not to squish the stems together. We want the pink background to peek through here.

- Now mix a little of your Payne's gray and sketch in a little more dark definition at the base of the stems where they meet the vase. We want a nice dark contrast here, and I went over the dark line a little when I was laying in the stems. I also dragged a little of the dark paint upward with the side of my knife to give the stems more definition.

**Step 7: Adding the blue flowers**

- Now the best part! Adding the super-textured flowers is always the joyful ending and really brings the piece to life. I'm usually eager to finish at this point. The momentum is moving everything along, and I'm ready to feel a sense of accomplishment.

- Drag down about 1 tablespoon of ultramarine blue and a couple of tablespoons of white and mix loosely. Drag down a dot of cadmium red, and mix it in with the blue to dull it down just a little. Streaks of blue and white are OK here, but try to blend in your cadmium red well.

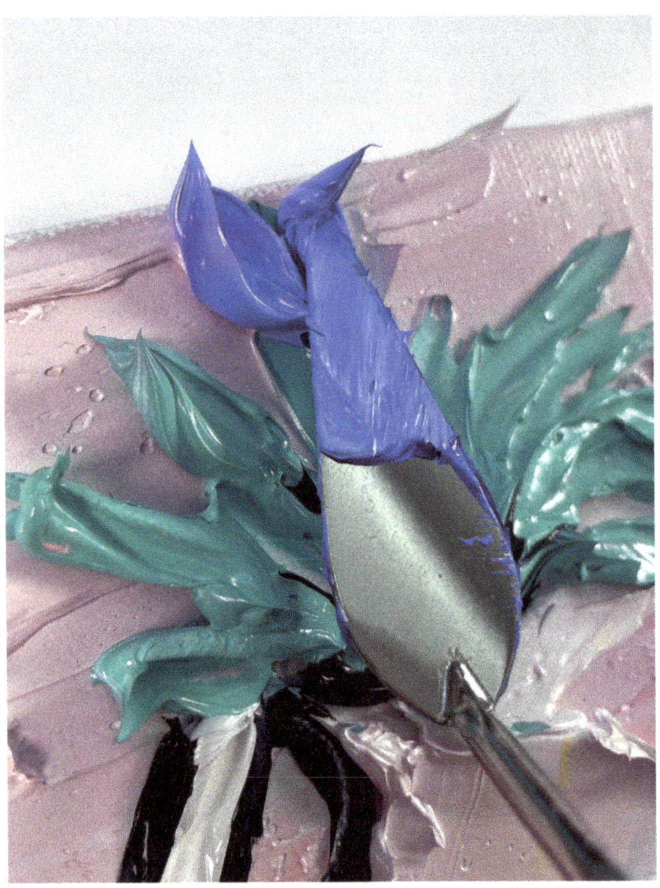

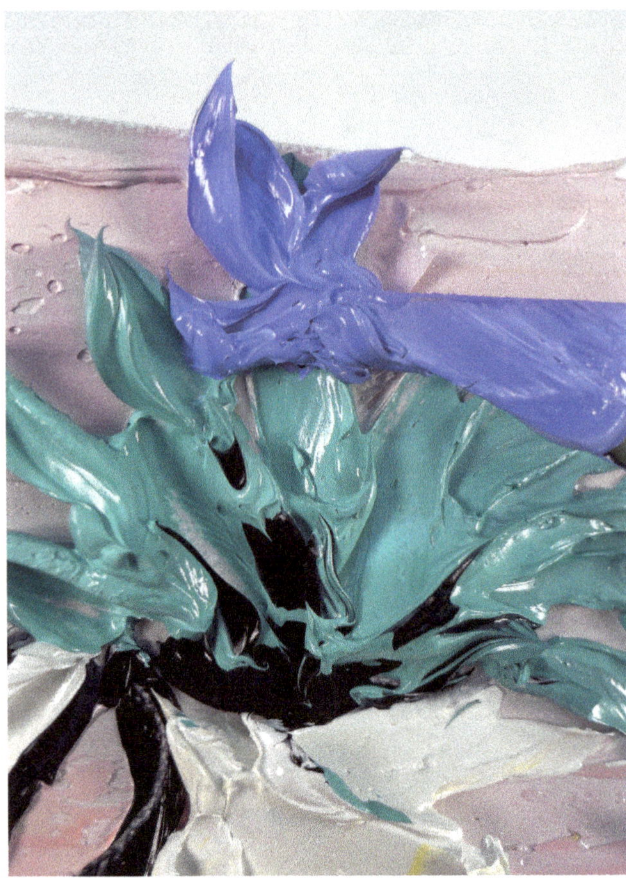

- Load your knife on the tip with ½ teaspoon of blue. We're detailing now, so we're using more of the tip of the knife. We're also wanting more of a sliver than a blob, so when you load your knife, you're dragging it down your palette for about ½ inch, as well as rotating your hand clockwise slightly and scooping, which will elongate the portion left on your knife.

- Starting in the center of your stems at the top, place (don't dab) in your first iris petal by laying the tip of your knife on the canvas and drag the knife down just a little bit before pulling it up, applying pressure so that the paint sticks to the canvas and you leave the blue sliver behind in a longish petal shape.

- It may help to switch to your smaller knife here. I've been doing this for a very long time, so I can maneuver the larger knife to accommodate the smaller details, but a smaller knife works really well here too and is easier to handle.

- Wipe your knife and reload, and continue with another petal next to the first one on the right, using the same technique.

- Note that mine are protruding from the top of the canvas somewhat. I do this by positioning the tip of my knife so that the paint sits just off the edge, then applying gentle pressure so that the paint sticks. I pull it down and then pull up the knife.

- Now we'll fill in the bottom petals. With a clean knife, and using the same technique to load the knife, position the tip of the knife slightly off to the left of your existing petals, but more horizontal and draw the knife sideways toward the center of the flower. If you have a lazy Susan, you can swivel it to position the canvas where it feels right to complete the angles and direction of the petals.

- For our last petal, we want to repeat this step, starting on the outside on the right and drawing the petal inward toward the center of the flower. Again, with a lazy Susan, you can turn the canvas upside down to complete this. It's a little tricky, and a good rule to remember is that you

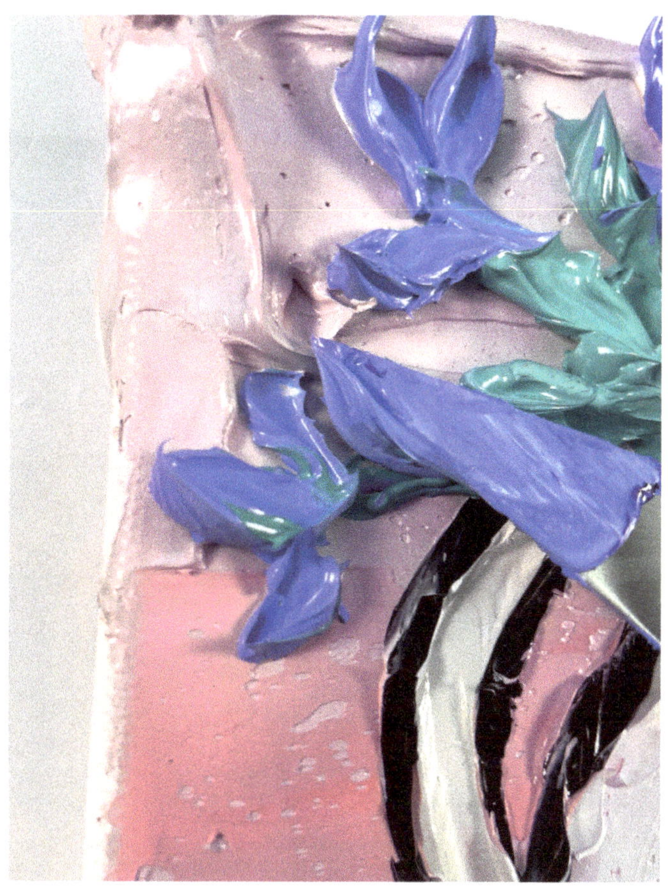

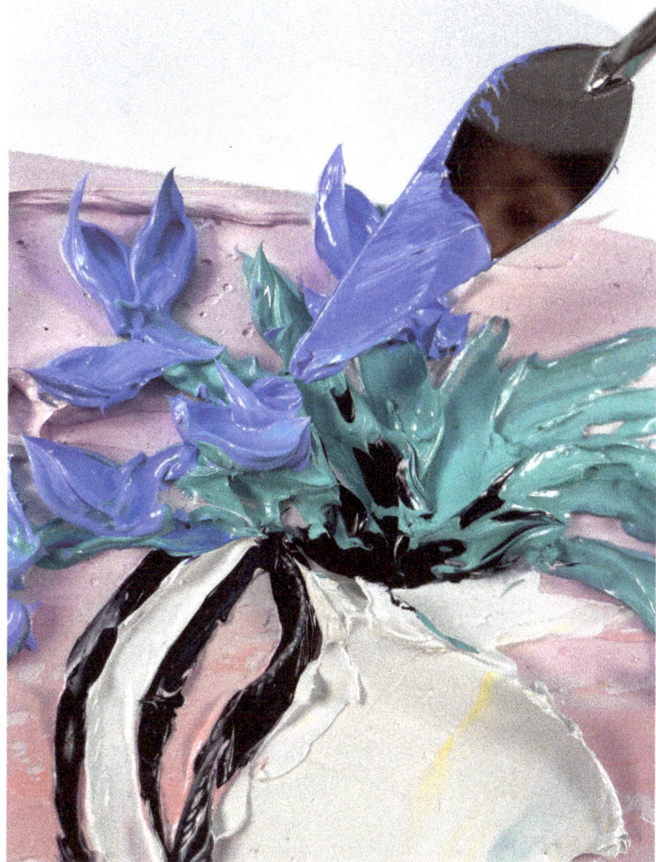

are mostly drawing the tip of the knife outward coming in toward the center of the flower, rather than the other way round. If you don't have a lazy Susan, I recommend picking up these smaller canvases and holding them upside down or swiveling them around to get at these more directional details. You can even paint them straight on a tabletop, flat.

- Repeat this technique, making another flower on the left. I made mine a little bigger, as we want some variation here.

- Then create another one right above the top of the handle, but take care not to go over the paint on the handle here. At this point, I start loosening the flowers up, so that they're not all the same or perfectly formed. So, my third one only has three petals before I start on the next flower right next to it. It's also important not to smoosh them all together. You'll end up with a mess of textured paint and lose the color-blocked effect.

- As we move over the highly textured green paint, it becomes harder to place the blue paint on top. Thick upon thick is tricky! When the paint underneath is very textured, I'm usually adding more of a suggestion on top, versus a perfectly formed and textured flower. Go ahead and dot them on, and leave them here. Fussing won't help. If you really don't like your blue petals, you can scoop them off with the tip of your knife, replace the green, and start over. If you do this, try to keep your strokes as large as you can to avoid a fussed-with appearance.

- Move on now to the right-hand stems. We've done enough on the left, and any more will start to muddy what we already have. I place another flower to the right of my very first one and then another to the right of this, at the tip of the stems, but not higher, as we don't want them to appear to be floating. These often only have around three petals and are quite fast and loose, dancing around the stems. We want them to be inconsistent, and I dot in a few singular petals that give the appearance of peeking through the stems as well.

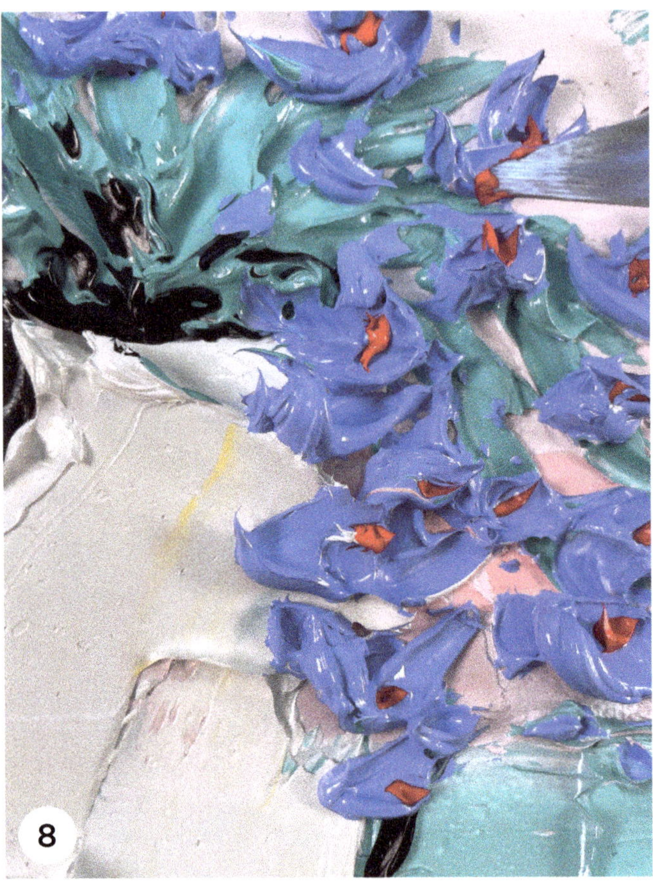


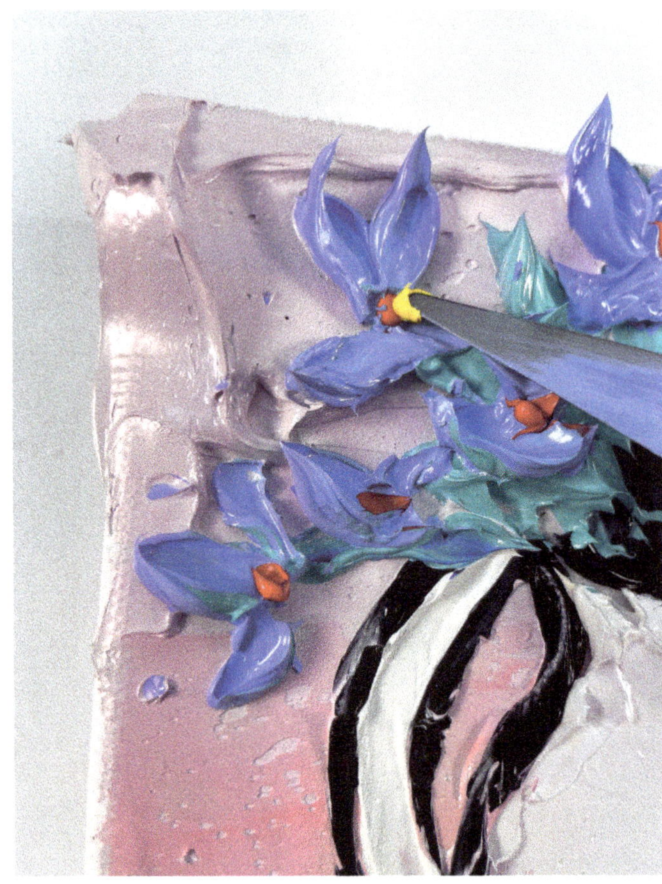

- I continue down the drooping stems, placing more petals here and there. We're getting small here, so instead of trying to paint in smaller complete flowers, I continue with the loose petals until I fill the green stem area with a good coverage of the petals, ending at the bottom of the vase where the white paint runs out.

**Step 8: Laying in the red & yellow flower details**

- Let's get these flowers done and finish the piece. Using the very end portion of your knife, load a tiny dot on the tip and dot it in the center of one of your blue flowers—gently placing it, without pressing it down too hard. Wipe your knife and repeat, placing a red dot in the center of every complete flower. Also add some to your broken up flowers, randomly placing dots throughout the textured blue petals. Don't overdo it here though. You can also use your smaller knife here if you prefer.
- Now repeat this with yellow paint, placing the dots slightly to the right of the little red ones and not directly on top.

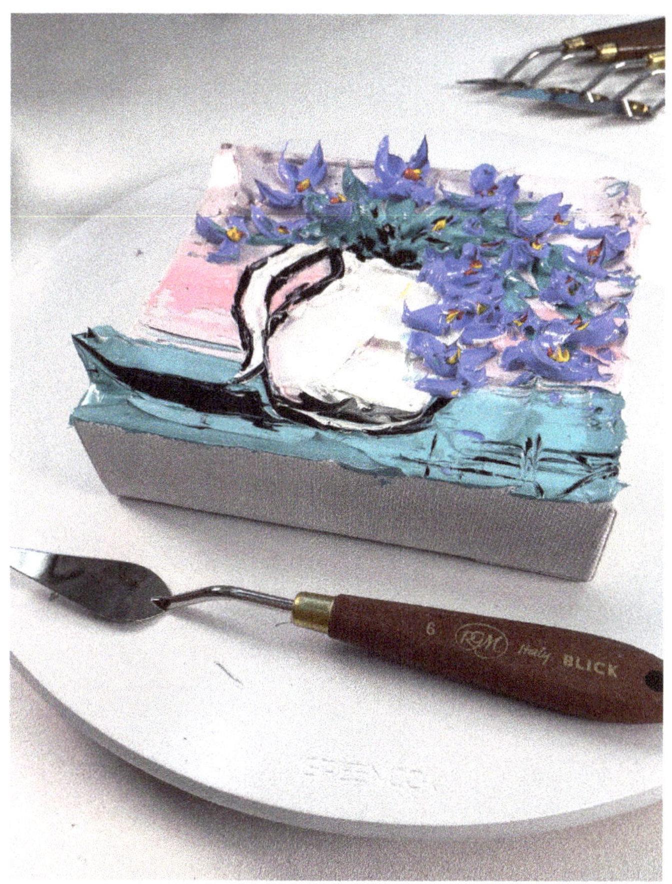


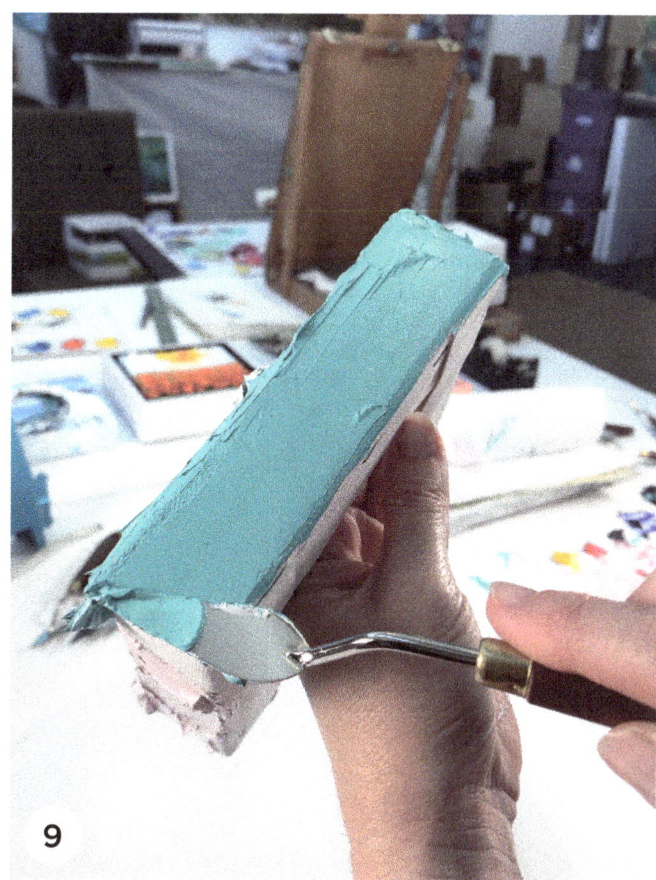

9

**Step 9: Paint the edges**

- Using up the last of my pink paint, I go ahead and finish the edges with back and forth and up and down strokes. It's important to follow the looseness of the painting and make the edges inconsistent and gestural, so I vary the types of strokes I use here a lot as I work quickly toward covering the white canvas. Again, with a tiny canvas, I find it's easier to pick it up and paint it while swiveling it around. Match up the green sides, not worrying about being exact, covering the entire canvas with your leftover paint. Finally, paint the bottom with large sideways strokes. I usually make the bottom edge fairly flat and less textured, so the painting can sit on a shelf if needed.

>>> Tip <<<

These little paintings look gorgeous on a bookshelf staged with other items.

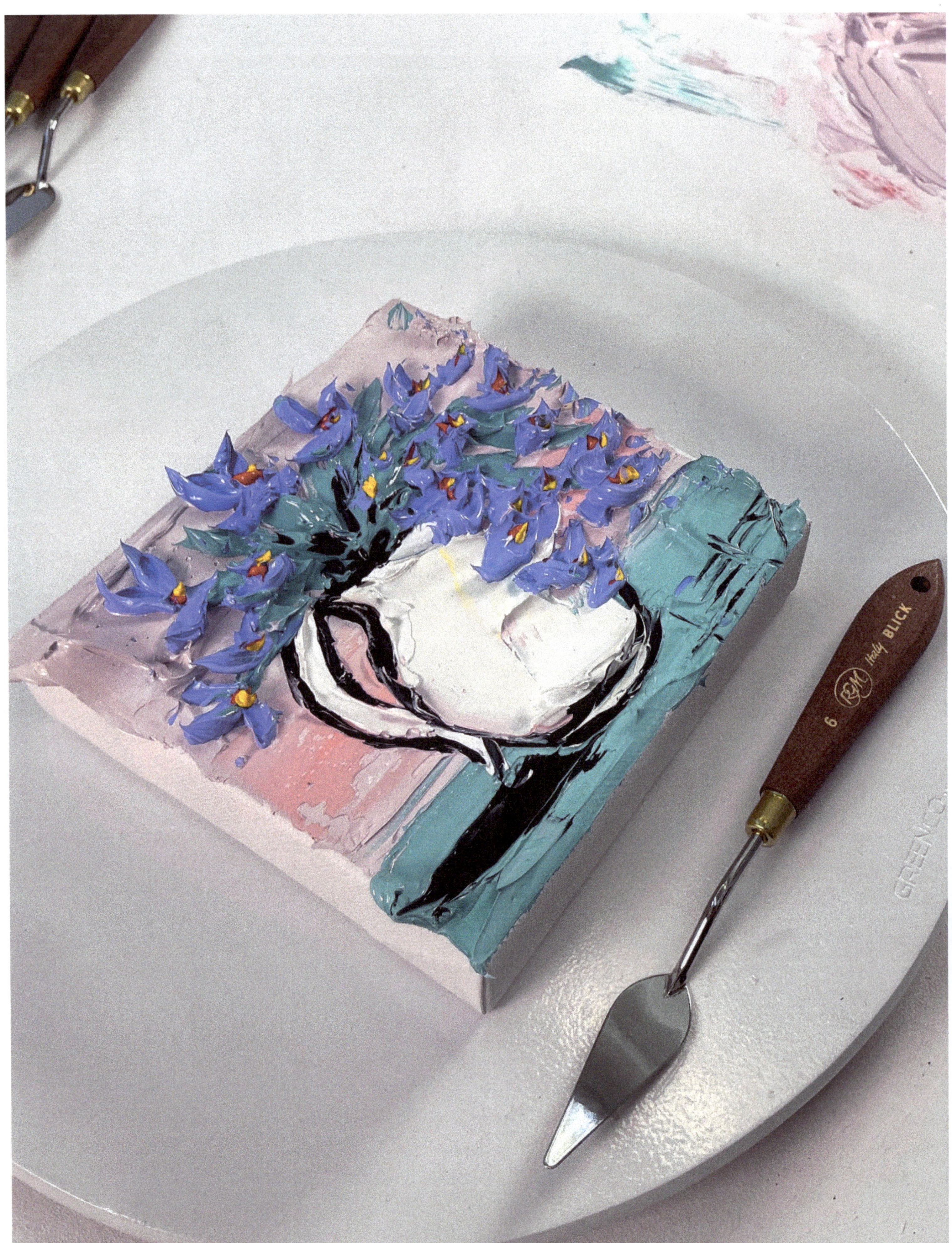
6 RGM Italy BLICK

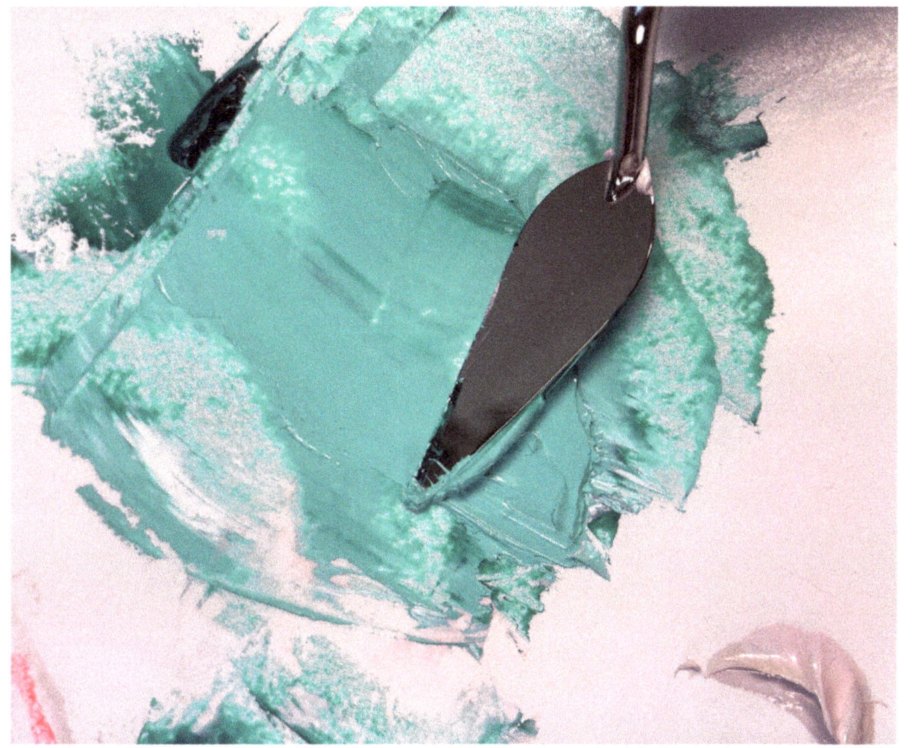

## SUMMARY:

### How'd it Gogh?

I hope you got your fix of Van Gogh–inspired irises with this piece. I just love the dreamy color palette with the complementary pink and green, and the way the blue flowers leap off the canvas.

As usual, this piece is harder than it looks, so my advice is to keep practicing as much as you can, doing little portions every day if possible. This is how I honed my skill over the years, by daily painting and making sure I'm enjoying what I'm doing.

Some paintings look better than others with heavy texture, and this one balances itself out perfectly with the textured vase, even more textured stems, and then extreme texture in the little flowers.

*"If you truly love nature, you will find beauty everywhere."*

—VINCENT VAN GOGH

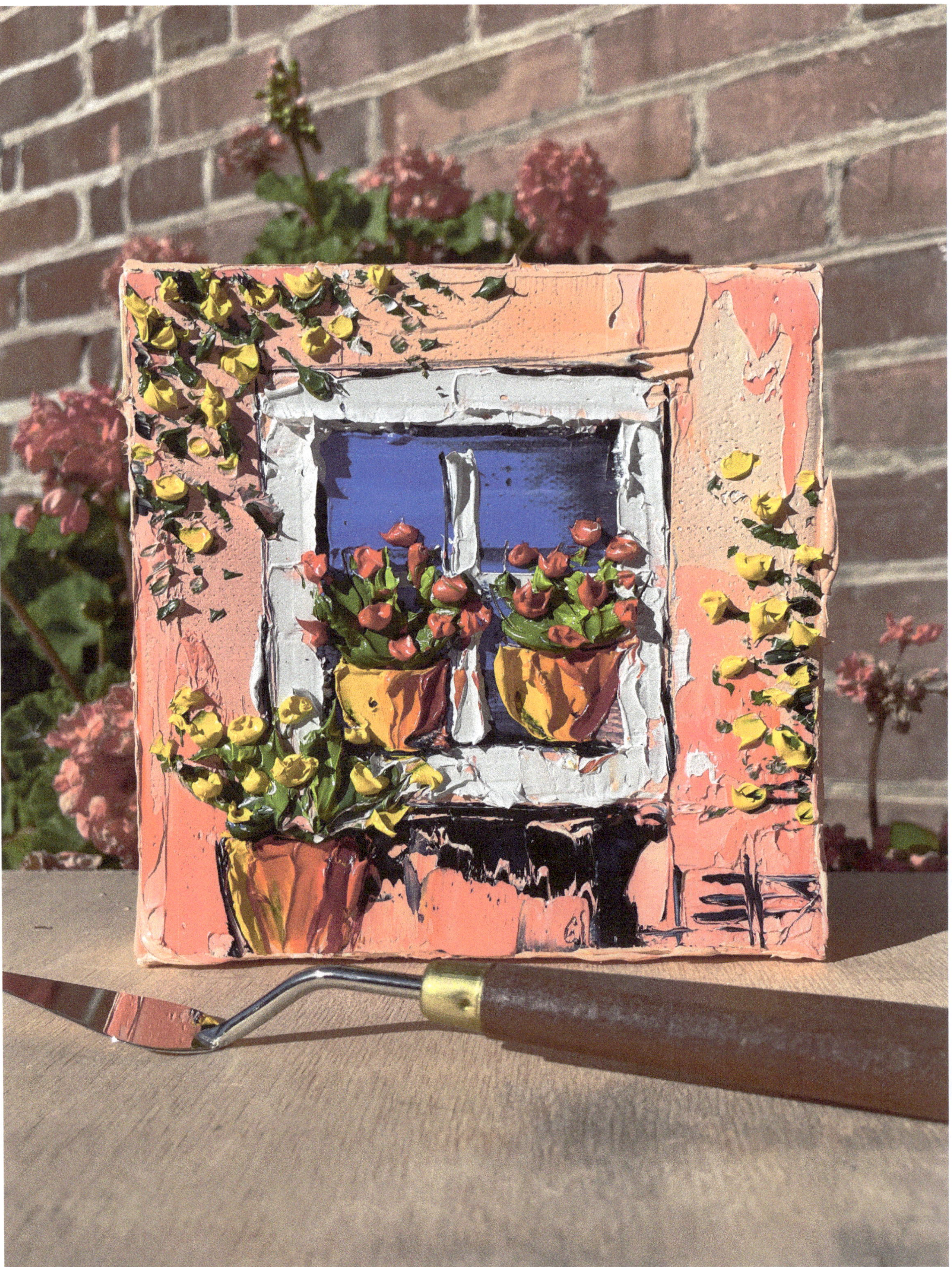

# (THE LITTLE HOUSE) PICCOLA CASA

| Tools & Materials | Color Palette | Difficulty Level |
|---|---|---|
| • Stretched canvas, size 6″ x 6″ with a 1½-inch depth<br>• Palette knife: Medium size, teardrop shape with rounded tip<br>• Palette knife: Small size, teardrop shape with rounded tip<br>• Palette knife; long, skinny blade (optional)<br>• Table easel or lazy Susan<br>• Palette paper<br>• Paper towel or rag for wiping your knife | Titanium white<br>Cadmium yellow<br>Cadmium red<br>Alizarin crimson<br>Ultramarine blue<br>Sap green<br>Payne's gray | <br> |





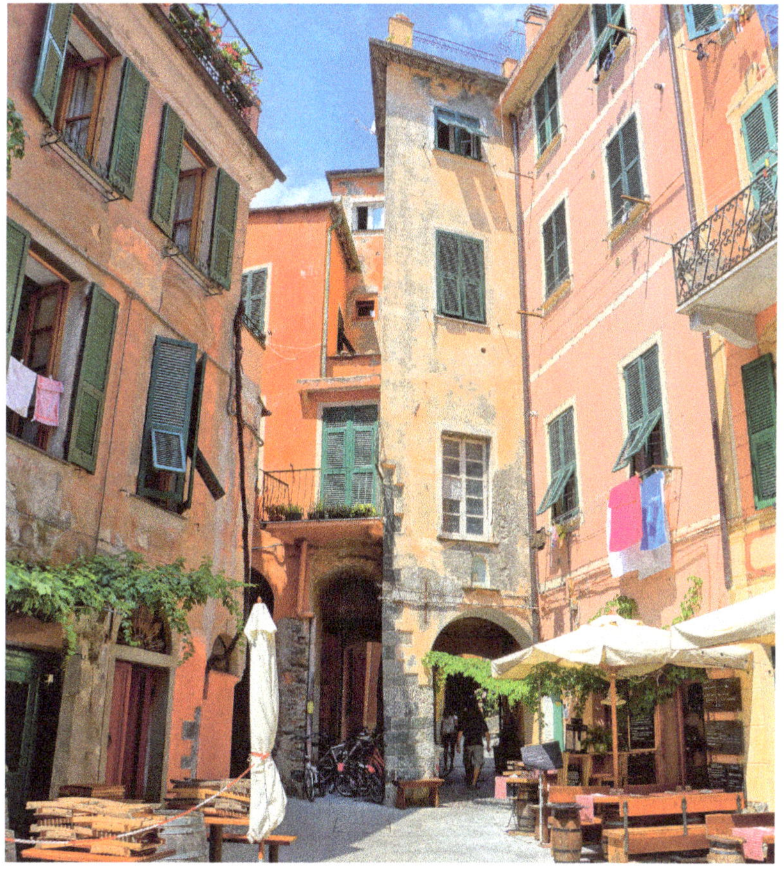

## Inspiration

This painting was inspired by my travels around Europe as a young college graduate. With a train ticket and my backpack, I went from London to Paris, then on to Barcelona, and back up the coast to the French Riviera. Monaco and Nice were sunbaked and glamorous, and everything I ever dreamed of. I then crossed the border to Italy and saw Genoa, Verona, Venice, Rome, and Pisa, ending up on the dreamy Amalfi Coast, before heading back to the UK via Switzerland. Nothing opens the mind quite like travel, and I still remember this experience very vividly, which is why it became the inspiration for so many of my cityscape and architectural pieces. I've always loved the melding of architecture and nature, so thick stone walls with pots of colorful geraniums are my happy place.

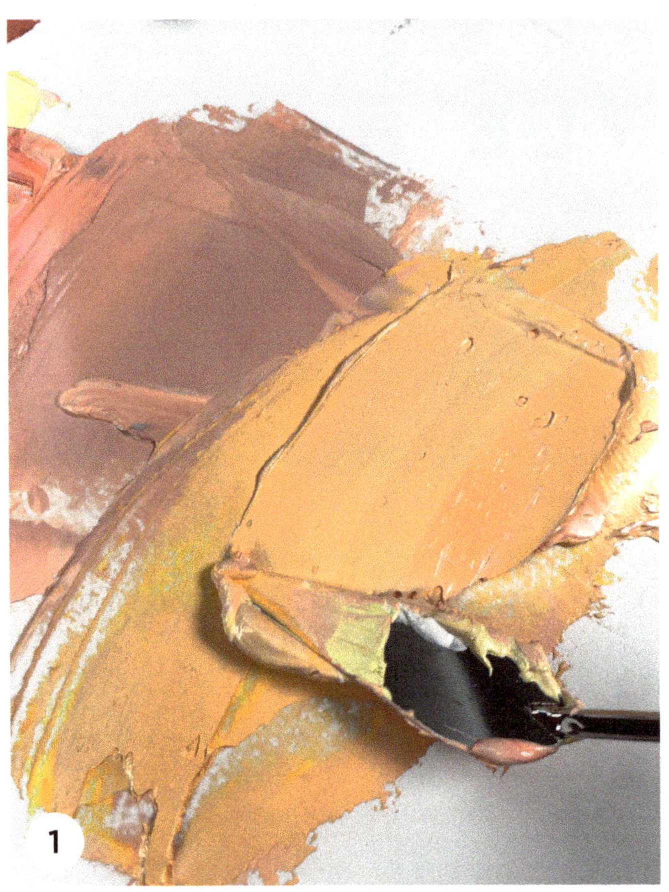

1

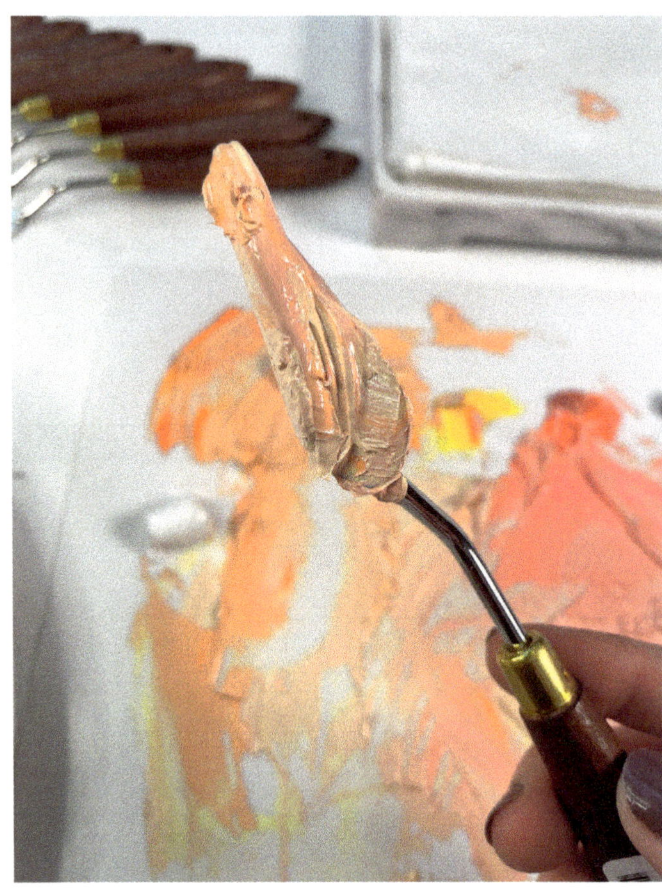

## Step-By-Step Instructions

**Step 1: Lay out your colors & mix your background peach color**

- Squeeze out a large blob of white paint, about the size of 3 heaped tablespoons on the top left of your palette. We are going to be filling in the entire background first on this piece, before laying the window and the flowers on top, so we want to mix the right amount of peach color with some variations in values to denote the stone texture.

- Here's where the palette knife is perfect for portraying old stone walls. You'll find (with practice) that skimming your knife along will naturally create an inconsistent and rustic look. It suggests you spent many hours fiddling with a brush to achieve the look of an old brick wall, and it actually only took you a few seconds!

- Squeeze out about 1 teaspoon each of cadmium yellow and cadmium red, alizarin crimson, sap green, ultramarine blue, and Payne's gray. Again, I like to put them in that order across the top of my palette from left to right so that I can drag the paint down to mix it with my palette knife, adding to it as I go.

- First, we are going to make the peach color. This is my go-to color base for a few different motifs, such as European buildings, beach sand (dulled down), sunsets, desertscapes, and flowers.

- Drag down around 2 tablespoons of white, and then drag down about 1 teaspoon each of cadmium yellow and cadmium red. Don't mix them all together immediately, but pull in pea-sized amounts of the yellow and mix. Then pull in a pea-sized amount of the cadmium red and mix until you have a light peach color.

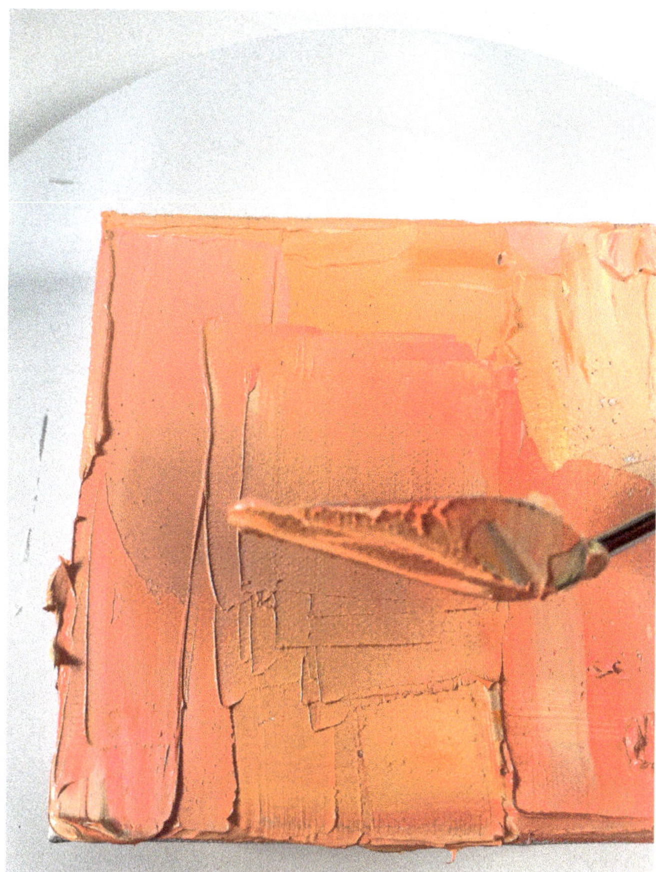

- We don't want to mix too dark here and have a batch of too-dark background color, so go slowly, and keep adding the colors to the white until you reach the shade you like. Old stone walls are faded and patchy, with worn bricks, scratches, and stains, so we want our paint to be a little streaky as well. I usually mix a variation of shades here and leave them on my palette ready to go. I pull in just a tiny dab of green into a portion of the light peach, to dull it down and make it less saturated. I also pull some alizarin crimson into a portion of the light peach to make a pinker variation and a more orange shade as well.

- Once we have these shades all mixed, we're ready to go!

**Step 2: Lay in your background**

- Load your knife with about 1 tablespoon of the midtone peach color, keeping the streaks and start at the top right of your canvas. Pull the paint down the canvas in one long sweep.

- We're starting vertically here, and with palette knife painting, it's important to always be thinking about the movement of the piece. Walls and structures go up and down, so the direction of your paint, especially with the streaks showing, gives the appearance of a vertical wall.

- Reload your knife with another smaller tablespoon, and here I'm swiping sideways from right to left on the top portion of the canvas. We don't want the entire painting to have up and down strokes. We also want some variation, so applying a couple of horizontal strokes gives it more interest and breaks up the vertical lines.

- Now reload your knife with the darker pink hue, again about a tablespoon, and do one long sweep on the left side of your canvas, as far down as you can go.

- Note the variations in color here, and the natural, textured look that the palette knife strokes are making organically.

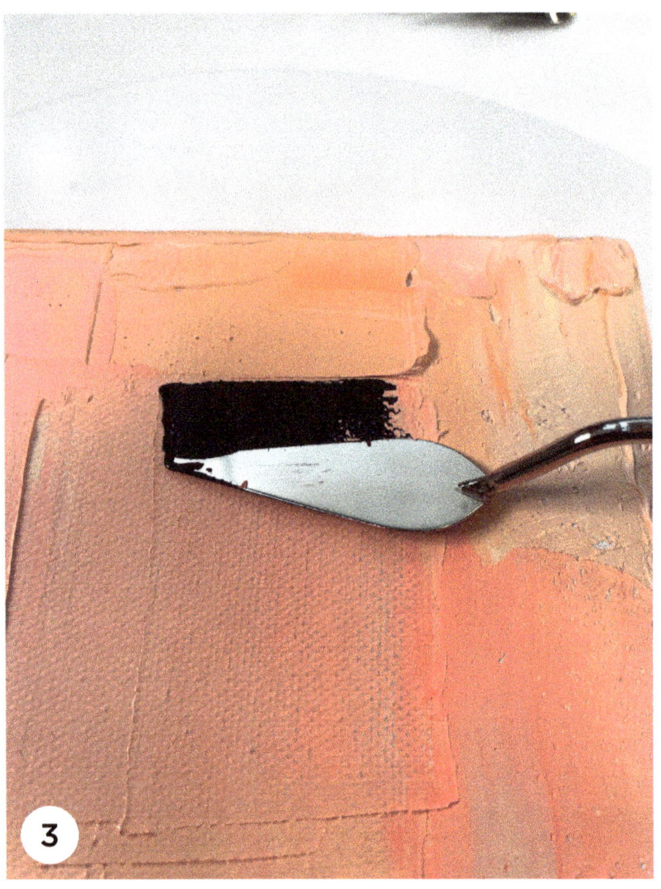

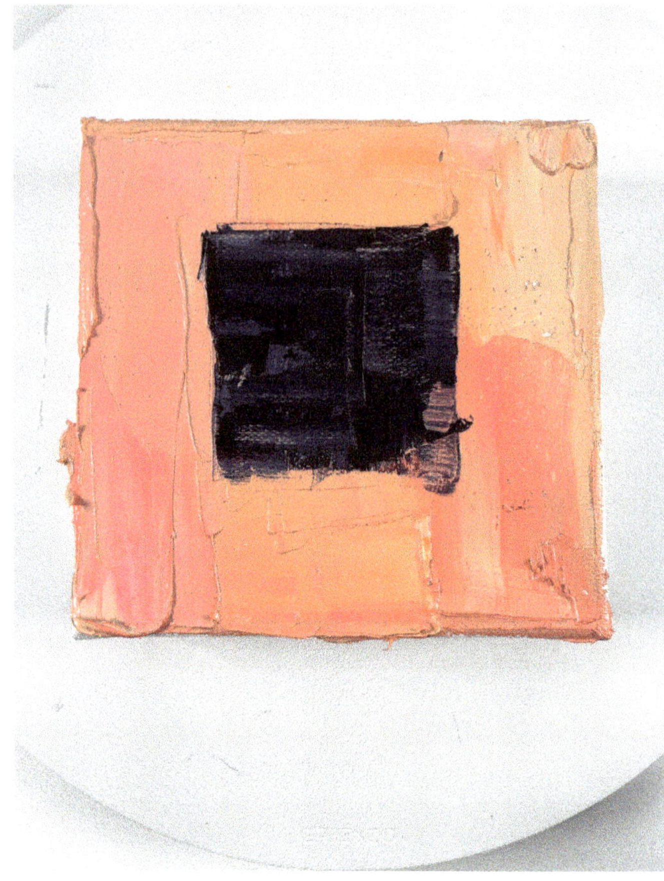

- So now we're going to fill in the rest of the canvas, starting with the bottom. Load your knife with 1 tablespoon of your darker, more pink shade, and starting at the bottom of the canvas, place your knife at the edge and swipe it up toward the center of the painting. To make this easier, I use the lazy Susan and swivel it around so that the painting is upside down, and I am pulling the stroke downward. This feels more natural and organic than starting at the bottom and going up, but if you're using an easel, go from bottom to top (unless you turn your canvas upside down on the easel—you can do that too).

- There's a distinct variation in the color here, and I'm leaving it just the way it is, as it's interesting and dynamic. Remember to leave the happy accidents alone! Don't give in to the lure of "fixing" them. It usually doesn't make them any better and just makes your painting look overworked and fiddled with.

- Repeat this motion on the left side, filling in the square canvas with a long swipe. Then using a sideways motion, fill in the last border portion with a large swipe from your reloaded knife.

- Lastly, we want to fill in the center portion, but keep the paint quite thin here. This is where our window is going to be situated, and we really just want to wet the canvas here, and not so much build up the texture.

**Step 3: Lay in your window**

- Now we are going to carve out our window, and things will start to take shape and get more exciting.

- Drag down your Payne's gray and mix it so that it's nice and pliable.

- Load your knife with about 1 teaspoon of the Payne's gray. Scoop up a ridge or sliver of paint on the edge of the blade. The object here is to cover the square portion of the window in the dark color, skimming it right over the top of the peach. We're not building up texture here, so we don't need a huge amount of paint.

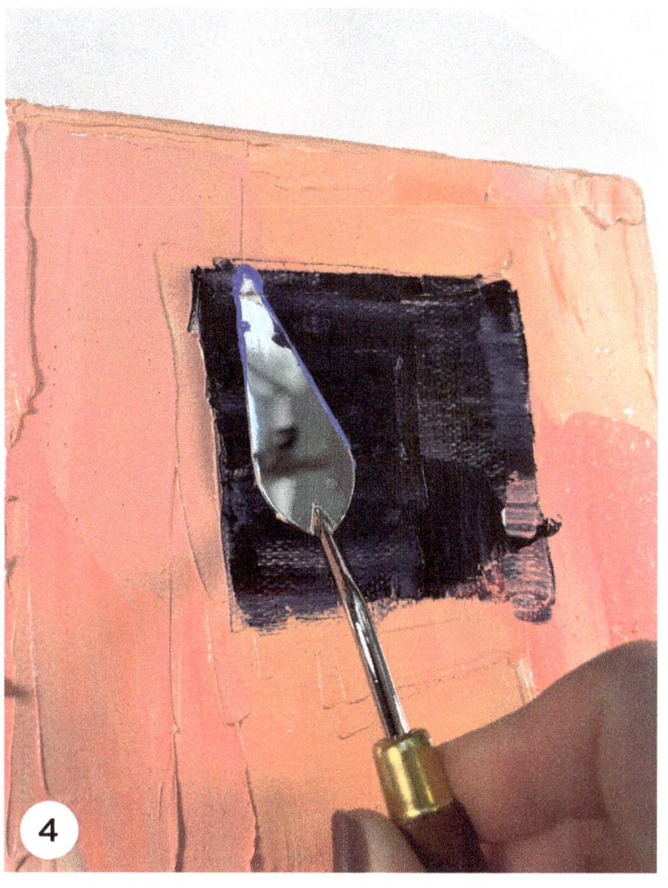


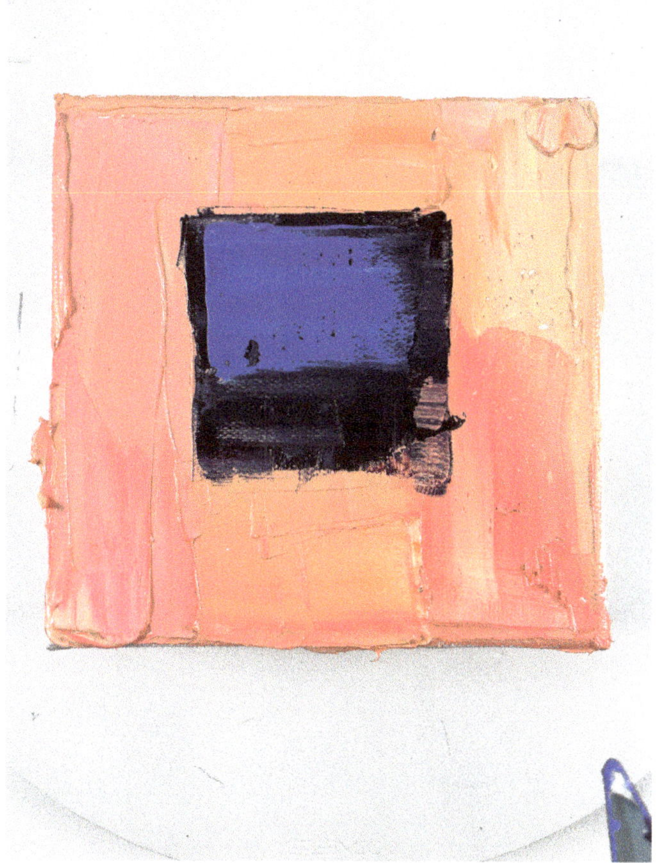

- Starting at the top, about 1½ inches from the edge of your canvas, and about 2 inches from the right edge, swipe down the dark color in one long stroke. Reload your clean knife, and repeat this on the left until you have a square in the center of your canvas. Don't worry if it's not perfect, and it doesn't have to be exactly in the center.
- Here I went ahead and touched up the right edge of the window and straightened it out a bit by using a sliver of the Payne's gray and pulling it across right to left. The advantage of the straight blade is apparent here with architecture. It's so easy and organic, correcting those pesky curved portions with the straight edge of the knife. If you see peach paint peeking through, or your edges are not straight at all, go ahead and load more Payne's gray paint and continue until you have your dark square. Remember, no fussing though!

**Step 4: Adding color & highlights**

- Next, we want to liven up the dark window with some colorful reflective light, to start bringing it to life. Drag down about 1 teaspoon of ultramarine blue and a pea-sized amount of white and mix thoroughly—no streaks of white allowed here.
- Using the technique similar to how you laid in the Payne's gray window, load your knife with a sliver of the blue on the edge, and starting from the left, swipe the knife right, letting the edges of the Payne's gray peeking through. Reload your knife and repeat a little further down. Again, the organic nature of the palette knife leaves portions of the darker color peeking through, looking rustic and uncontrived.
- Now that our window is starting to come together, it's time to add some more color highlights to the walls before we move on to the plants.
- Using some of the darker, more orange shade of peach on your palette, load a sliver on your knife and skim it across your lighter peach, starting at the bottom, going with the vertical perspective of the stone wall. Repeat on both sides, making sure to really skim it across the top. Try not to overdo it here, and let the lighter peach

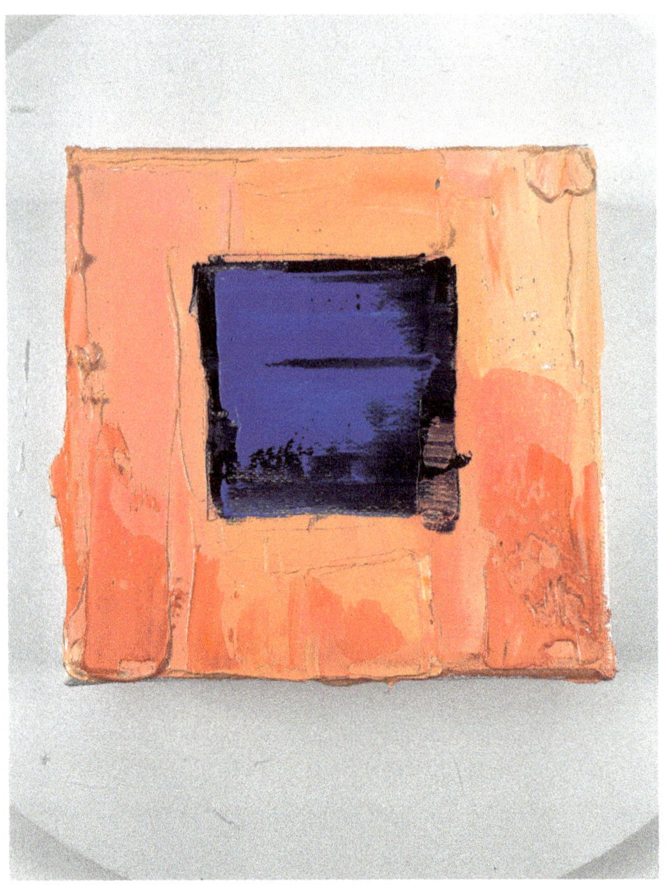

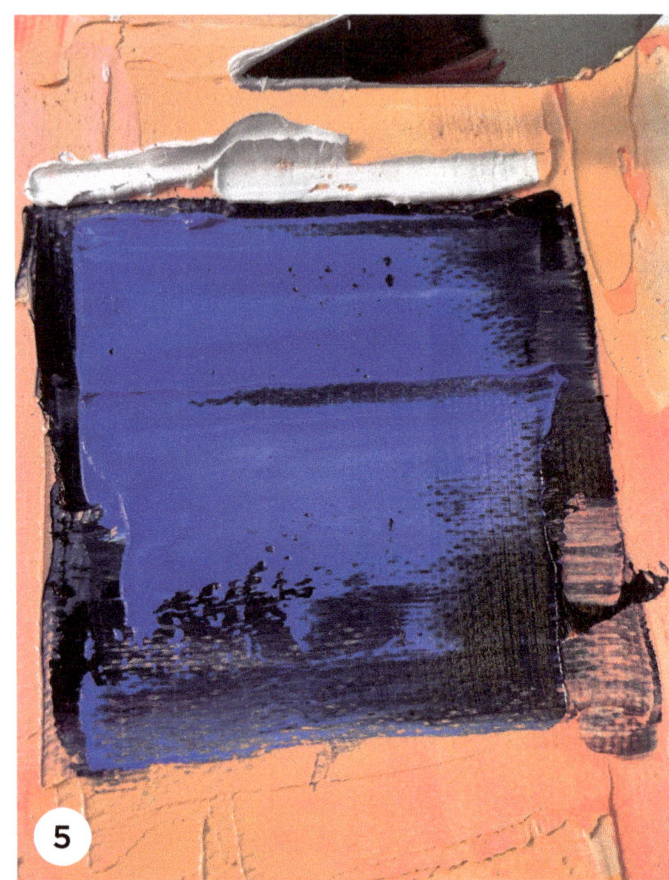

peek through. This creates a dynamic upper layer, looking just like a crumbling wall.

- Now I add a few highlights to the top of the walls in the same hue, skimming my knife very gently across the top of the existing paint layer. Repeat this on the left and right, making sure it is subtle.

**Step 5: Adding windowsills & shadows**

- Drag down a large tablespoon of white and mix until it is very pliable.
- Load your knife with a portion on the underside of your blade, and then load a sliver or a ridge by running your knife down through the paint and picking it up by rotating your hand.
- Placing your knife gently but firmly on the canvas, at the edge of the window, and gently pressing on the edge, lay in portions of white in strips around the window frame, pulling your knife up so as not to make the line too thick. Clean and reload your knife as you go, finishing a complete border around the window. Don't worry about the edges. We're going to tidy them up next.
- Using a clean knife and Payne's gray, we're going to tidy up the edges by running the knife gently around the sides.
- Load a thin sliver onto the edge of your knife, making sure it's pliable and not too thick.
- Drag it gently and fairly quickly around the edges, trying to keep the straight edge of the window. Wipe and reload your knife each time the Payne's gray runs out.
- Now using the last of the Payne's gray, we're going to create a shadow under the window, which will really give it depth.
- Load the Payne's gray on your knife, and placing the edge gently against the bottom windowsill, skim the knife over the paint to create the shadow. Repeat this across the bottom of the windowsill, being careful not to go beyond the side edges of the white.

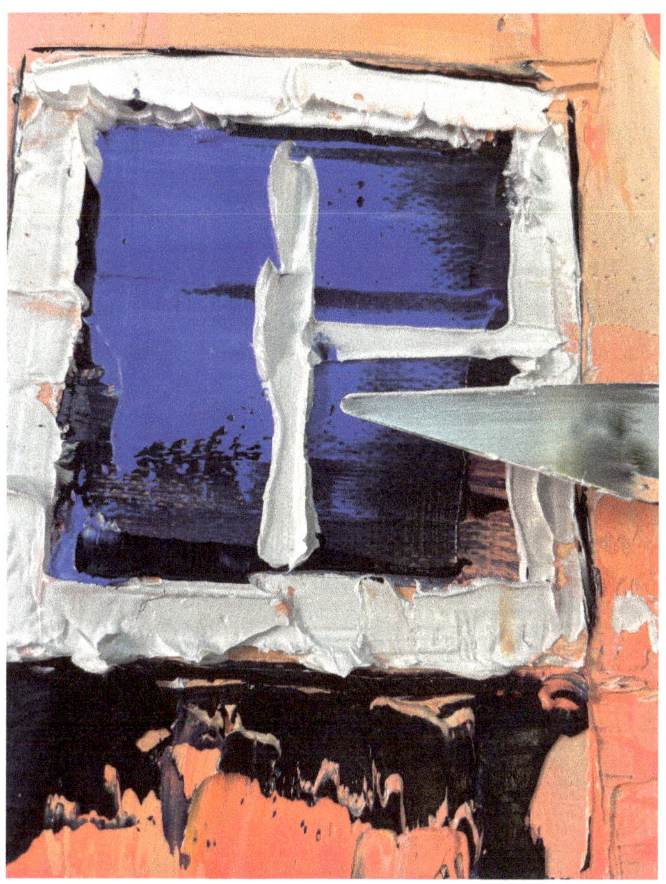

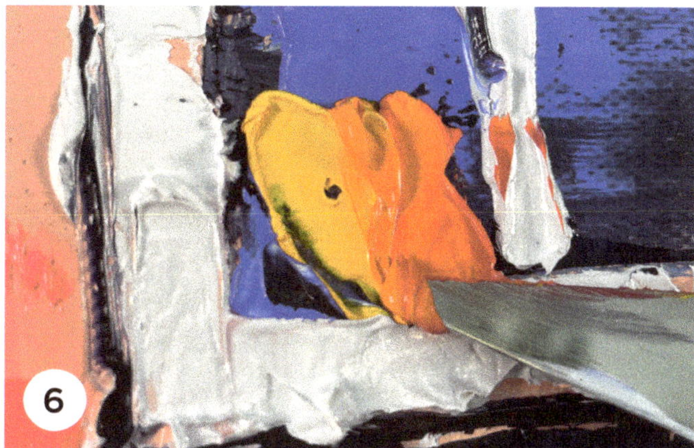


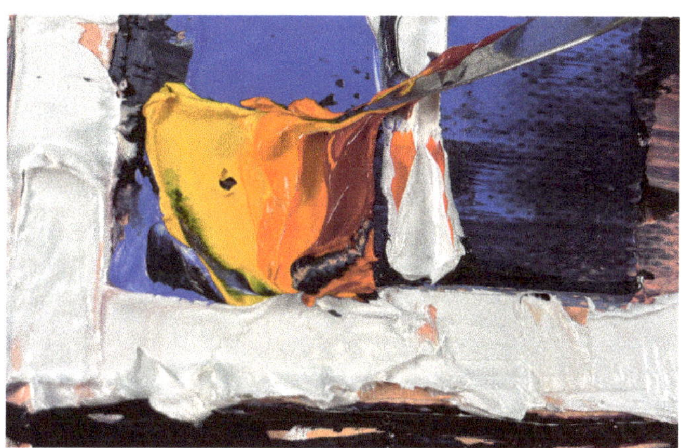

- Now let's put in the rest of the window details. Loading the knife with a sliver of white on the edge, gently place it in a cross formation in the center. Don't worry if it doesn't match up and touch the edges. It is meant to be a suggestion and certainly not perfect. Reload your knife and repeat this on either side. Here, I'm using my lazy Susan to swivel the canvas so that I can maneuver around more easily.

**Step 6: Adding the plant pots & flowers**

- Drag down 1 teaspoon each of cadmium yellow, cadmium red, and alizarin crimson.
- Load your knife with a small portion of yellow on the tip, and place it gently on the canvas just above the window-sill. Press down in a curved shape and draw the knife up. Next, mix a little yellow with just a dab of cadmium red to make orange and repeat the first step, gently laying a strip of orange paint right next to the yellow. Lastly, mix a small amount of cadmium red with alizarin crimson and lay in another small strip right next to the orange to complete the shape of the plant pot.
- Lastly, to tidy up the form of the pot, with the tip of my knife I smooth out the top edge into a gentle curve.
- Go ahead and repeat these steps and create another plant pot on the right side of the windowsill. Make sure it's not exactly the same size, so make it a little smaller or larger. I made my one on the right slightly taller.
- Repeat this all again on the bottom right, with a larger plant pot sitting on the ground. On this one, I also added a thin line of Payne's gray on the top, and on the right side by loading a small sliver on the edge of the knife and gently pulling it down.
- The next step with our plant pots is to mix some yellow and green together. Drag down 1 tablespoon of each and mix thoroughly.

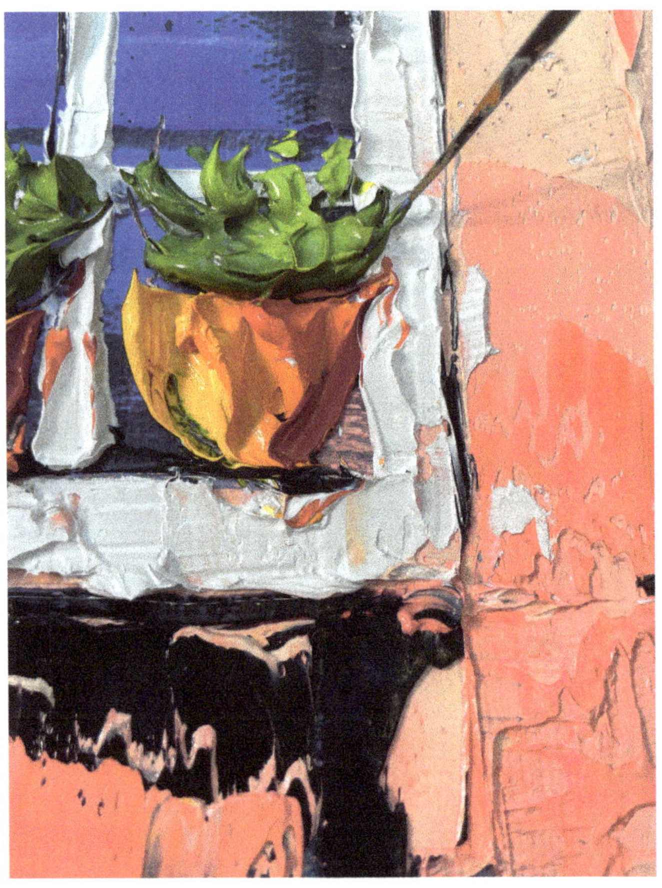

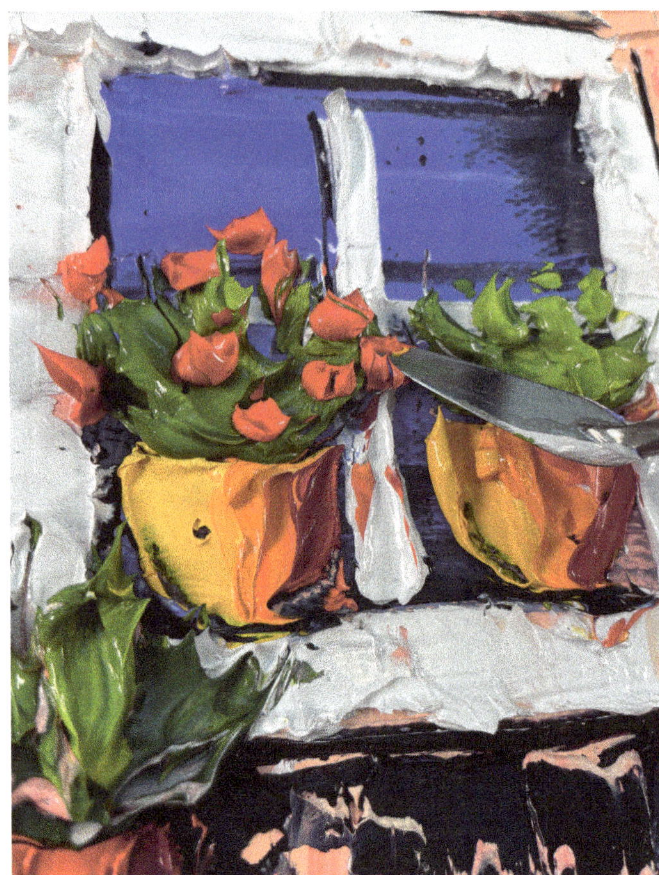

- I'm switching to my smaller knife in order to get the details here.
- Load your knife with about 1 teaspoon on the tip and dot in the plant foliage starting at the base of the pot and drawing it upward.
- Repeat this a few times on both plant pots, and again on the bottom pot on the ground, until you have very thick foliage on all three plants. I mixed in a little extra yellow to lighten up the tips of the plants as well, which creates a more organic look. If you're using a lazy Susan, it's often easier to swivel the canvas upside down to complete the plant foliage.
- Next, I'm using my long skinny palette knife to give the plants more structure and movement upward. I gently pull up the paint, starting from the base and making stems and grass-like strands. It's tempting to overdo this, but make sure you stop after you've done a few. If you don't have this knife, don't worry! You can do all these details with your standard knife twisted sideways so that you are using the skinny side of the blade. It's just a little easier to do it with the sharper knife. (Not to mention fun!)
- Finally, the flowers! This part is the most fun, adding such pizazz to the piece.
- Using your little knife and cadmium red straight out of the tube, scoop up little dots and gently place them on your plant foliage, pulling the knife up quickly. Make sure not to squish them into the green paint underneath. Place about eight or 10 flowers on each of the two top plants, making sure you use a clean knife and a fresh, generously textured blob for each flower.
- Repeat this for the last pot, this time using yellow straight out of the tube.

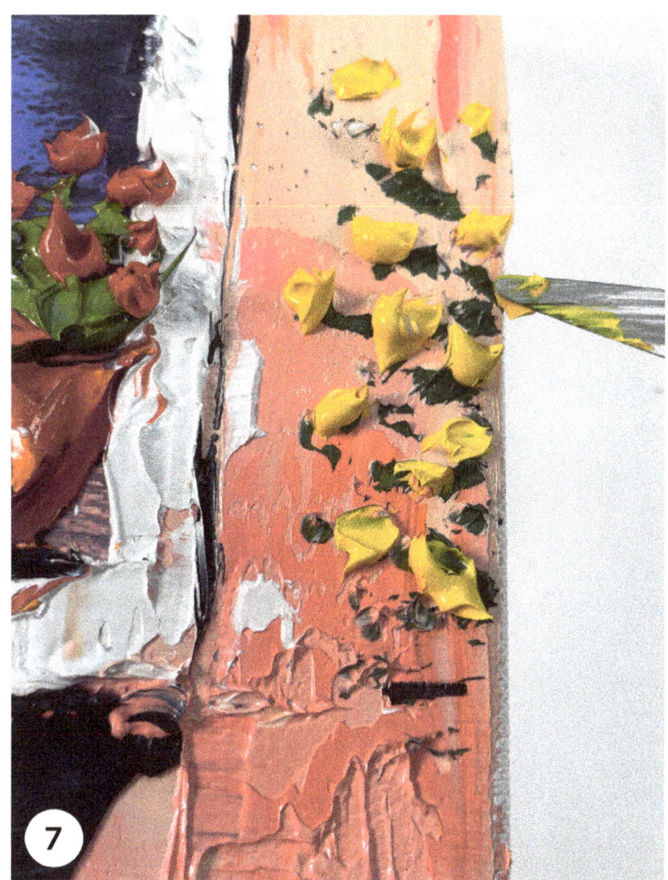

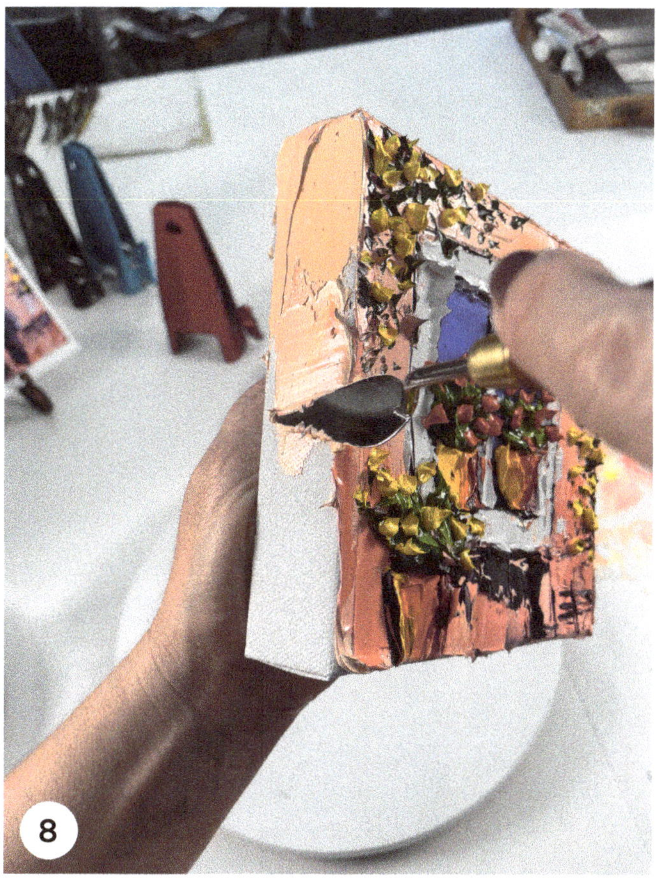

**Step 7: Laying in the vines & flowers**

- Our last step, which really brings the project to life, is to liven up the stone wall with a lovely creeper.

- Drag down 1 tablespoon of green and load the edge of your knife with a sliver. At this point, I swiveled my lazy Susan so that the painting was upside down to give myself some elbow room.

- Using the edge of your knife, in the top-left corner, dot in slivers to resemble creeping vines. Make sure you don't add too many straight lines here, breaking them up with the tip of the knife as you go. Also add a few vines on the opposite side, but not in the corner.

- Lastly, add some little yellow flowers the same way you did with the plant pots. With yellow straight out of the tube, dot flowers over the vines, using your small knife.

**Step 8: Sign your painting & paint the edges (optional)**

- Go ahead and sign your painting, either on the front or on the painted edge if you prefer. I signed mine on the front right.

- I found it easier to just pick the painting up to paint the sides, swiveling it around on my fingers. After covering the canvas with leftover peach-colored paint, I then created a suggestion of the vines on the edges as well.

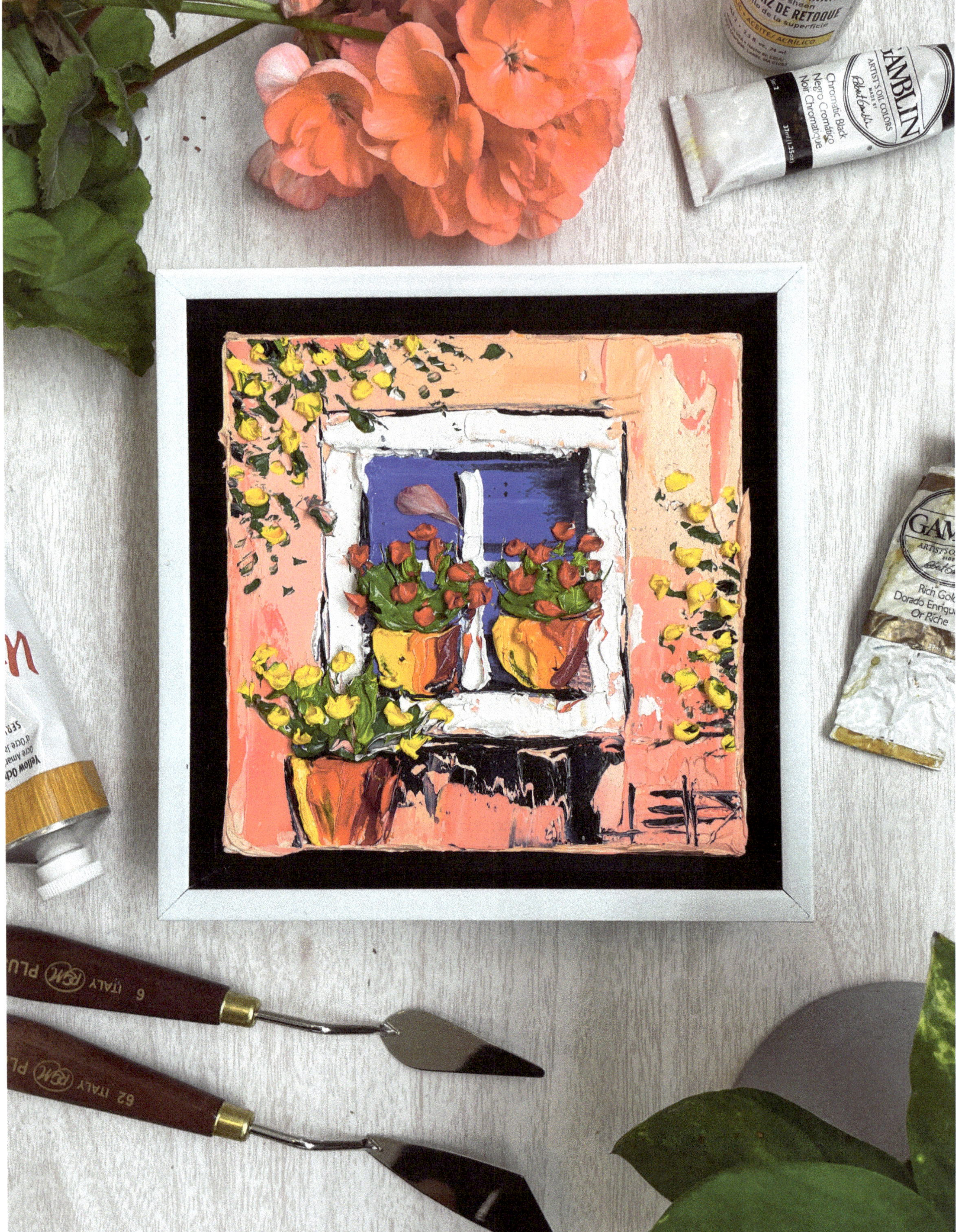

ARTIST'S OIL COLORS
Chromatic Black
Negro Cromático
Noir Chromatique

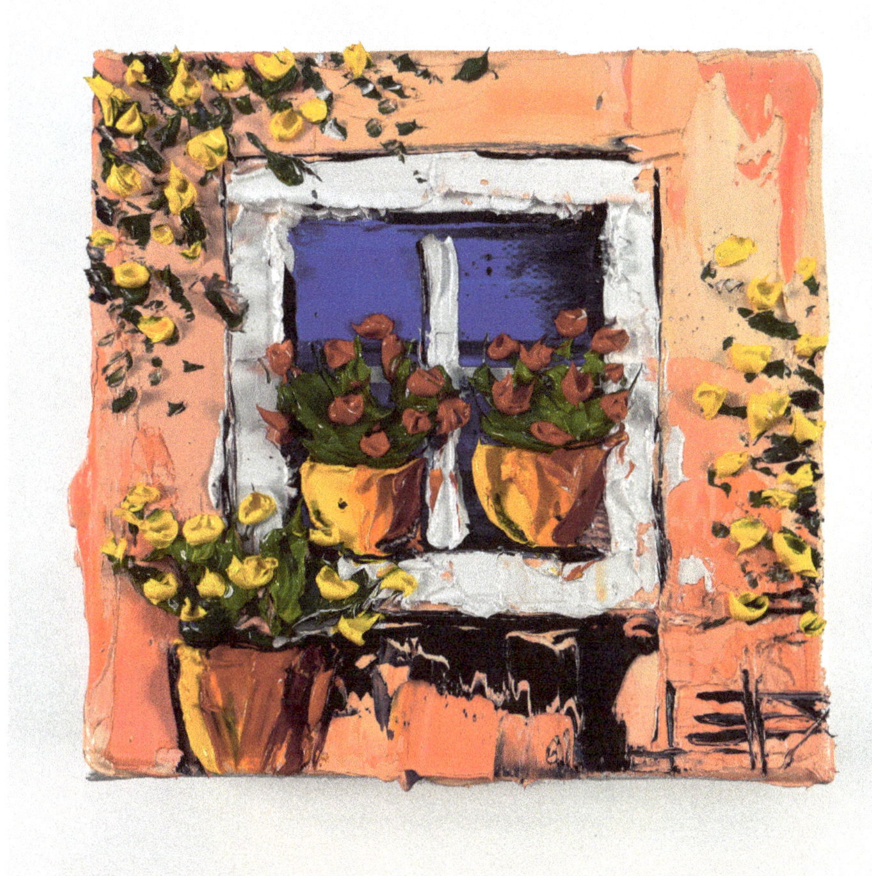

## SUMMARY:
## Did You Capture the Emotion of the Piece?

This little piece just oozes charm. It reflects warm afternoons basking in the Mediterranean summer sun and glasses of wine under the vines while you enjoy the buzz of the bees around the sweet-smelling flowers. Time seems to stand still in Italy, and this little piece perfectly captures the essence of that timeless quality.

Italy has inspired artists for centuries with its charming architecture, and the palette knife naturally captures the texture of the old stone walls. When you practice the technique of skimming the knife over the underlayer of paint to create shadows, imperfections, and a streaky stone effect, you'll be well on your way to mastering the art of palette knife painting.

*"The Creator made Italy from designs by Michelangelo."*

—MARK TWAIN

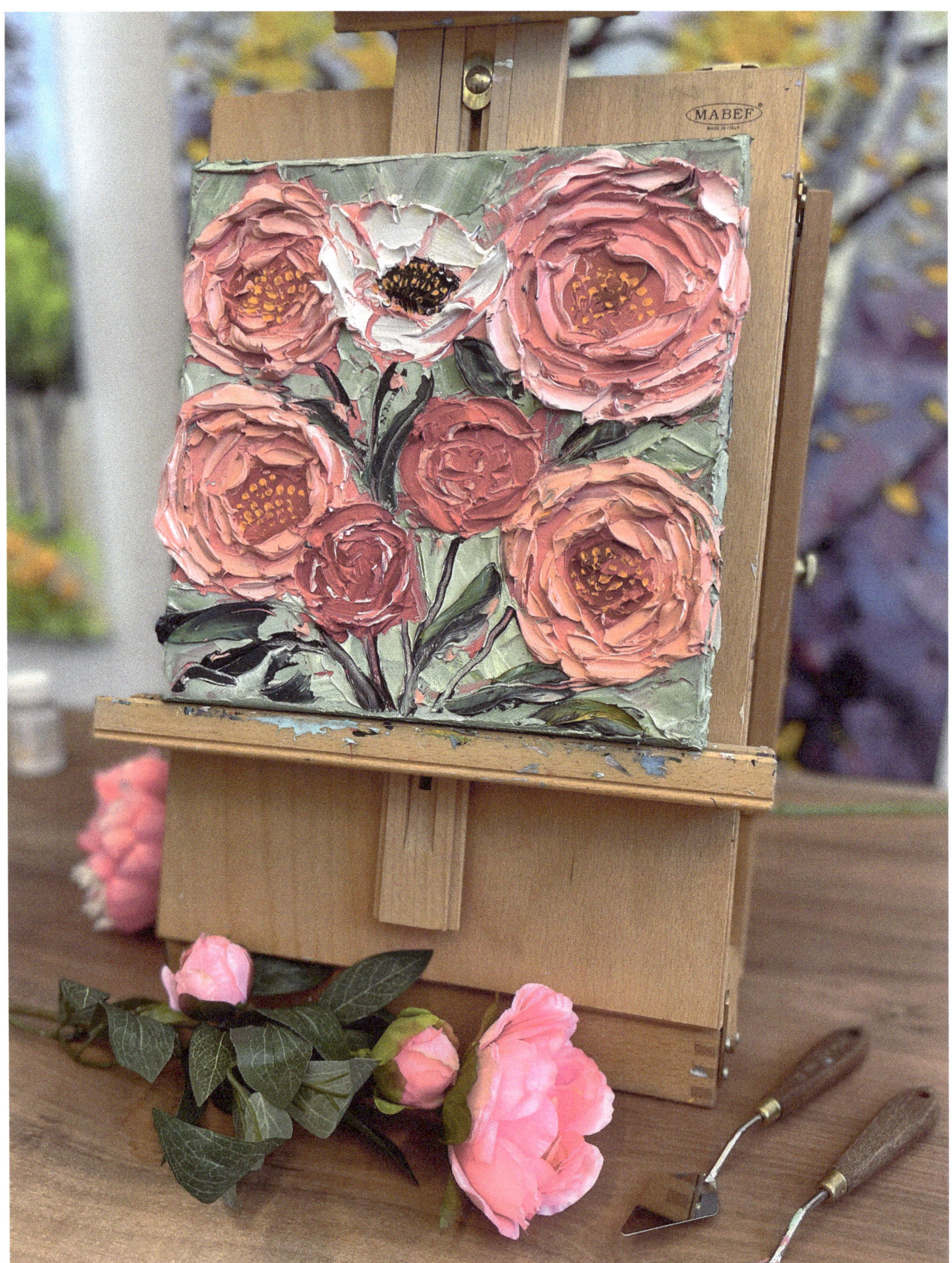
MABEF

# SUMMER PEONIES

**Tools & Materials**

- Stretched canvas, size 10″ x 10″ with a 1½-inch depth
- Palette knife: medium size, teardrop shape with rounded tip
- Palette knife: fancy tip with dot details (optional)
- Palette knife: angled top (optional)
- Palette knife: long, skinny tip (optional)
- Table easel
- Palette paper
- Paper towel or rag for wiping your knife

**Color Palette**

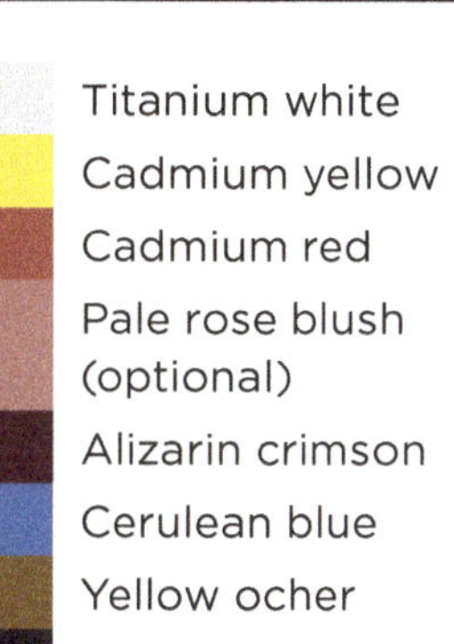

- Titanium white
- Cadmium yellow
- Cadmium red
- Pale rose blush (optional)
- Alizarin crimson
- Cerulean blue
- Yellow ocher
- Payne's gray
- Prussian blue

**Difficulty Level**

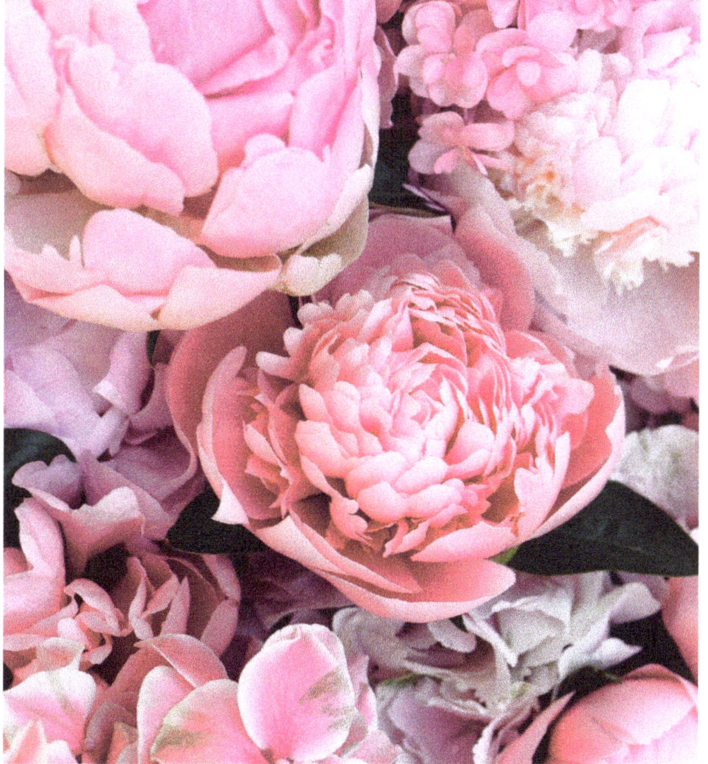

## *Inspiration*

I was inspired to paint this piece with the onset of peony season in the late spring and early summer. Bouquets of every type and color of peony are available at this time of year, and I chose one with a lovely saturated deeper pink, with quite a few yellow hues in it. What a gorgeous color! Combined with those fluttery petals and ethereal glow, it's nature and ballet all wrapped up in a bow. Let's go ahead and paint it.

With this slightly larger canvas, I'm now using a table easel, with my palette paper and paper towels for wiping my knives laid out on my righthand side. The lazy Susan works great for smaller pieces, but with a bigger canvas I recommend an easel that allows for access to the sides as well. I have several easels in my studio, including two tabletop versions that allow me to stand or sit and also maneuver around them with my knives, with plenty of elbow room.

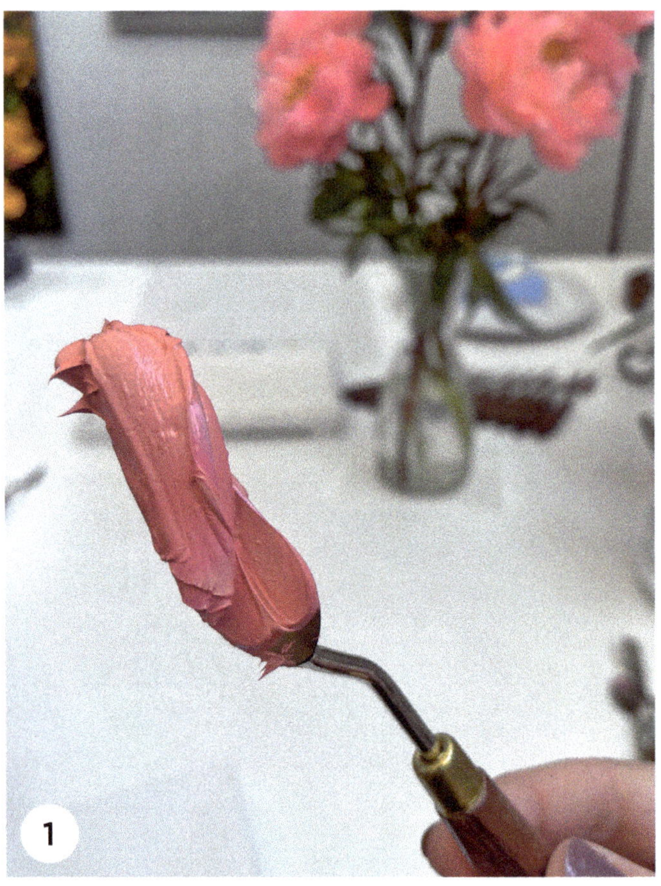


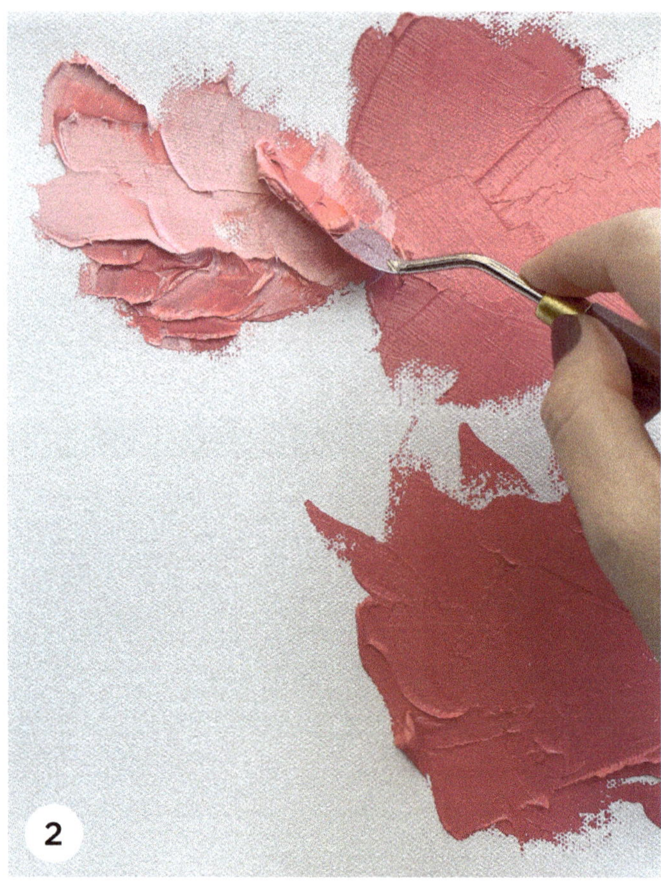


## Step-By-Step Instructions

**Step 1: Lay out your colors & mix your basic peony hues**

- Squeeze out a large blob of white paint, about the size of 3 heaped tablespoons on the top left of your palette. We are going to be blocking in the basic shapes of the pink flowers before filling in the green background on this piece, so we want to mix various shades of pink with some variations in colors to accentuate the diversity of the many different types of peonies.

- Squeeze out about 1 teaspoon each of cadium yellow, cadmium red, and alizarin crimson. Again, I like to put them in that order across the top of my palette from left to right so that I can drag the paint down to mix it with my palette knife, adding to it as I go.

- Start by dragging down 1 tablespoon of white and 1 teaspoon of crimson. Mix them together, and then add smaller portions of cadmium red and cadmium yellow until you get to the pink hue with an orange tint to it. We're going to use quite a bit of this color, adding to it as we go, so there's not really an issue with too much paint here—it just means your blooms will be even more 3D in appearance!

- I'm also mixing darker and lighter shades, adding a little more crimson and keeping it off to one side. A great premixed color for peonies is pale rose blush, or light pink, which I'm using here for bulk. Don't worry if you don't have this color. You can easily mix it with the other colors here on your palette. It's just a bit quicker and easier to have the tube ready to go.

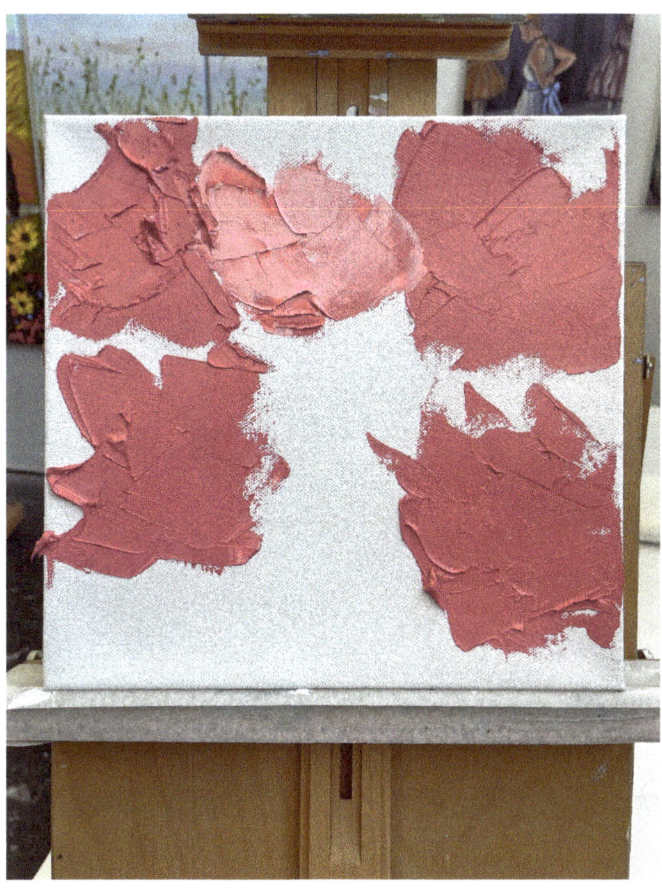

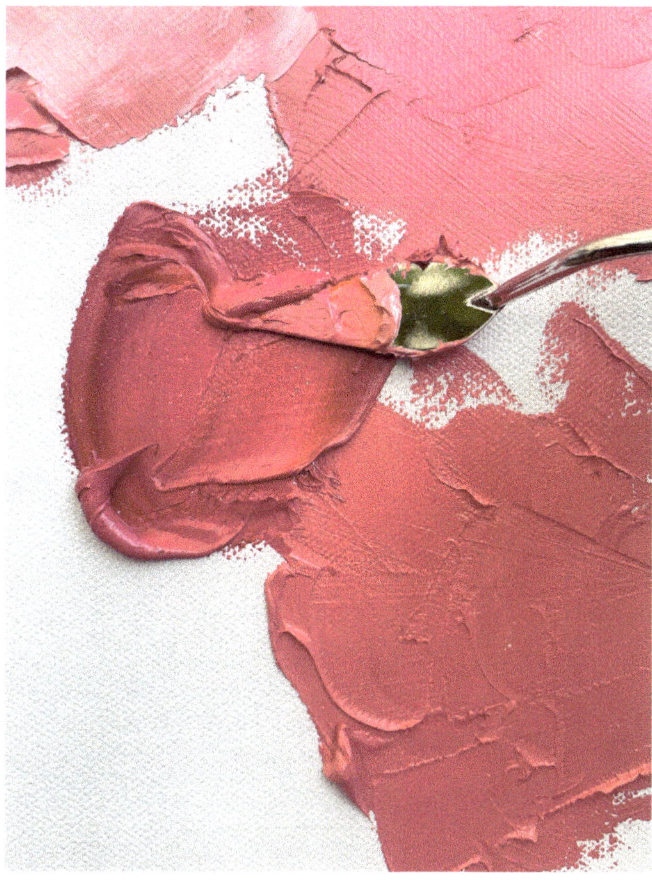

**Step 2: Lay in your bloom shapes**

- Starting at the top of your canvas, start blocking in where you want your blooms to sit. This is a contemporary square canvas, so I usually would go with around five good-sized blooms (not four—that's too symmetrical) and then a couple of little buds and/or smaller blooms for variation and interest.

- Load your knife with about 1 tablespoon of the pink color, and block in the shapes in a circular motion, not worrying about building up the texture too much here.

- Place another bloom with your lighter pink in the top middle (but not exactly in the middle).

- I'm taking care here to make them organic and fluffy with wisps and inconsistencies. This creates movement and interest, and keeps them from feeling static. We want them to dance around the canvas and bring it to life.

- Load your knife again with about 1 tablespoon of the darker pink, and lay in two shapes on the top left, and another underneath, again using large strokes to smooth out the paint and moving outward in the shape of petals protruding from the center. You should have five nicely sized bloom shapes around the edges of your canvas.

- Lastly, for variation, and to break up the uniform size of the five large blooms, we want to place in a couple of smaller buds. These we will make a little smaller, and also more of an oval shape to denote more of a bud shape, with the flowers about to open. Pull down a pea-sized amount of crimson with your knife and add it to your darker shade of pink to make a rich red. Then go ahead and block in a smaller bud shape in the center area, but just off to the right (never in the exact center).

- Lastly, load your knife with a smaller tablespoon of darkest pink, and add another bloom in the center left, slightly below the last one. We now have a lovely mix of shapes and sizes, placed naturally, and not too contrived.

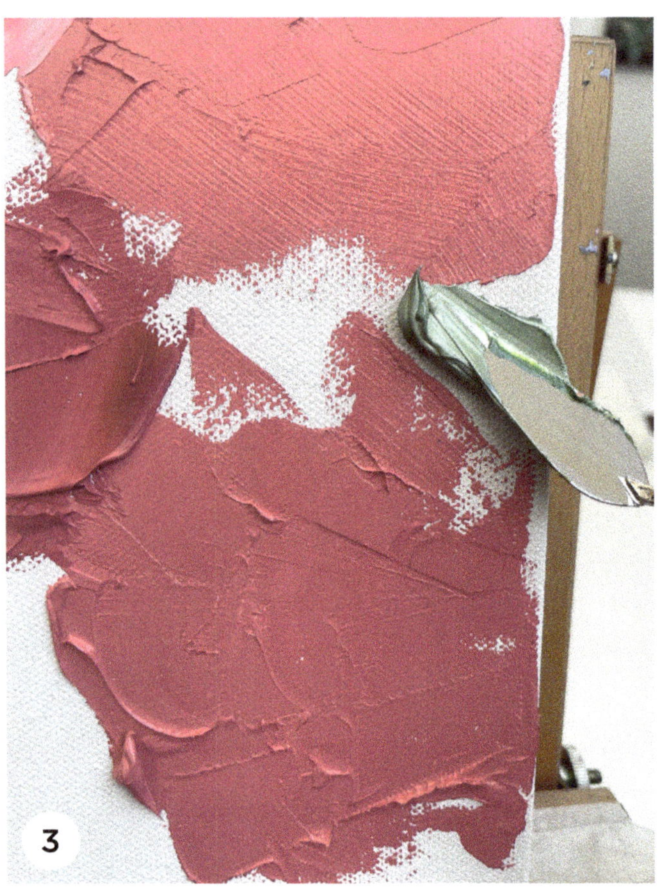


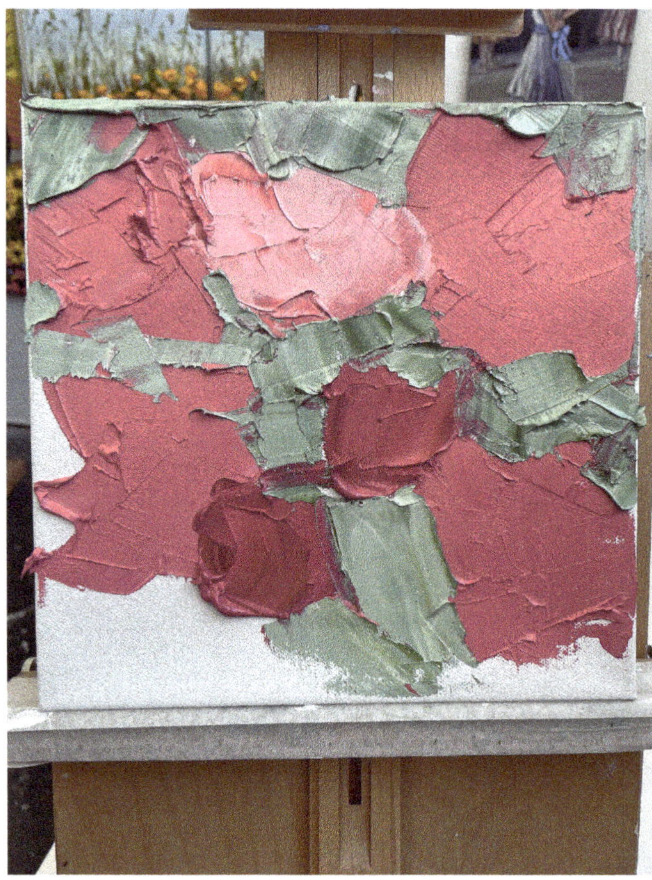

**Step 3: Lay in your green background**

- Now we are going to fill in our green background, and things will start to take shape and get more dynamic and exciting.

- Drag down a generous teaspoon of your cerulean blue and about the same amount of yellow ocher, and mix it so that you have a nice Van Gogh–inspired light teal color. We want to mix and have different shades ready here, so keep some darker using more cerulean blue, keep some browner with more ocher, and lighten some up with white. Keep them all together on your palette ready to go.

- Start laying in your green background, moving around the pink flower shapes that you have already blocked in. I'm using fairly large choppy strokes here, side to side, to lay in the texture. I'm keeping it loose and gestural, covering the white canvas, but not blending or fussing. The aim is to fill in all of the white canvas.

- Continue to fill in all the gaps, reloading the knife as you go. You also want to pull in a few variations of green from your palette here. Streaks and inconsistencies are not only allowed but encouraged here, as they add to the abandonment of your piece and make it look more natural.

- I went super chunky on the top-left edge here and decided to leave it for interest and a 3D effect. Continue around the canvas until you have filled in all the white canvas with green. If you're not sure which direction to use with your knife strokes, think about the subject matter we are portraying here. A bouquet has a circular shape, so if you move your knife (roughly) outwards toward the edges from the center, you'll capture the shape of a bouquet. Don't go side to side or up and down with every stroke. It won't have the same effect as the more circular movement. Remember not to make all your strokes outward, though. We don't want a Ferris wheel effect either! There's a sweet spot here, so break them up with a few sideways strokes here and there.

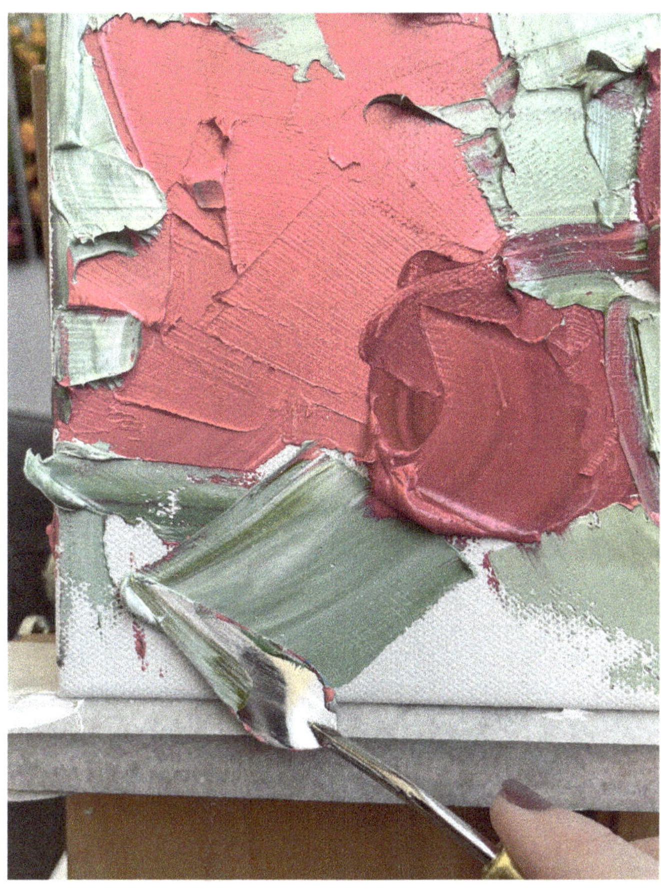

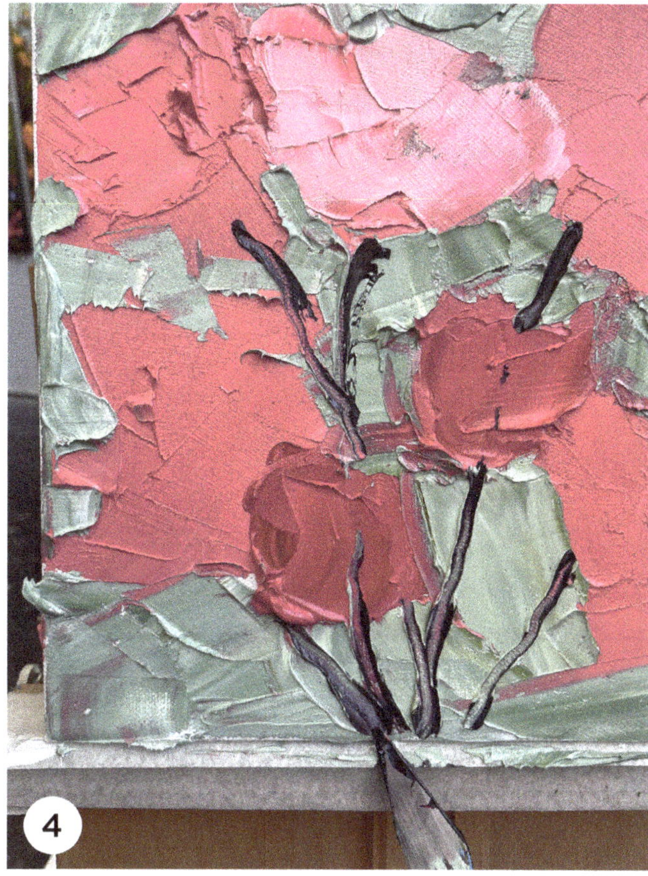


**Step 4: Adding stems & leaves**

- Now we're going to start giving the piece more structure, so we'll start putting some stems on our blooms and leaves.

- Drag down about 1 tablespoon of your Prussian blue, and mix it with the darker teal you have left on your palette. Starting at the base of your top-center bloom, gently sketch (not carving out) in a dark line, not worrying about exactly matching the ends. Wipe your knife and repeat this for every bloom and bud. I'm right-handed, so my stems often take on a slight arc to the left, but you can arc them right if you prefer. Always do what feels more natural and right for you. If it feels natural and you're having fun, use that as your North Star, and keep going.

- You'll notice at the bottom that the stems are starting to clump together and look like more of a bunch or bouquet.

- Next, we're going to use our more angular palette knife to create leaves. If you don't have this knife, don't worry. You can use your regular knife, but it just won't have quite the definition on the tips of the leaves. Using the same dark green you used for the stems, load your knife by scraping it along your palette with the sharp blade edge, with about a teaspoon on the bottom of your knife, toward the tip, lifting it up.

- Now place the blade edge down starting at the tip of your leaf, and draw the blade toward the stem, applying a little pressure on the tip, while twisting it to the right and then left in a little wriggle as you pull it along, before pulling it up where it meets the stem. Repeat this again with a clean, reloaded knife at least once for each stem, aiming for the light green, and being careful not to muddy the leaves/stem/flower together.

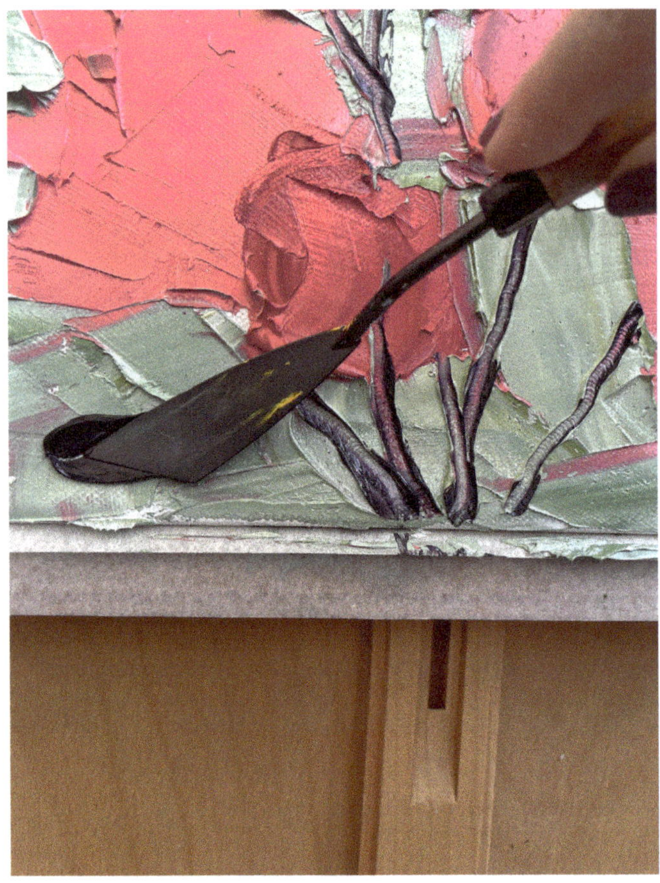

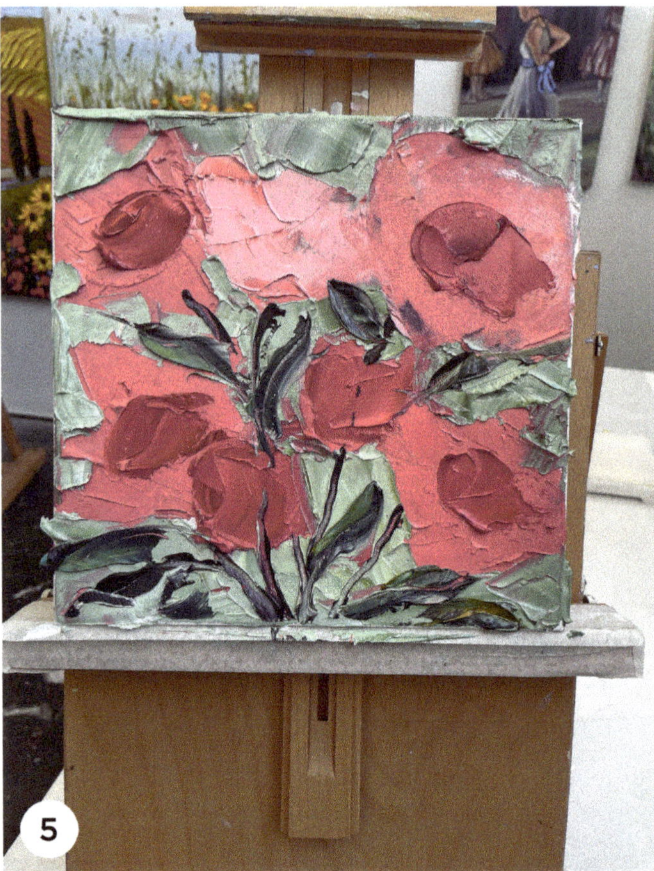


- Palette knife painting is a color-blocking technique, so keeping colors separate is important, and it's where using striking complementary colors and shapes is key to marrying good technique with whimsy and flair.

- You should end up with a good mix of stems, blooms, and leaves, making sure there are no white canvas "holes" and that it looks balanced.

**Step 5: Adding the pink blooms**

- Let's start building up that gorgeous flamingo-ballet pink! The blooms need more structure before we continue to build up the texture, so I'm going to go ahead and place some darker pink in the middle of each one, to give us something to aim at and to help make them look nice and round.

- Drag down a large tablespoon of darker pink and lay it in a round center in each of the four large blooms in each corner, wiping and reloading your knife every time. Don't worry about the lighter bloom in the center top. We're going to make that one a different color, just to break things up so that the blooms are not the same.

- Now we get to start on the texture. Drag down 1 tablespoon of a medium value pink. If you don't have enough, mix some more as we're getting very textured now. This is the part where the painting really starts to shine. We want to do some color blocking here and create a difference in value between the darker pink center and the petals. This will really make our bloom pop.

- We also want our medium pink to have streaks of white. Peony petals get lighter on the tips, so the streaks of white help to make the blooms look ethereal and wispy. Pull down some white paint, and mix it loosely into your medium pink, so that the streaks show.

- Scooping up a tablespoon on the edge of your knife, lay it down in a strip, going clockwise around the edge of the dark pink in the middle of the bloom. You'll have to apply a little pressure with the tip of your knife and lift it up.

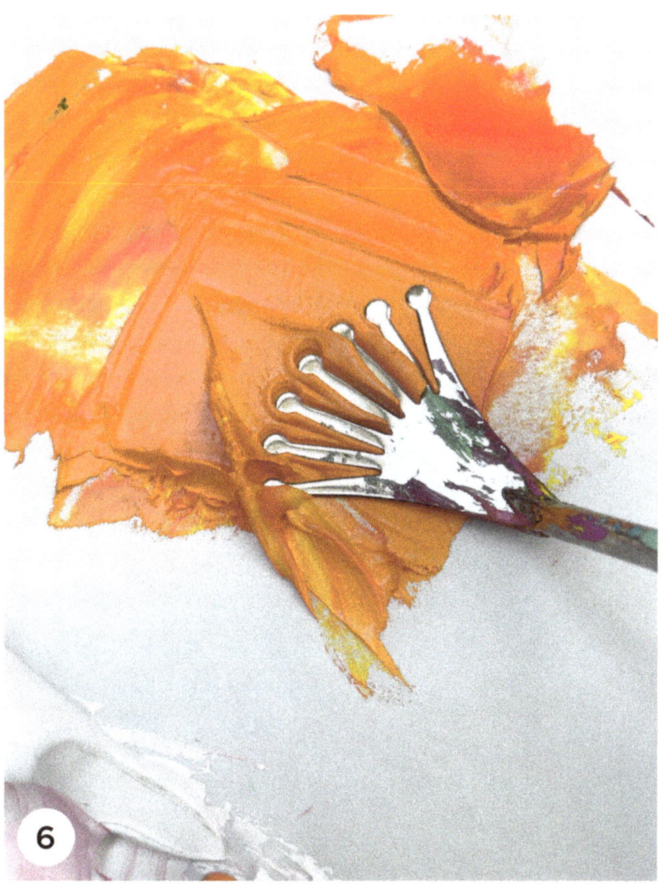


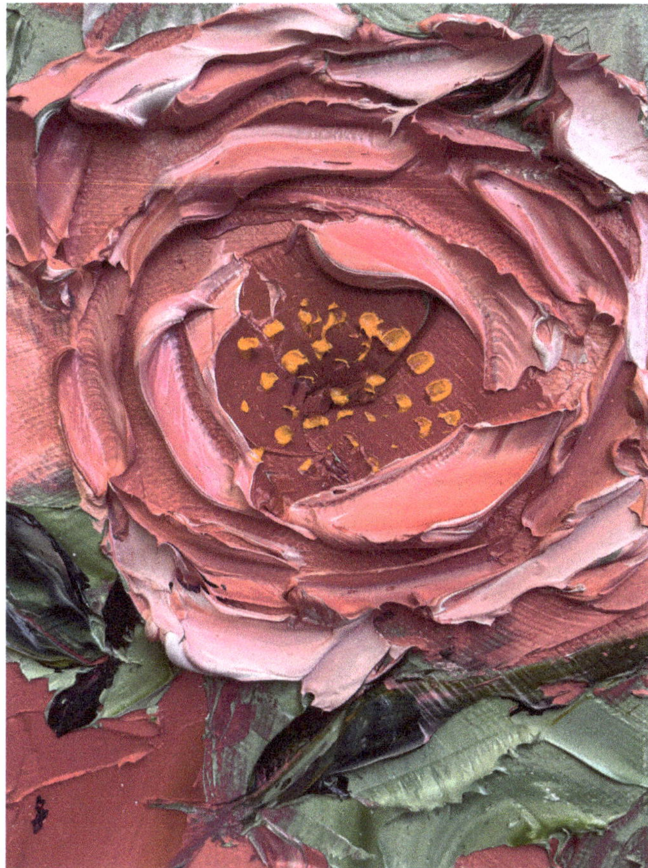

Do not squish the paint into the canvas too much here; just gently place it on. We're wanting strips here, as we want the paint underneath to show through. Lay strips around the outside, making sure to leave little gaps here and there between the strips. Clean your knife and reload with the same color. Lay in another outer circle of petals using the same technique with laying down thick strips of medium value pink. Make sure to leave a gap between the first and second rows of circular petal strokes.

- Clean your knife and reload, and lay in a third row of petals, leaving a gap in between the second and third row. Try to make sure your gaps between the strips of petals don't all fall in the same place and stagger them somewhat. Also, pull in a little more white for your third row of petals, as peonies get lighter on the tips, keeping it streaky and inconsistent.

- I also decided to go somewhat off the canvas here, laying in a petal that protrudes from the edge for interest and using the same circular motion to place it on and draw the knife up without pressing down too hard.

**Step 6: Adding the orange to the center of the bloom**

- Drag down ½ teaspoon each of cadmium yellow and cadmium red, and mix well to make a rich, saturated orange.

- Using your fancy tip knife if you have it, dot the tip with orange, not worrying too much about texture here. This knife is more for mark-making than building up texture. If you don't have the fancy tip knife, you can use the tip of your regular knife with little singular dots.

- Carefully, and with not too much pressure, dot in the details in the center of the flower, making sure not to blend, or place in too many. We want the dots to really pop against the pink center. You can also pivot the knife sideways so that you are just using the tips on the edges, rather than all six tips at once. Stop when you have a good amount of dot coverage within your pink center.

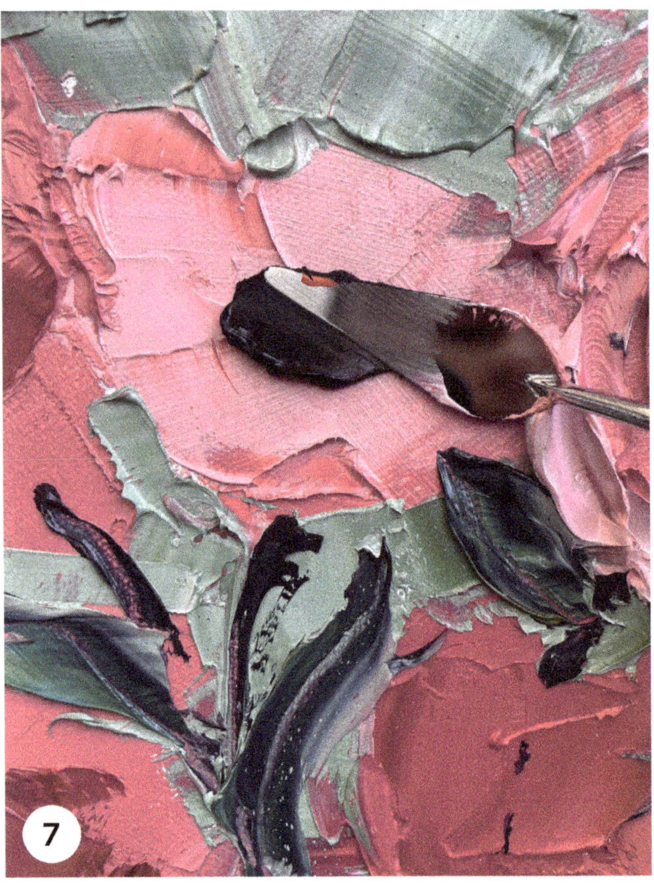

7

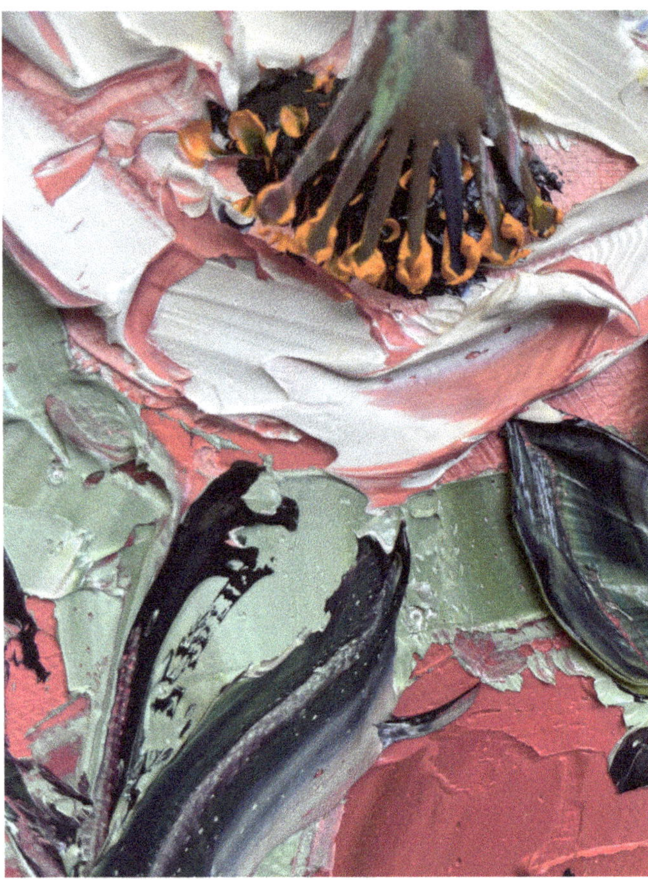

- Note that at this point, I could have completed all my textured blooms before moving on to mixing the orange and dotting in the center of the flowers, but sometimes it's good to jump ahead a little and complete a portion. Little feelings of accomplishment are important, and feeling like your painting is progressing nicely gives you confidence and momentum to finish the piece. Nothing will derail you faster than frustration or boredom when it comes to painting, so make sure that you're giving yourself little wins along the way. When you complete a bloom and it's really starting to shine, make sure you are consciously enjoying it. Stop, make a cup of tea, step back from your piece, and pat yourself on the back—you're doing just fine!
- I'm quite intentional with my painting, and I also want to be a lifelong, dedicated painter. To sustain my excitement over painting over the long term, I really try to make sure that I'm actually enjoying what I'm doing. If I'm really not feeling a painting, I'll usually finish it up, step away, and move on to another the next day. It's funny that painting is so subjective that often the paintings you don't like will be other people's favorites!
- The last little detail on the orange dots is to create little stems to anchor them a tiny bit. If you have the long skinny knife, it's perfect for this detail. Otherwise, you can use the tip of your regular knife by pivoting it sideways and using the sharper edge of the blade. Pull down a tiny amount of the orange paint from each dot to suggest a little stem.

**Step 7: Finishing the large textured blooms**

- Moving on to the next bloom, we're going to make this one a little lighter. With a clean knife, pull down 1 teaspoon of Payne's gray, and place in a roundish shape in the center of your middle bloom.

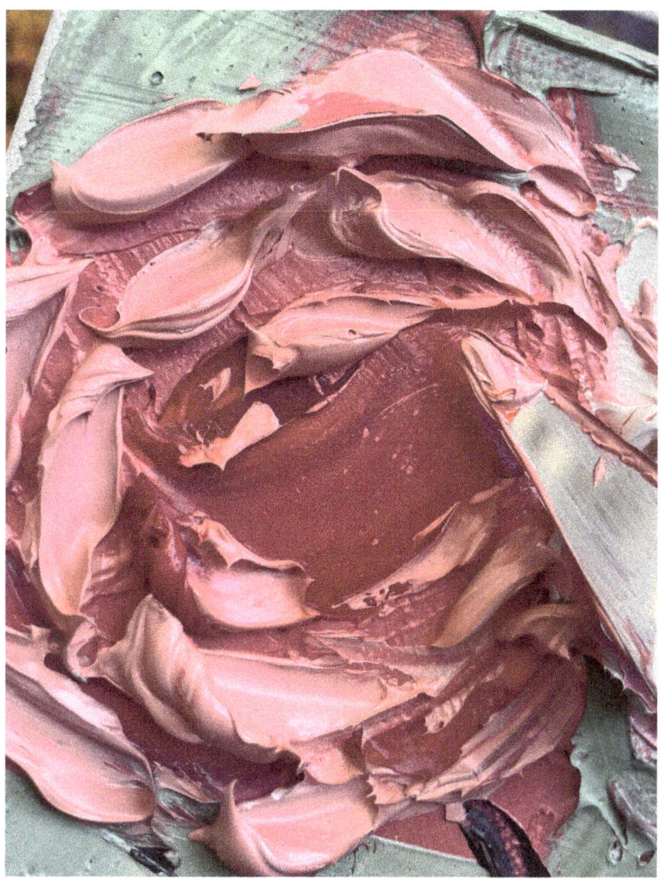

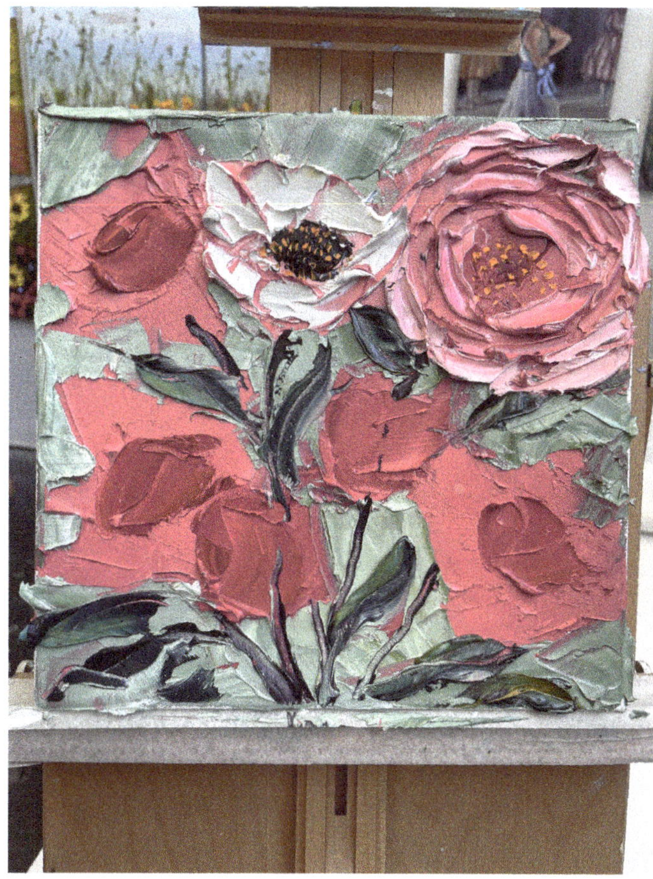

- Next, with a clean knife, pull down about 3 tablespoons of white. Load your knife with 1 tablespoon of the white, and then pull the knife down through the medium pink paint to create a small ridge of pink that sits just on the side of the white. This is going to create lovely pink tips on your petals. Start laying in the petals of the white bloom by starting at the outer edge. Push the paint down, gently applying pressure, and draw the knife inwards. Stop at the black and pull the knife up. Repeat this several times around the bloom until you've covered all the pink underneath. Make sure your petals on the sides are more of an oval shape, and make sure your petals on the bottom are a little smaller than the top ones. This will help with a more natural shape. We can also sketch in some petal edges. With the tip of your knife and some medium pink paint, draw in the petal edges using the natural edge of the paint where it protrudes as a guide.
- Now we'll repeat the step with the orange dots in the center. With your fancy tip knife, dot in a few orange accents, and then use your skinny knife to create some subtle stems as well.
- Continuing with the blooms, load your knife with a 1 table-spoon of pink, and start on the left bloom, laying in strips of pink in a circular pattern, starting on the outside of the dark pink center. Make sure not to go over the white paint of your neighboring white bloom, as we want to keep the color-blocking contrast here, and when there is already a lot of texture, less texture next to it often works better on these edges. Continue with your strips until you have about three circles. Then use your fancy tip knife to dot in some orange details in the center.
- I decided that I had now covered up too much of the right edge of my white flower, and that it needed a little more color blocking, so I went back and added a little more white on the edge to create more definition and a boundary between the blooms.

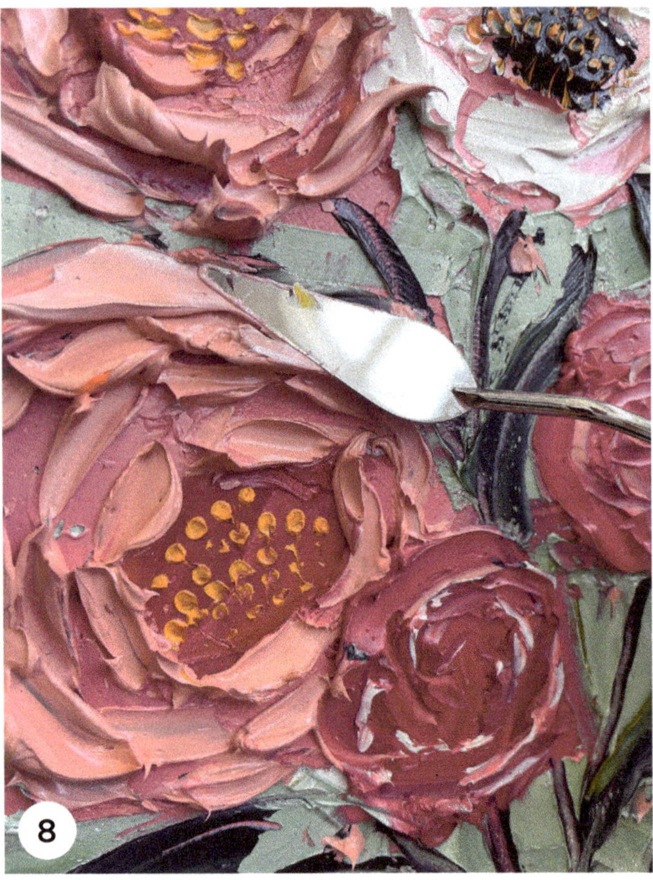


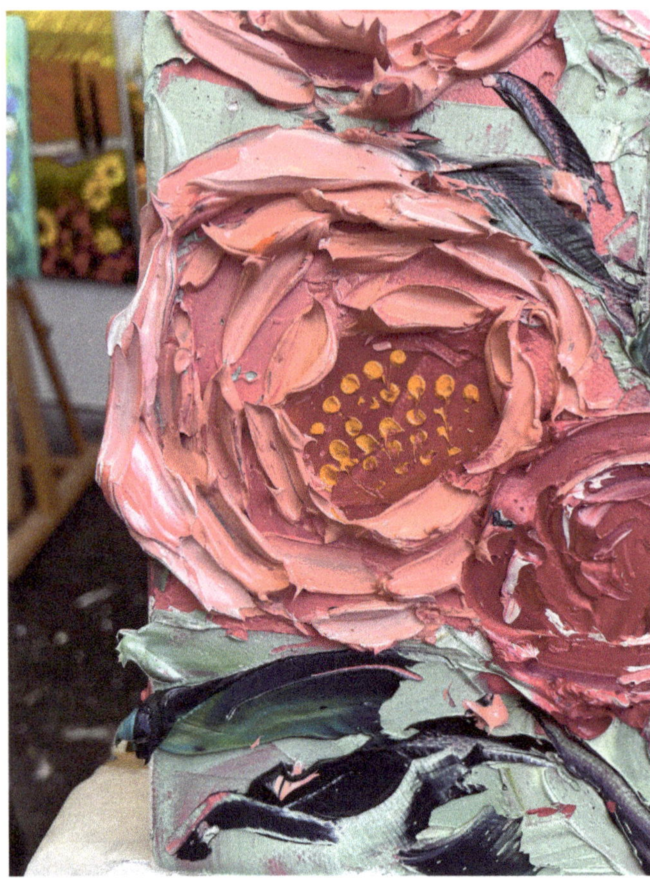

- Now start on your third large bloom on the bottom right, using the same technique with the three rows of petals and ending with the orange dot details in the center.
- Repeat this step with your fourth large bloom on the bottom left, laying in three rows of petals and the orange dot details.

**Step 8: Laying in the dark pink buds**

- The last details we are going to add here are the two smaller blooms, which are more budlike, and help to balance out the composition. Drag down some crimson, about ½ teaspoon, and add it to your medium pink. You may have to mix a little more paint here, to keep the texture consistent with the rest of the painting. Load your knife and lay in the dark pink with up and down strokes. Repeat this for the second bud.
- Using the tip of your knife, load a small dab of lighter pink and gently run it over the top of the dark pink paint to sketch in some petal variations. Repeat this with a lighter shade on the other bud to color block in the petals. Don't put the orange dot details on these two buds.
- One last detail here is to pull in some of your leftover pink paint to dot in pink details on the green background, which helps to tie the whole piece together and create equilibrium with your composition. Load your knife with a small amount of medium or light pink, and dot a few places quickly here and there, blending slightly by dragging your knife sideways just a little as you move along, rather than dabbing the knife straight down and lifting up.

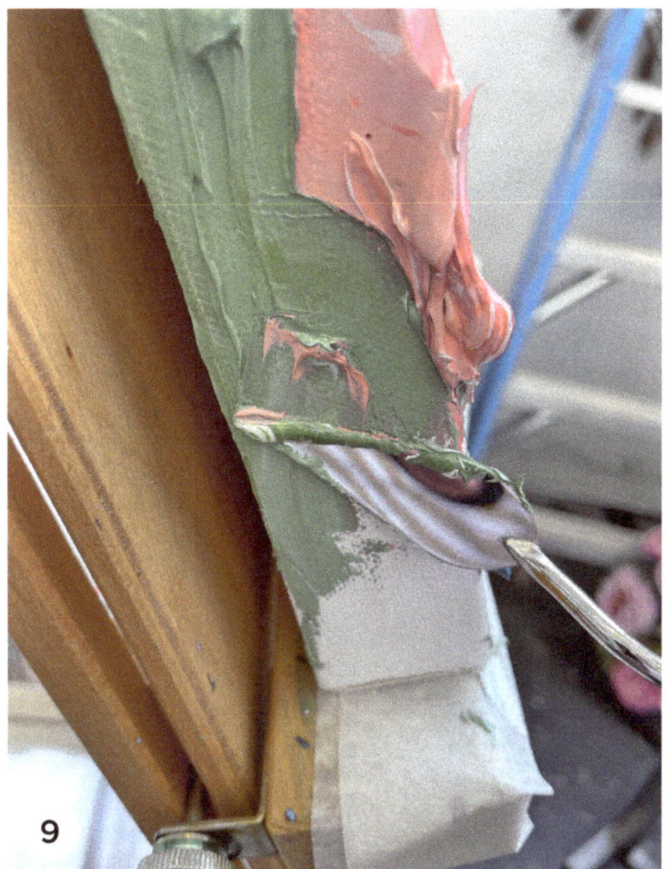


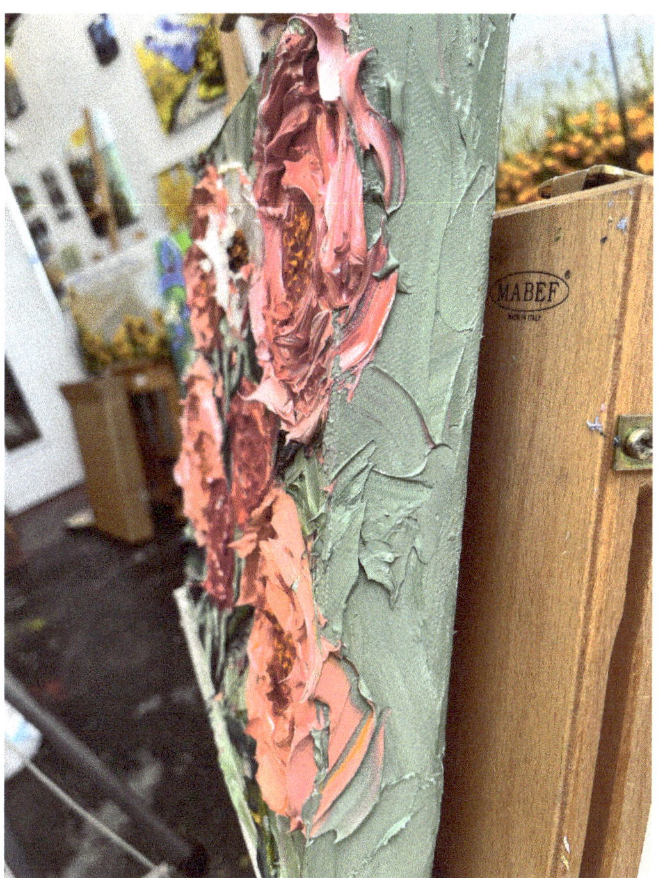


**Step 9: Paint the edges**

- This time, I painted the top three edges while the painting was on the easel. After covering the edge of the canvas with leftover green-colored paint, I then created a suggestion of the pink blooms on the edges as well. I ran out of space for signing this one on the front, so I signed it on the right edge later. It's a good idea here to also pick your canvas up and finish the bottom edge, then lay the piece down flat to dry somewhere away from dust. It's always easier to mix and to match the paint colors while they're fresh in your mind, and much harder to come back at a later date and try to match up the green to finish the bottom edge, so I always try and finish it completely. Not to mention the fact that it just always feels great to complete a project!

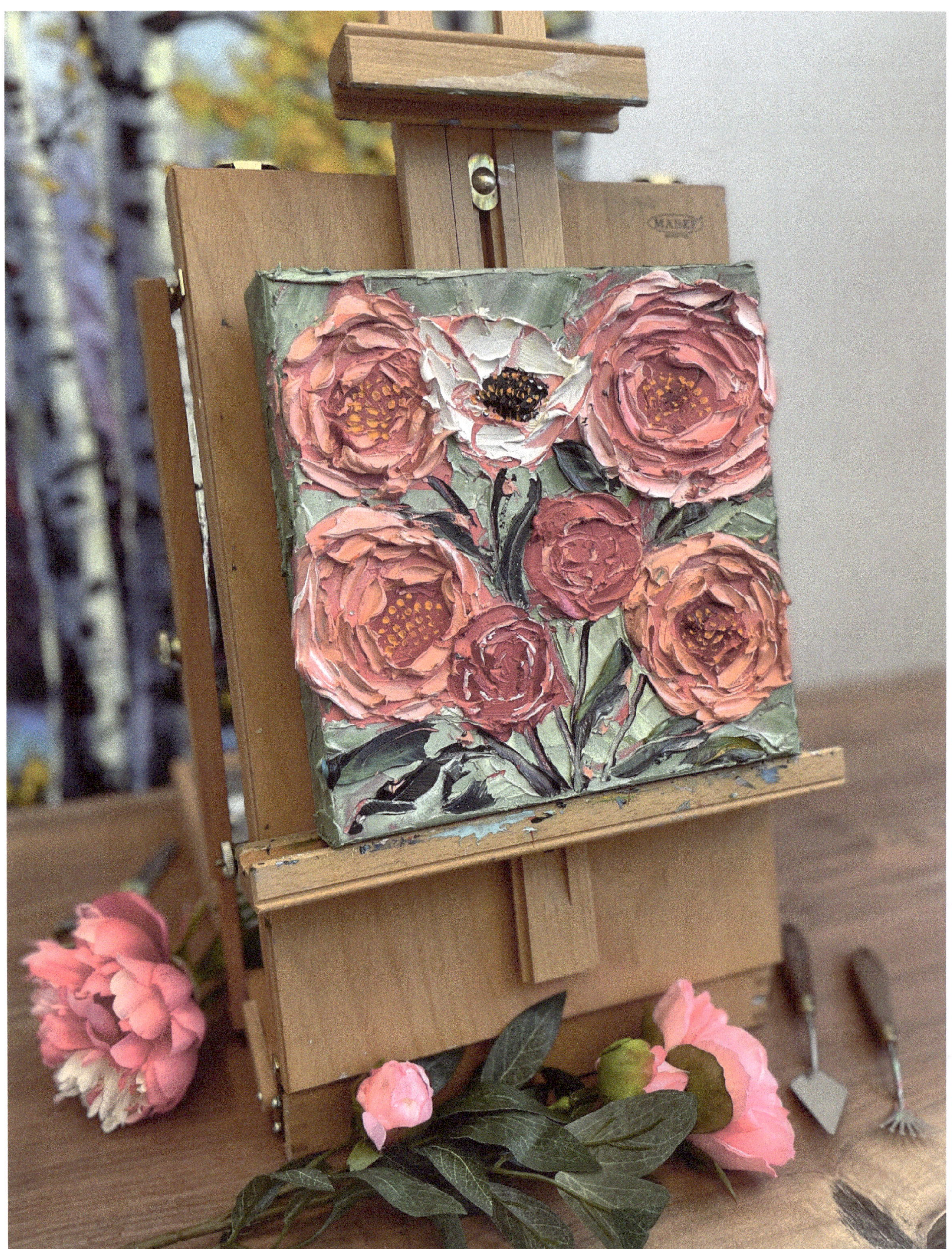
MABEF

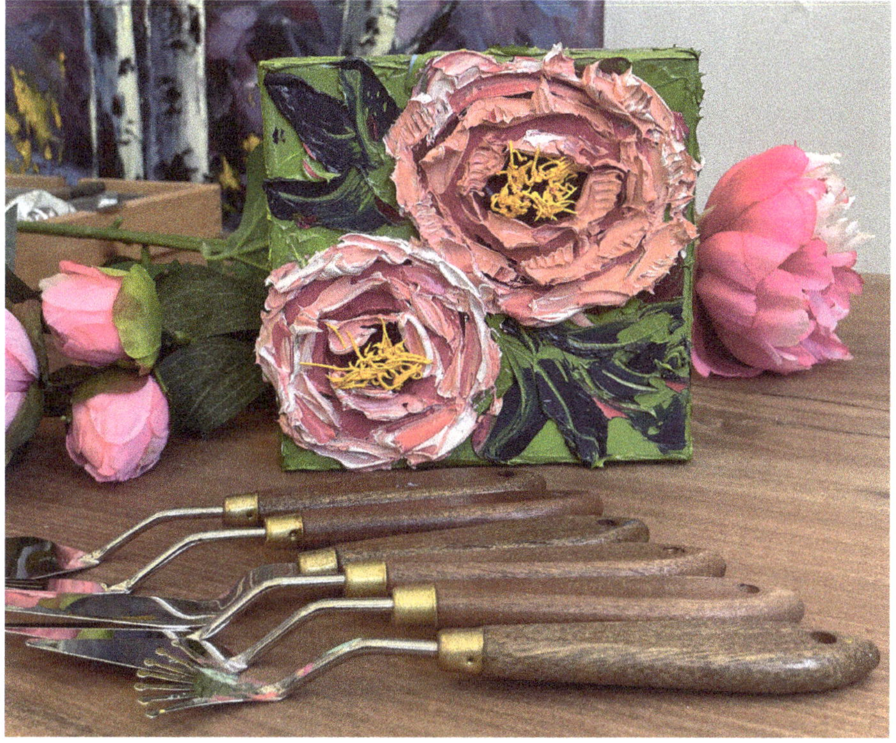

## SUMMARY:

## Did This Inspire You to Find the Perfect Bunch of Peonies to Paint?

There are more than 30 different species of peonies, but the window for enjoying them is small. They only bloom in the late spring and early summer, and for a few days at best. But it's worth the wait!

They turn out beautifully with the palette knife, which captures the fluffy and ethereal qualities nicely with texture, creating ridges, dips, and shadows, as well as movement and interest.

"I must have flowers, always and always."

—CLAUDE MONET

>>> Tip <<<

If you take your palette knife painting outside in the early evening (when it's dry) and hold it in direct light, you'll be mesmerized by the way the texture dances and glows. It's a great time of day, with the golden light to photograph your piece to show off the texture better as well.

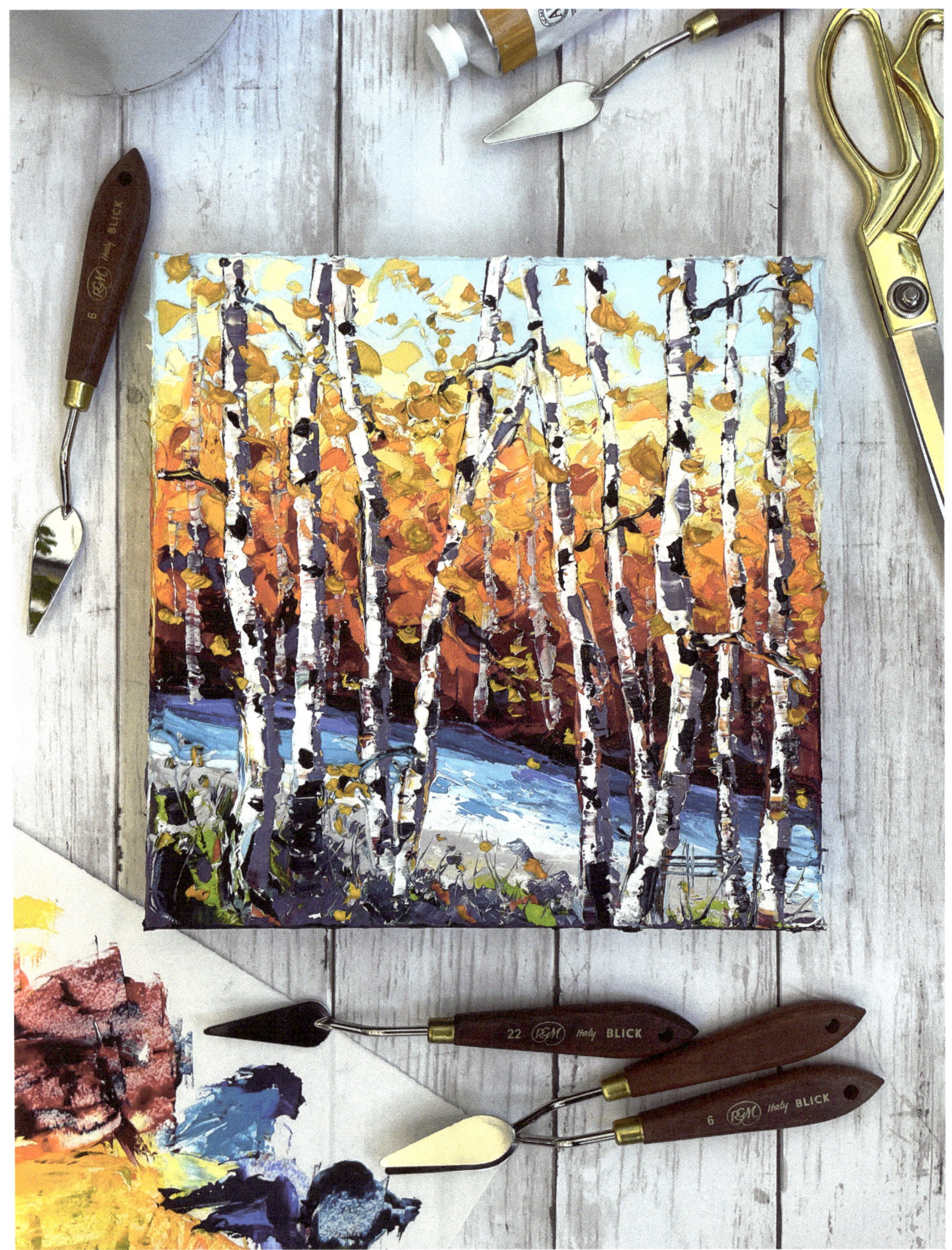
22 RGM Italy BLICK
6 RGM Italy BLICK

# BIRCH TREE FOREST IN THE FALL

| Tools & Materials | Color Palette | Difficulty Level |
|---|---|---|
| • Stretched canvas, size 10″ x 10″ with a 1½-inch depth | Titanium white | |
| • Palette knife: medium size, teardrop shape with rounded tip | Cadmium yellow | |
| • Palette knife: small size, teardrop shape with rounded tip | Cadmium red | |
| • Palette knife: skinny tip (optional) | Alizarin crimson | |
| • Table easel | Cerulean blue | |
| • Palette paper | Ultramarine or French ultramarine blue | |
| • Paper towel or rag for wiping your knife | Prussian blue | |

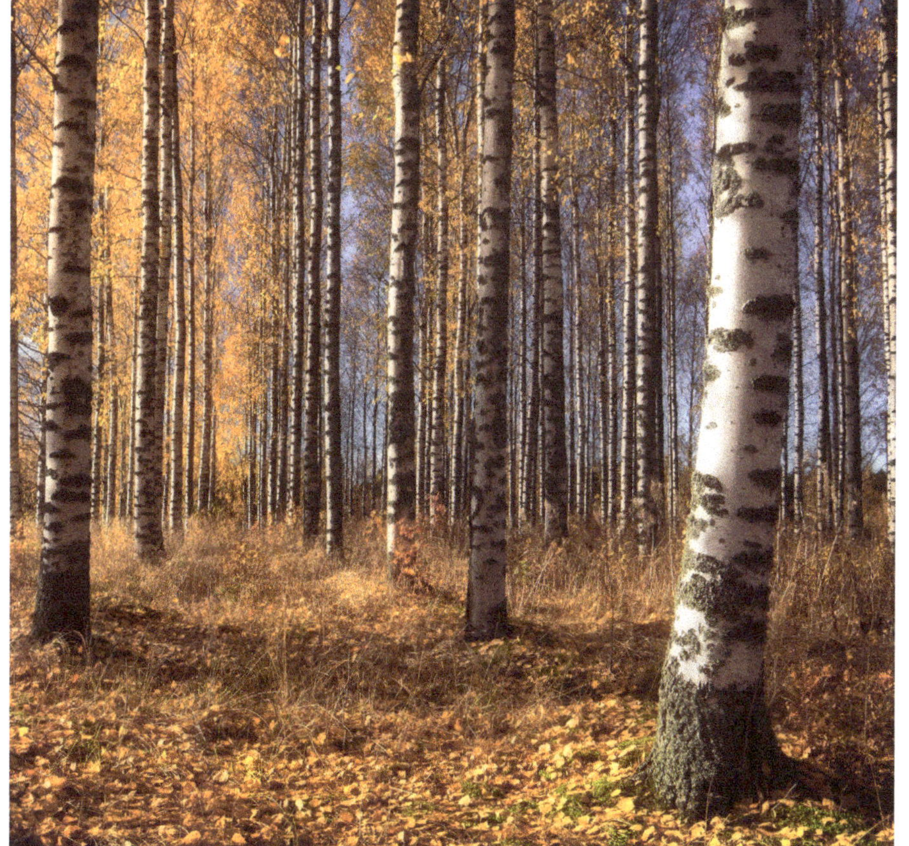

*Inspiration*

My very first palette knife painting in 2012 was of a tree in our backyard in Florida. My instructor at the oil painting course I was enrolled in had inspired me to Google "palette knife painting," after explaining how Gustave Courbet had used the palette knife to paint an entire piece, rather than portions of a painting. I was transfixed by the sculptural quality of the process, and my obsession with palette knives was born. I have not put my knives down since, and I still adore the quick abandon and the striking effect of painting with a knife. Birch and aspen trees are my favorite, with their stark white trunks overlaid on a colorful background.

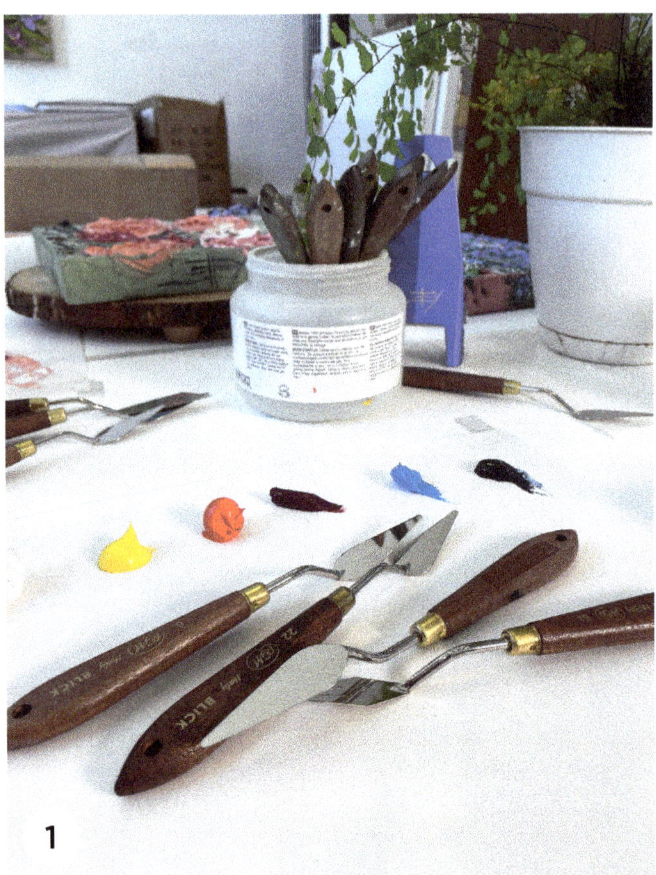


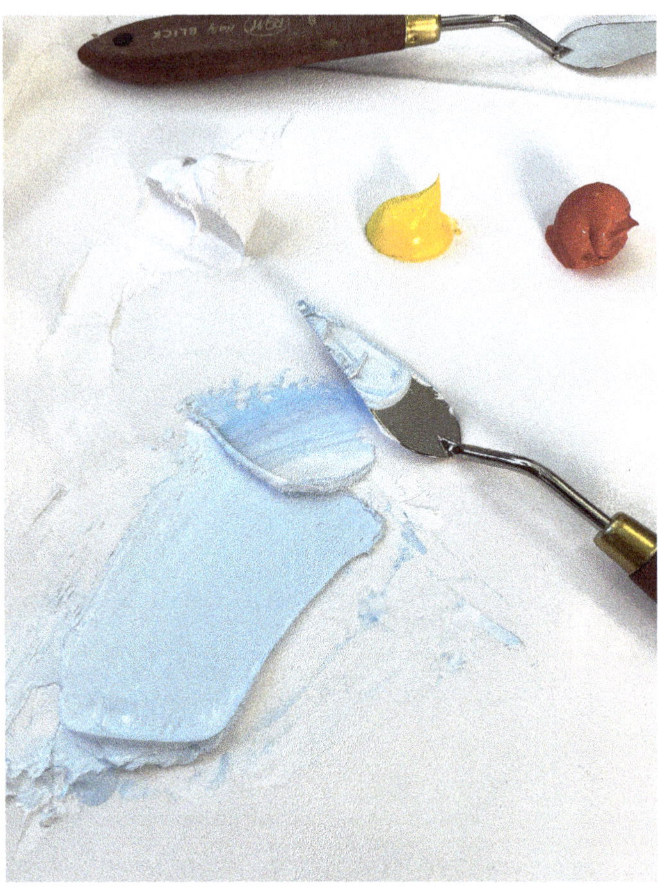

## Step-By-Step Instructions

**Step 1: Lay out your colors & mix your basic sky and treetop hues**

- Squeeze out a large portion of white paint, about the size of 2 heaped tablespoons on the top left of your palette. We are going to be blocking in the background color here again, before filling in the trunks on this piece. Are you noticing a pattern here? Fill in the background first, and then the elements in the foreground.

- Squeeze out around 1 teaspoon each of cadmium yellow, cadmium red, alizarin crimson, cerulean blue, ultramarine blue, and Prussian blue in that order.

- Start by dragging down 1 tablespoon of white, and ½ teaspoon of cerulean blue. Mix them together until very light blue. Then add a dot of orange mixed from red and yellow to dull it down a little.

- Now drag down 1 tablespoon of white with a clean knife and ½ teaspoon of yellow, and mix. These two colors are going to sit side by side and overlap somewhat, but we are not blending the background. This painting is mostly an overlay effect without much blending and is a great example of the wet-into-wet technique.

**Step 2: Lay in your blue sky & yellow treetops foliage**

- Load your knife with 1 tablespoon of light blue, and starting at the top right of your canvas, start blocking in your sky with a large sweep side to side, right across the top of your canvas. We are creating a sky peeking through the foliage here, so we want it more patchy as we go down. Repeat this by reloading your knife with more tablespoons of blue, until you've filled in about 2 inches.

- Wipe your knife and reload with 1 tablespoon of your light yellow color. Now we're going to start laying the blue and

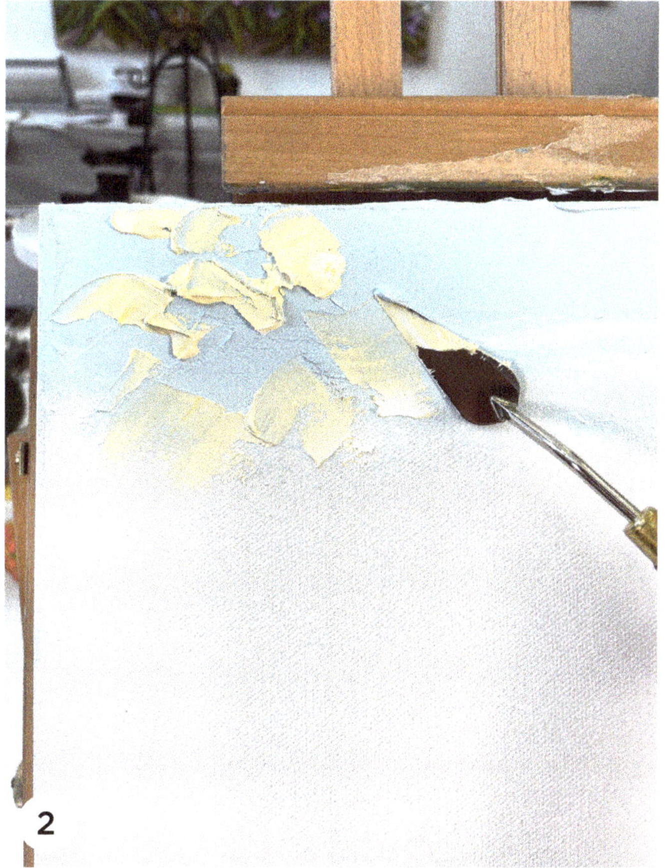

yellow colors together without blending. Using shorter, choppy side-to-side around 1-inch strokes, start placing the yellow on the canvas in sweeps, starting at the top and moving down, with random strokes. Make sure you vary the direction of these strokes. Some are right to left, some are left to right, some tilt upward at the end as you lift your knife, and some tilt downward. The yellow is the tree foliage and the very tips of the trees in the background, so we want the effect of leaves, which are very inconsistent. In general, I like to give my leaf foliage a little swoop down and up in a U shape. Let's call it the inward U and the outward U, rotating the wrist toward and away from the body. This motion gives the paint blobs movement and makes the leaves look like they are dancing around, being blown by the wind and drifting to the forest floor.

- I started at the top left of the canvas, but you could start anywhere at the top. When you get to the area where the blue paint runs out, reload your knife and start filling in this portion with the same type of strokes of yellow. The trees gain volume as they do down, so our treetops are more sparse. This is where you can blend a little more if needed, to fill in the white canvas gaps.

- Continue across the canvas with this U technique until you've filled in the top portion with light yellow strokes, leaving plenty of blue peeking through and filling in the portion that meets the white canvas so that there are no more gaps.

**Step 3: Lay in your orange & red tree foliage**

- Now we are going to fill in the rest of our colorful tree background, and you'll start to see your piece coming to life.

- Drag down 1 tablespoon of your yellow, and about 1 teaspoon of cadmium red. Mix it so that you have a yellow color that is a darker than your previous one. Add a dot of cerulean blue right there next to it to dull it down just a little. Now drag down 1 teaspoon of white, and mix with a little of

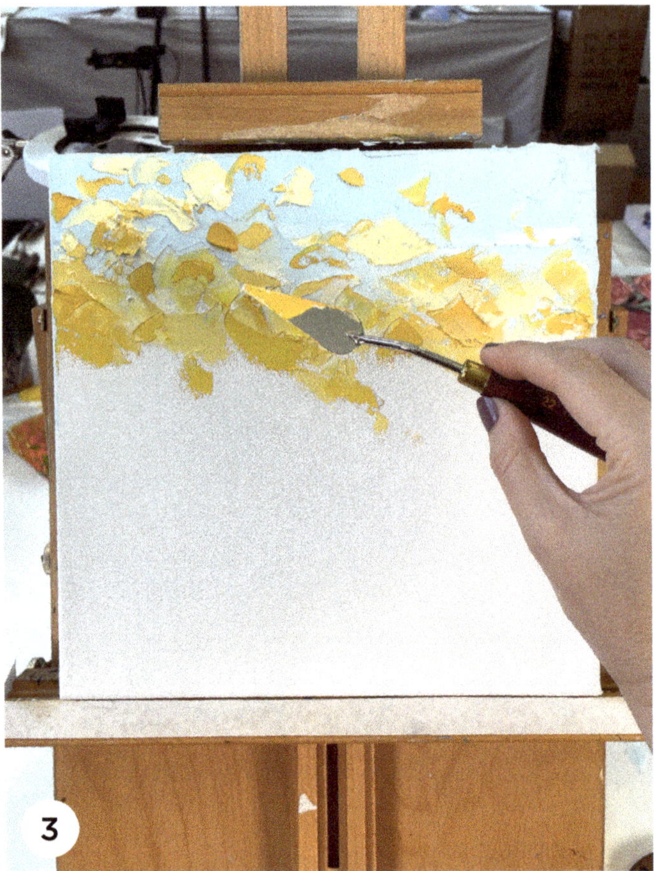


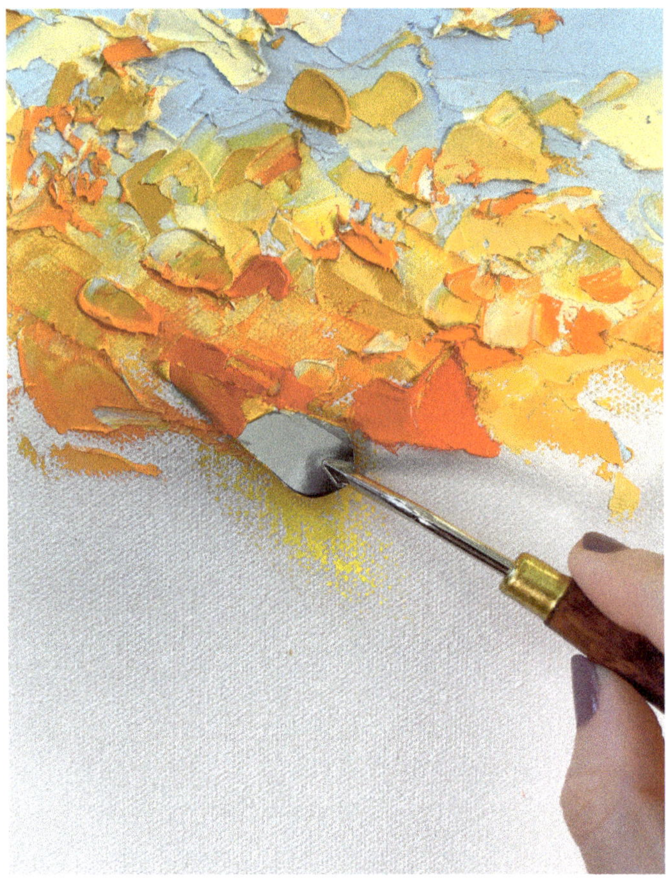

your yellow to lighten it up a bit. We're going for somewhat of a gradient here with our fall colors, so we want the colors to flow into each other. It's good to have them mixed and ready to go.

- Start placing in your darker yellow with side-to-side sweeps, in the same way you did with the U technique. In some places I'm also skimming the knife over the top of the light yellow paint to catch some on the edges. I'm also wanting to go darker as I go down the canvas, so I just add a few highlights at the top, with more as I go down, and fill in the area where the light yellow stops at the white canvas.
- Now I move on to my darker yellow, using the same technique and placing in the darker portions with a few higher, but most lower, moving my way down the canvas.
- It's time to bring it up a notch and start on the orange. Drag down ½ teaspoon of cadmium red and 1 teaspoon of yellow, and mix.
- Start adding sweeps of orange using the same U technique. Lightly sweep your knife across the tops of the darker yellow, getting larger as you move down the canvas and filling in the lower portions by the white canvas.
- Now drag down another teaspoon of cadmium red and add it to the existing orange until you have a very vibrant and saturated orange, and repeat this all again, dotting in some smaller leaves and adding more as you go down.
- Note here that I'm not laying these colors straight across the canvas like a fence. I've started higher on the left and let it fade out a little on the right.
- Now I drag down another teaspoon of cadmium red, and make a slightly darker shade of orange, mixing it with a little yellow. Repeat the U technique, adding the darker orange in smaller portions, and ending just below the white canvas. Don't go overboard here. It's a very bright color, and we don't need a ton of this.

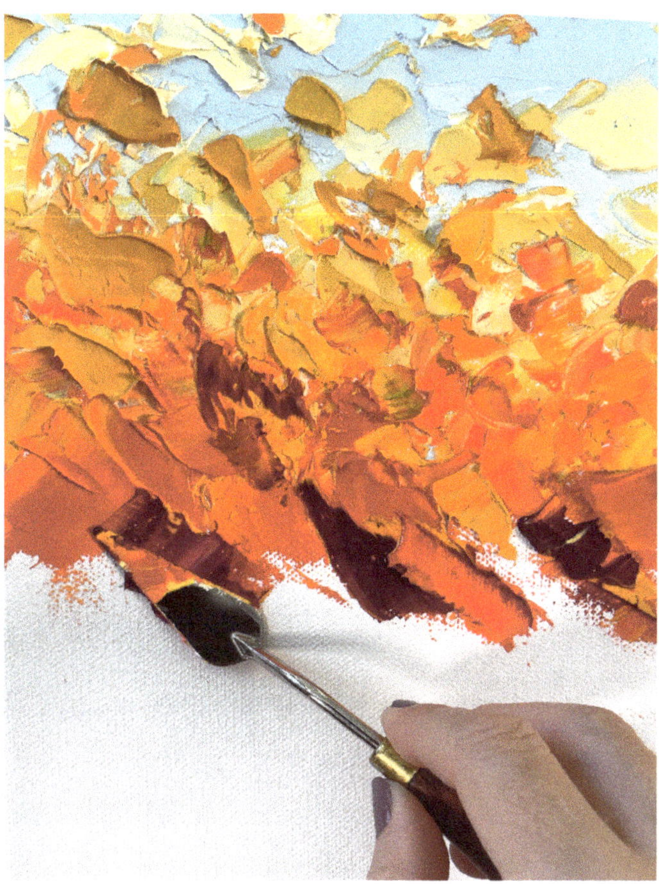

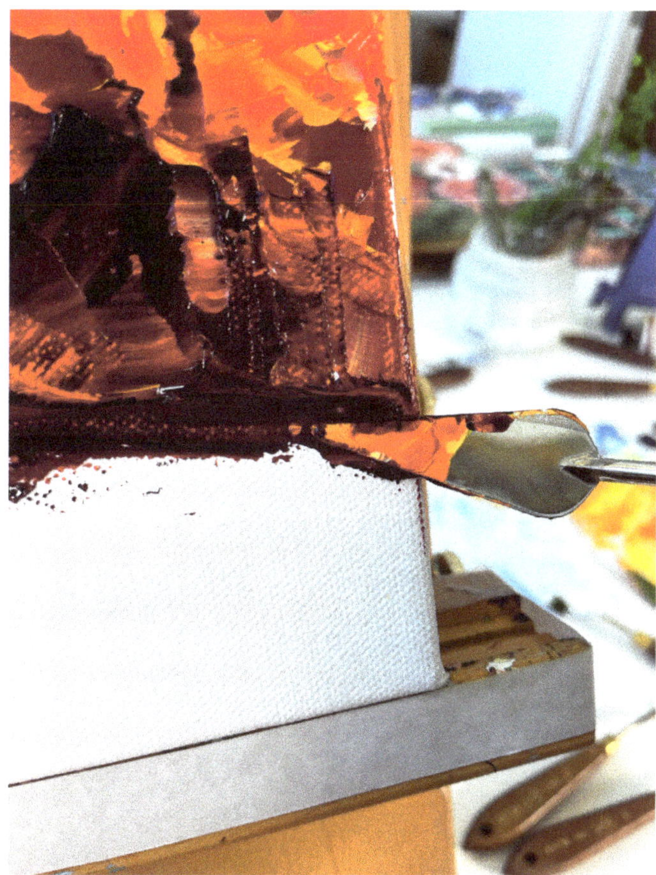

- I decided at this point that it needed a little more medium value orange to balance it out. Now is the time to adjust this portion, as you can't go back and do it after you've put in the trunks. We're going for a nice balance of colors, not too much of any one, so I adjusted it a little by adding some strokes of medium orange right over the top. This also adds more texture, exactly what we're going for.

- Now we're going to add our red, and then we'll be done with the background foliage. Drag down 1 teaspoon of crimson, and mix it with around 1 teaspoon of cadmium red, or just whatever is left on your palette. It's OK to be streaky here with these darker colors, so don't worry about mixing it thoroughly.

- Now start placing in your red using the same U technique, being careful not to overwhelm the piece with too much red and keeping a nice, balanced gradient, in keeping with your previous shades.

- We're also wanting to start shaping our mountain stream, so I start pulling down my red on the right more, to make the downstream composition.

- Now, using pure crimson, my darkest shade in my foliage, I place in some strokes at the bottom, again, not using so much that I overwhelm things, but making sure I end my foliage with the darkest shade across the bottom. I then drag down around ½ teaspoon of Prussian blue and mix it with 1 teaspoon of crimson. Repeating this technique, I finish the bottom strip, with a gentle slope down on the right.

- My final detail here is to add a few purple highlights to the darkest red areas to suggest cooler shadows. Using your existing crimson, add a little cerulean blue and mix. Then place in a few small random strokes, right over your darkest reds.

- Now is a good time to take a break if you feel like you need it. I'm a tea drinker, so off I go to reset a bit and gain some perspective. When you step back and look at your piece, you'll often see fresh things to adjust, versus staring at the same piece for too long, creating tunnel vision.

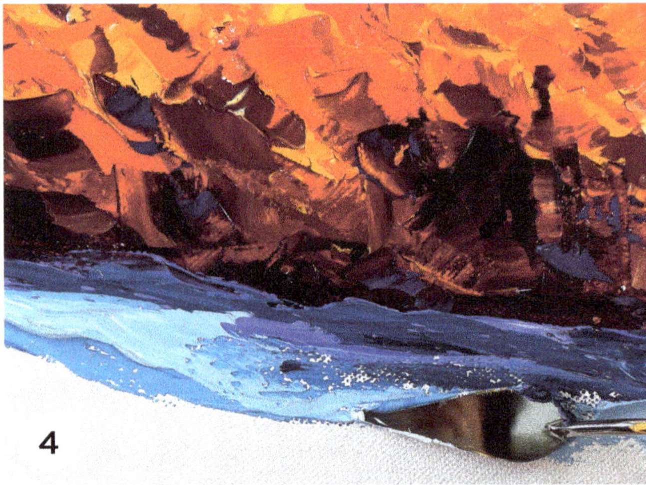

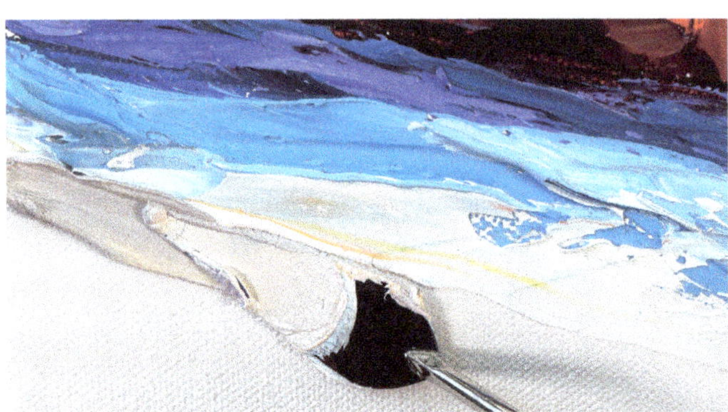

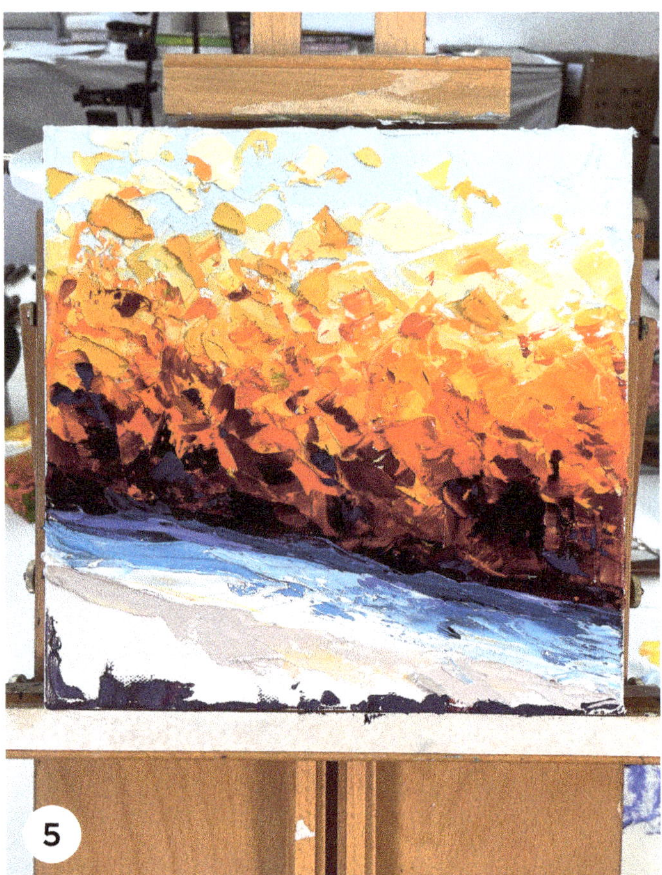

- Go ahead and check for too-large areas of any one color. Break these up with strokes of opposing colors if needed.

**Step 4: Sketching in the river**

- Drag down 1 teaspoon of ultramarine blue, and using the tip and middle portion of the blade, load and start laying in the water with a sideways motion, pulling the knife along in the direction of the water, matching up the dark reds and moving down the canvas from left to right. Try not to blend the reds and blue here too much; just gently match up the two colors with the tip of your knife.
- Once you've done a strip of ultramarine blue right across, drag down 1 teaspoon of cerulean blue, and add another streak in the same motion, matching it up with the ultramarine blue above and going in the direction of the flowing water.
- Lighten up the water a little to suggest some whitewater areas where the water is moving faster. Add a little white to your cerulean blue and mix loosely. Now add another strip of lighter blue with white under your cerulean blue. You can play around here with skimming your knife lightly over the top of the other colors, and as the paint "sticks" to the underlayer, it creates natural-looking rivulets and frothy portions.
- Now lighten it up a little more by adding another teaspoon of white to your cerulean blue, hardly mixing it, and create a lighter portion where the water pools a little on the right side of your stream. We don't want the stream to be the same width all the way across, so making it wider on the right makes it look more natural as well.

**Step 5: Filling in the ground**

- Now we're going to fill in the ground portion before laying our trees over the top of the background.
- I want a suggestion of a bank below my stream, so I go ahead and make a sandy color by mixing 1 teaspoon of white with around a pea-sized portion of yellow and cadmium

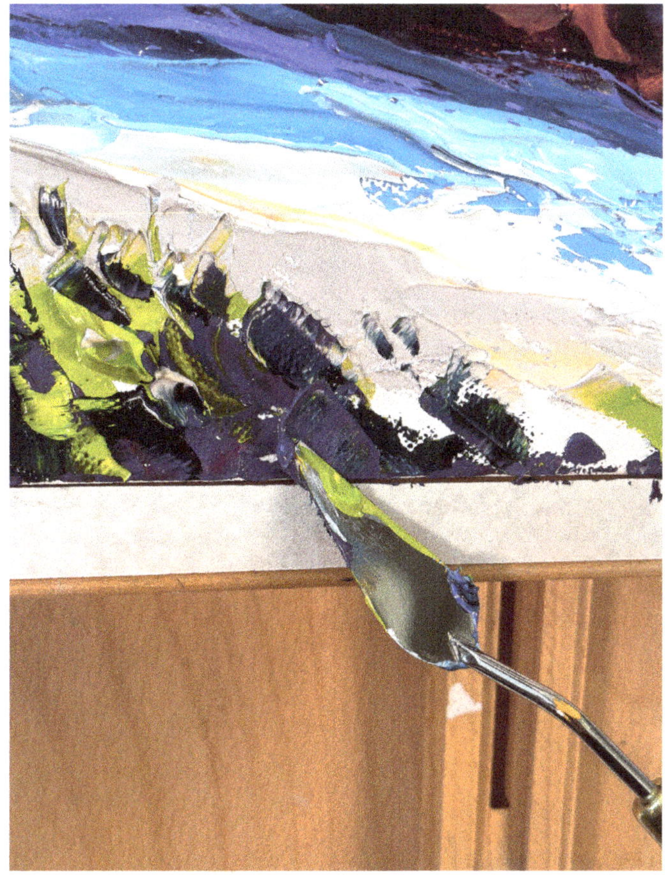

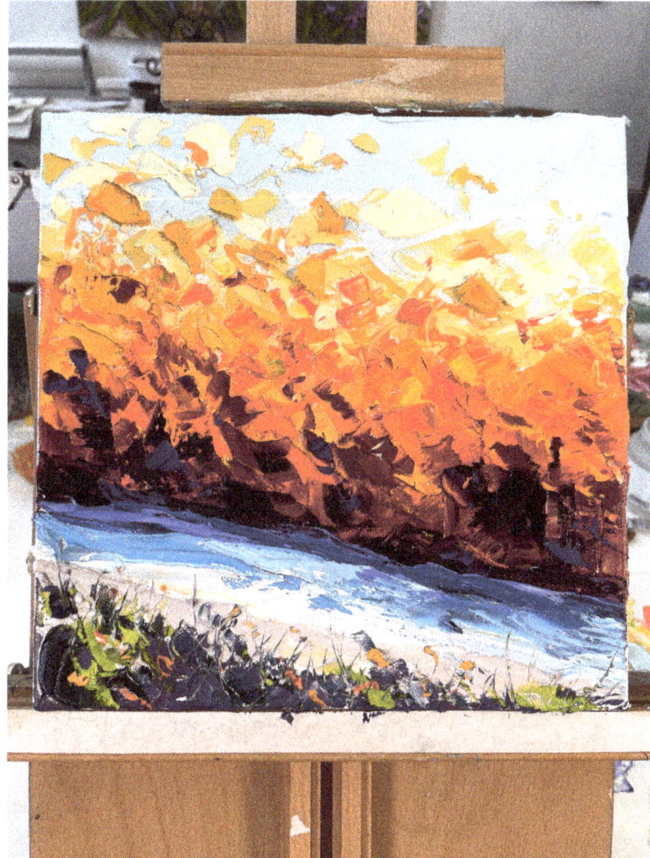

red. Add just a dot of your left-over purple if it needs dulling down a little. Using mostly the tip of the knife, I sketch in a strip below my white water, making sure I'm keeping it loose and not finicky, the same way I did the water, pulling the knife along in the same direction.

- I'm now going to lay in the darkest ground portion where the trees end, before blocking in the green. Using your left-over purple (add some yellow if it's too bright), and the edge of the knife, cover the bottom edge of your canvas with upwards strokes to fill it in.
- Now we need some under-growth, and I really love a little pop of green here. We have to be careful not to overdo it, as this is an autumn scene, which in real life would not have much green.
- Drag down 1 teaspoon of yellow, and mix with your cerulean blue left on your palette. Start laying in your grassy foliage with side-to-side strokes across the canvas, overlapping the sandy color and the dark purple. We're not blending here, but color blocking to fill in the white canvas.
- I don't want my green all the way across the bottom, so I break it up with dark purple strokes to fill in the white canvas, keeping it sponta-neous and gestural, and with the movement and strokes flowing upwards like the natural movement of the grassy undergrowth.
- Once I have the white canvas filled in, I then use my long skinny palette knife to create more grasslike strands by scraping the paint upward in different directions. You can use your regular knife for this if needed.
- Then switch back to your regular knife and add a few little dot highlights of red and yellow here and there in the ground portion to pull all the colors together.
- Let's pause and assess things before we move on to the trunks. Now is the time to fix things if needed. There's no

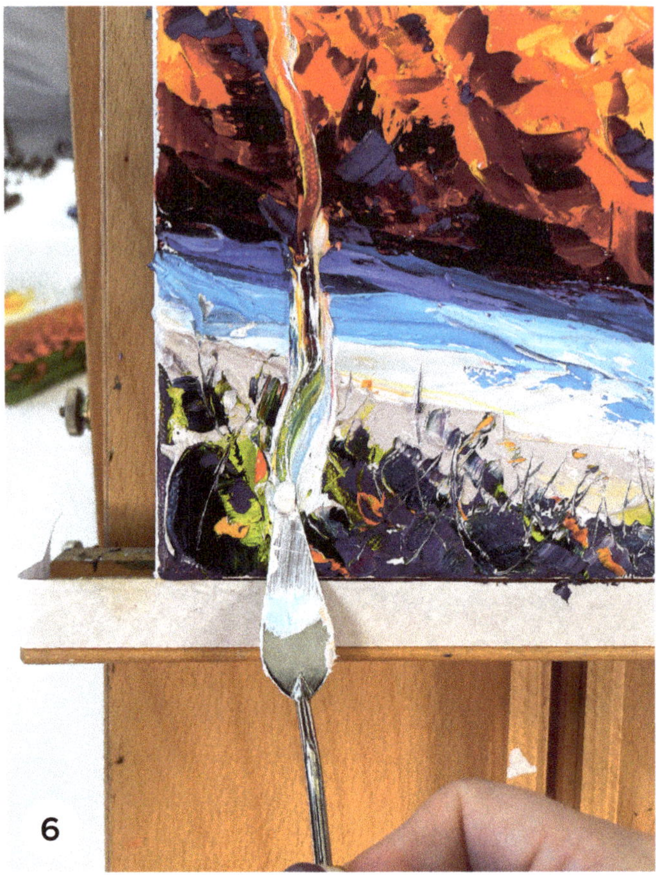

6

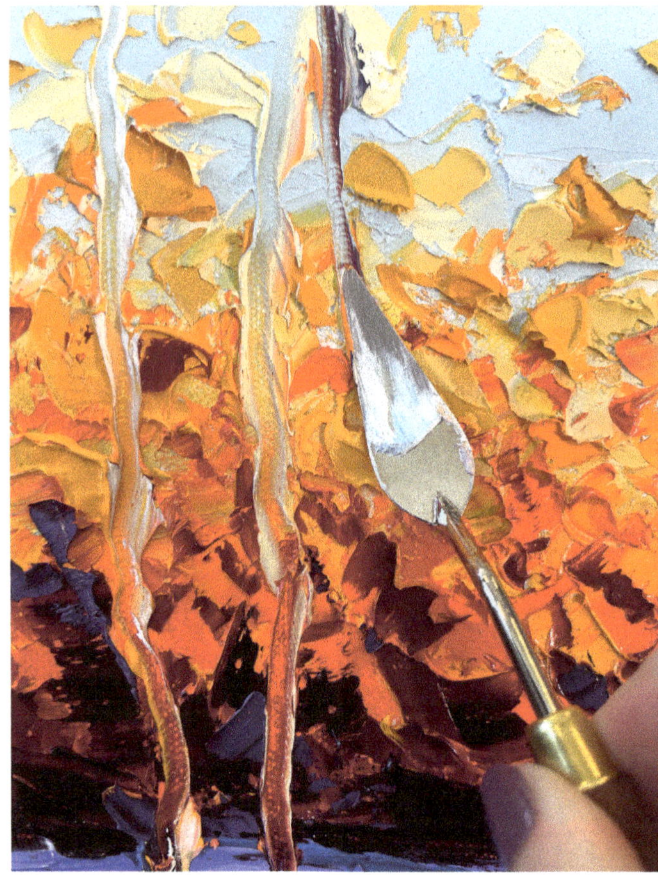

going back once the trunks are on. I don't think we need to. It's looking good! We could stop now, and this could be a painting all by itself. If you're thinking that, it's a good indicator you're doing a great job. Also, remember that fiddling doesn't usually result in a better piece, so it's mostly just better to move on and finish.

**Step 6: Adding the white trunks**

- With a clean knife, drag down 1 tablespoon of white, and add a dot of yellow, mixing until it's nice and pliable.

- We're going to be sketching in the trunks and also kind of carving them out at the same time. Don't worry—it sounds complicated, but it's super easy and it's fun!

- Leaving just a thin layer of white on your knife, begin sketching in your first trunk on the left, about 1 inch from the edge on the canvas. Starting at the top and using mostly the tip, sketch down loosely making sure not to keep it absolutely straight, but more meandering and flowy down the canvas to the bottom, ending where the grass stops. Do this all in one stroke, gently but firmly.

- We're not really carving out the underlayer of paint, but applying gentle pressure to create a natural line in the indented underpainting.

- Wipe your knife, and repeat this technique across your canvas, making sure to keep the distance between trees varied, and to make some veer off-center when you start at the top, so they're not all uniform. I went and placed four trunks on the right. These birch trees cluster somewhat, so try to make some of them group at the bottom. I left a natural gap in the middle before continuing across the canvas.

- On the right, I place in five trees, making sure to keep them varied and clustered somewhat.

- I now add a tiny detail in the background in the form of smaller trunks across the river. Using a tiny amount of white paint, and the edge of your knife, lay in some very gestural trunks in the red areas

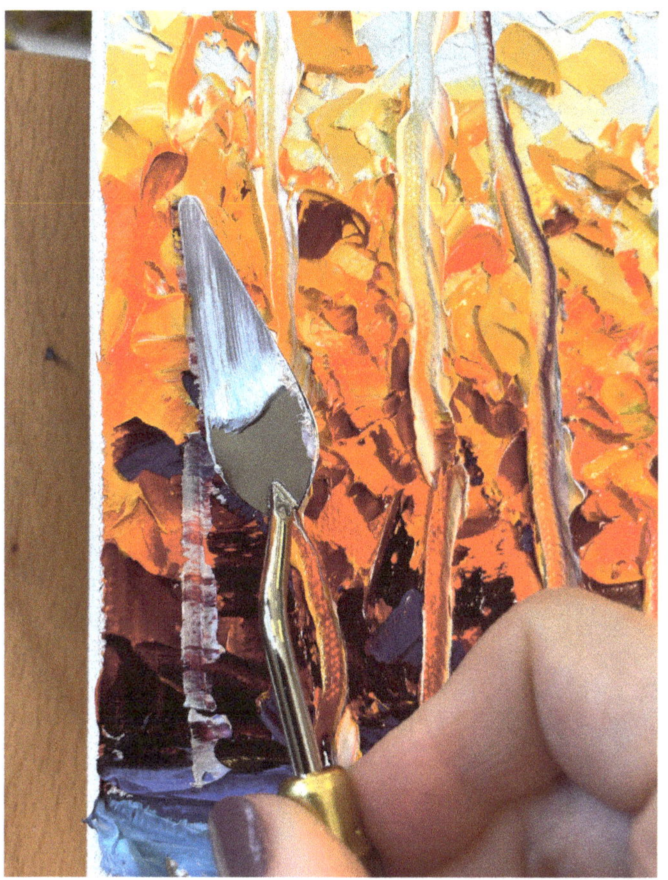

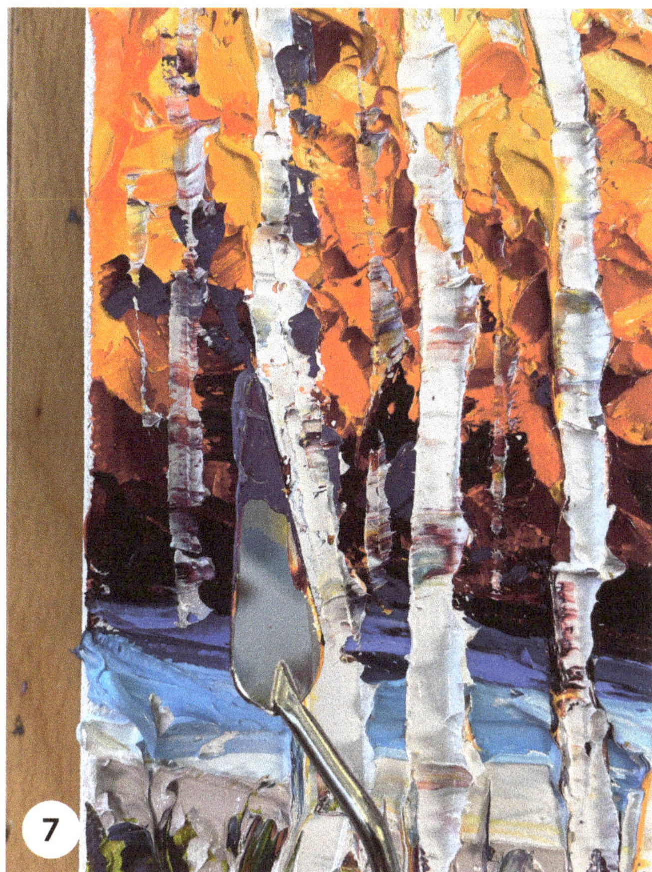


between your trunks in the foreground. Don't do them all the way up, but let them taper off and disappear. We want these trunks to stay in the background, so don't do them too dark, but make them a mere suggestion. They will add to the depth of the piece.

- Now we'll start building up the texture on the trunks, and you'll really see them start to come to life and pop forward in the composition.
- Load your clean knife with about ½ tablespoon sliver of white on the left edge, and starting at the top left, lay in your white using the edge of your knife with a sideways stroke, placing the paint on gently so that it sticks. Pull the knife up and repeat the stroke underneath several times until you've done the entire trunk, wiping and reloading your knife as you go.
- Repeat this technique for all trunks in the foreground, making sure you leave some portions thicker, and not worrying too much about the red paint underneath showing through.

**Step 7: Adding the shadows on the trunks**

- Drag down what you have left of your dark purple and add just a little white to it if needed. We're going to be creating a shadowy side of the trunks, to make them appear round. In this painting, the sun is on the left, so the light hits the trunks on their left side, then recedes into shadows on the right side.
- Load your knife with a small portion of dark purple. With darker colors, we are sketching more than building up texture, so we're really just skimming the knife over the white rather than adding bulk.
- Using the same sideways motion you used to lay in the white, start laying in your dark purple starting on the right side of the trunk, with the right edge of the blade, moving the knife toward the left and pulling it up.

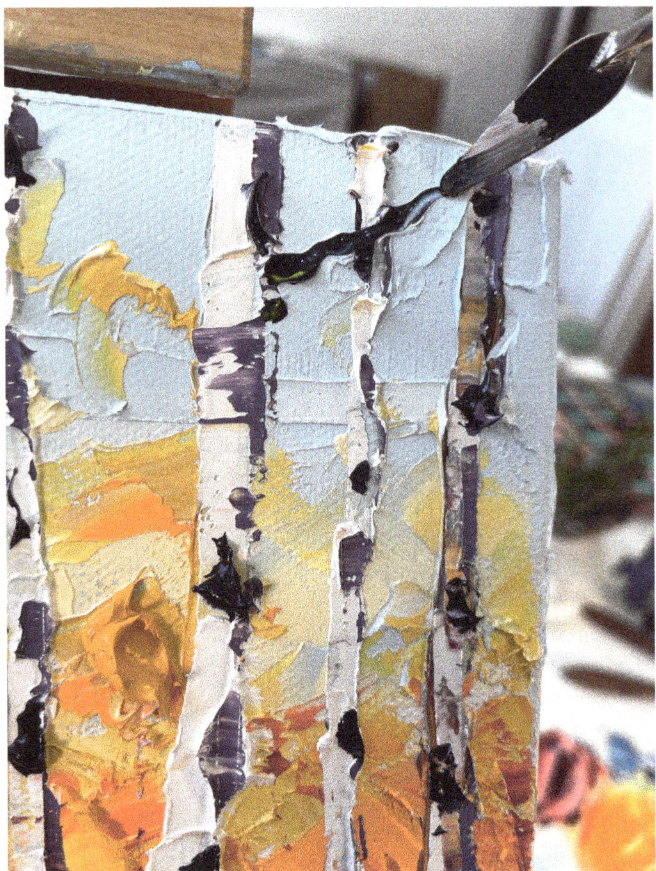

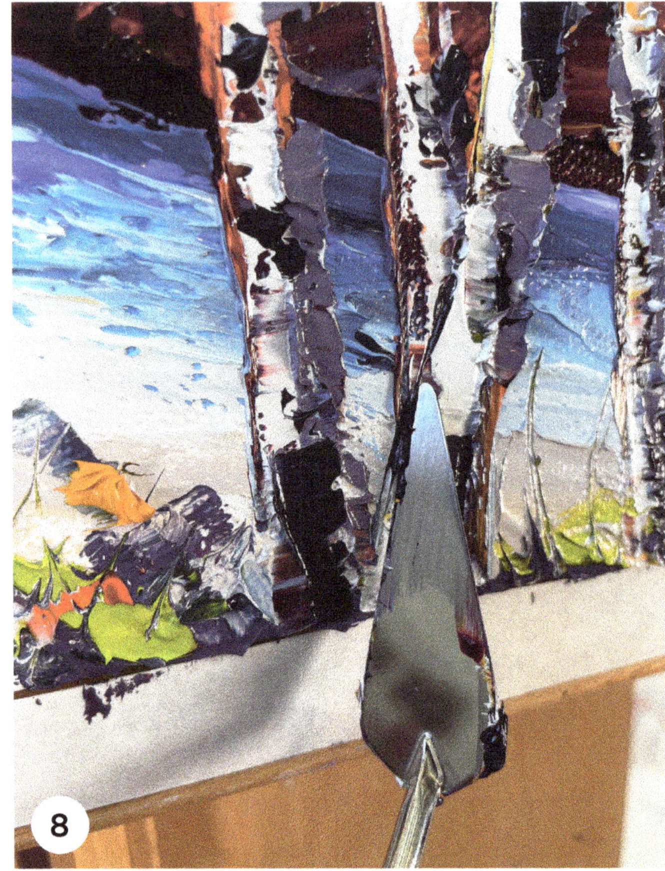


- Be careful here not to cover the entire trunk with your dark color. We want lots of variations here, so make sure to leave a lot of white peeking through to create the patchy effect.
- Continue wiping and reloading and adding the dark purple to all your trees in the foreground.

**Step 8: Laying in the black bark details**

- This is my favorite part! Adding the black details here really shapes the piece and makes the trees recognizable. You get to sketch and create little knots and branches and twigs and hollows that give your piece tons of personality.
- We're nearly there—you got this. Let's get these trunks done and finish the piece!
- I often use Prussian blue, cadmium red, and alizarin crimson to mix a very dark color. You can also use Payne's gray instead if you have it.
- Using the tip of your knife, start dotting in the tree knots and ridges with a quick dab, applying a little pressure to make sure it sticks to the paint below and pulling up the knife. You can switch to your smaller knife here if you prefer, if it feels easier to maneuver.
- It's a good idea to start at the top left and make your way right, but I often get excited and place dots wherever I feel like here, making sure to space them out about an inch, but also clustering a couple here and there to keep them inconsistent.
- Once you've filled in a few black dots on each trunk, you then want to add a few little branches here and there by loading the tip of the knife with your dark color and dragging the tip of your knife through the paint. These can be mostly at the top, or midway down the trunks, and I usually place them where there is a gap, or an area that could use a little extra interest or balance.
- I also switched to my smaller knife here, as the tip is smaller.

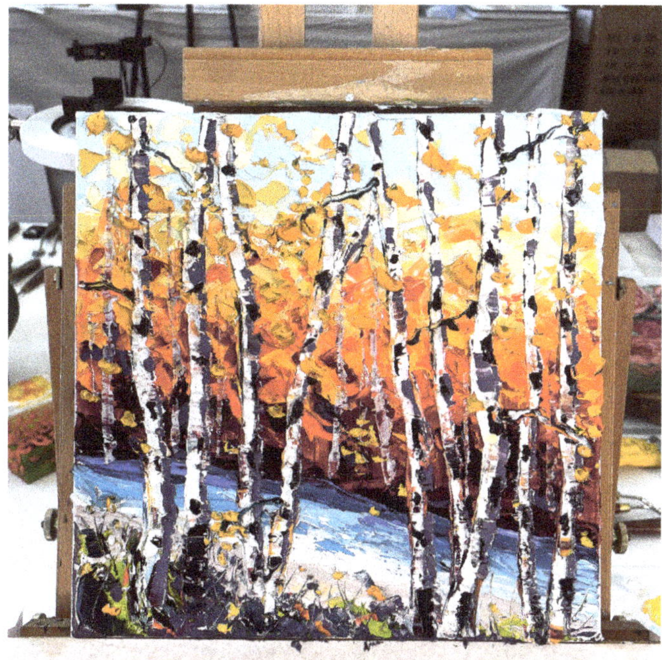

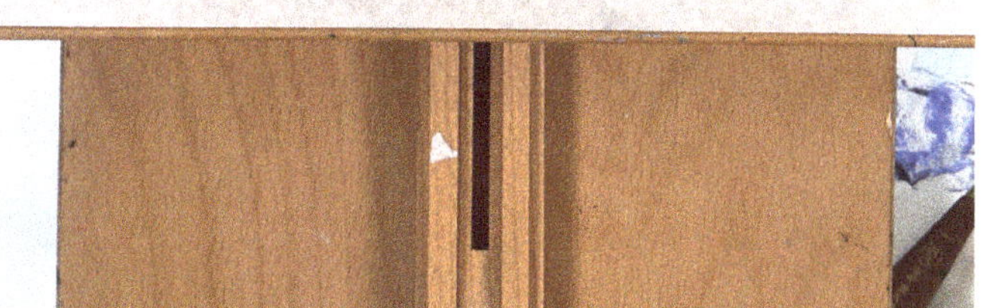

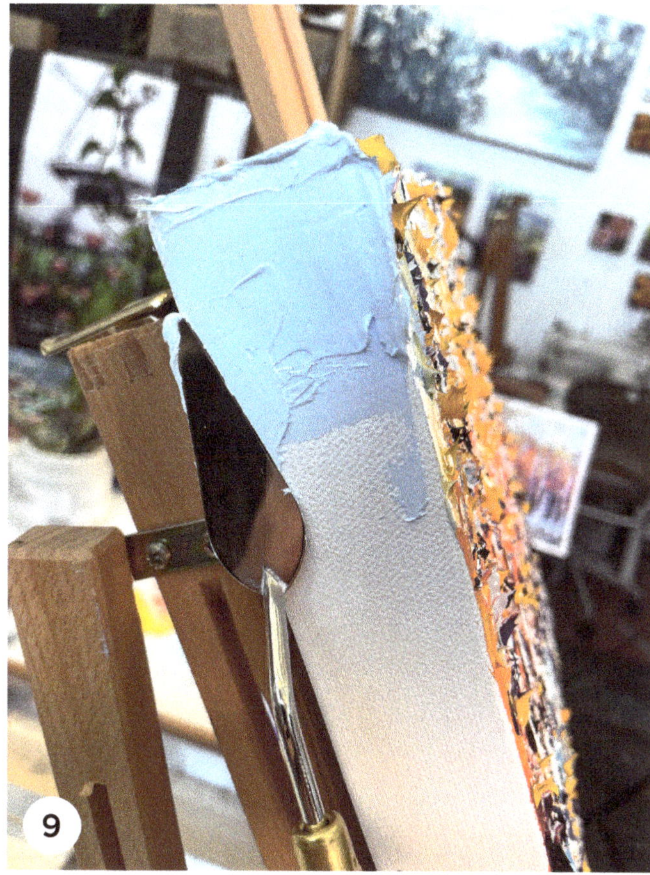

9

We don't want to carve out huge branches here, just little suggestions of branchlets where we can then add foliage. I added about 10 smaller branches before deciding that was enough to balance out the composition.

- The last detail to add with the dark paint is some lines on the edges of the trunks to tidy them up and create just a little more definition.
- Using the edge of your knife, draw it through the dark paint sideways with the edge of the blade, so the edge is covered with a sliver, and go ahead and add a few thin lines where the white paint is messy on the edges of your trunks, or where the trunks need a little more definition. This will have the most effect over the blue sky area and the river. Don't overdo it, and make sure you don't draw a line all the way down the trunks. Only do this in portions to keep it subtle.
- The last detail here is little pops of yellow foliage on the ends of our little branches and a few dots here and there to suggest falling leaves. These dots can cover the white trunks in places. Go ahead and use up the yellow and orange paint on your palette by dotting in these little falling leaves. They add to the texture and the overall effect and really make your painting leap off the canvas.

**Step 9: Paint the edges**

- It's nice to match up the pattern on these fall tree pieces, so I may have to mix a little more of the colors. Starting with cerulean blue on top and the top portion of both sides, I loosely lay in strokes of blue, filling in the white. Where the tree trunks stop at the top, I add little suggestions of white at the top, so that the edge isn't so stark.
- I then match up the pale yellow, darker yellow, cadmium red, and crimson on both sides, before moving on to the river and the ground.

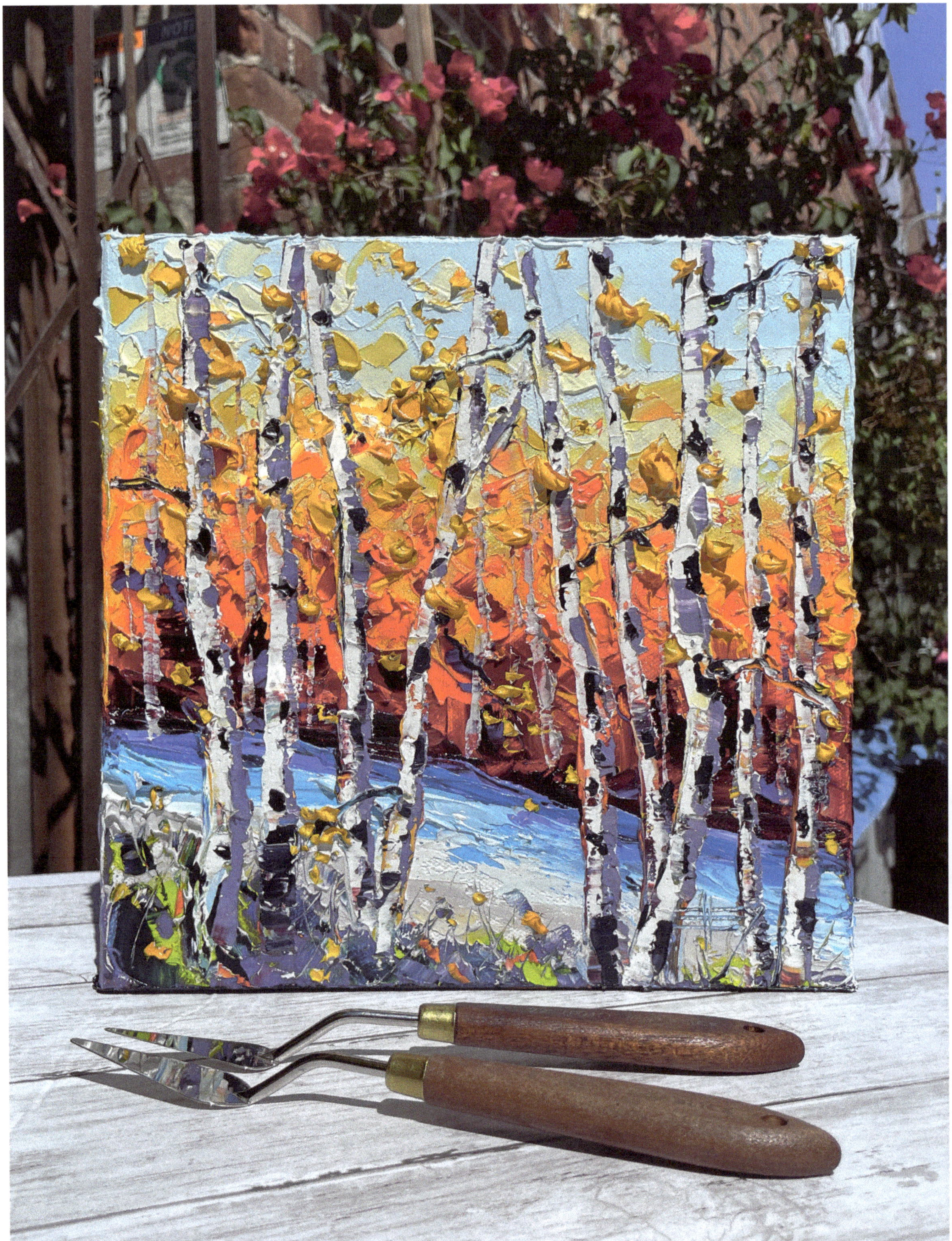

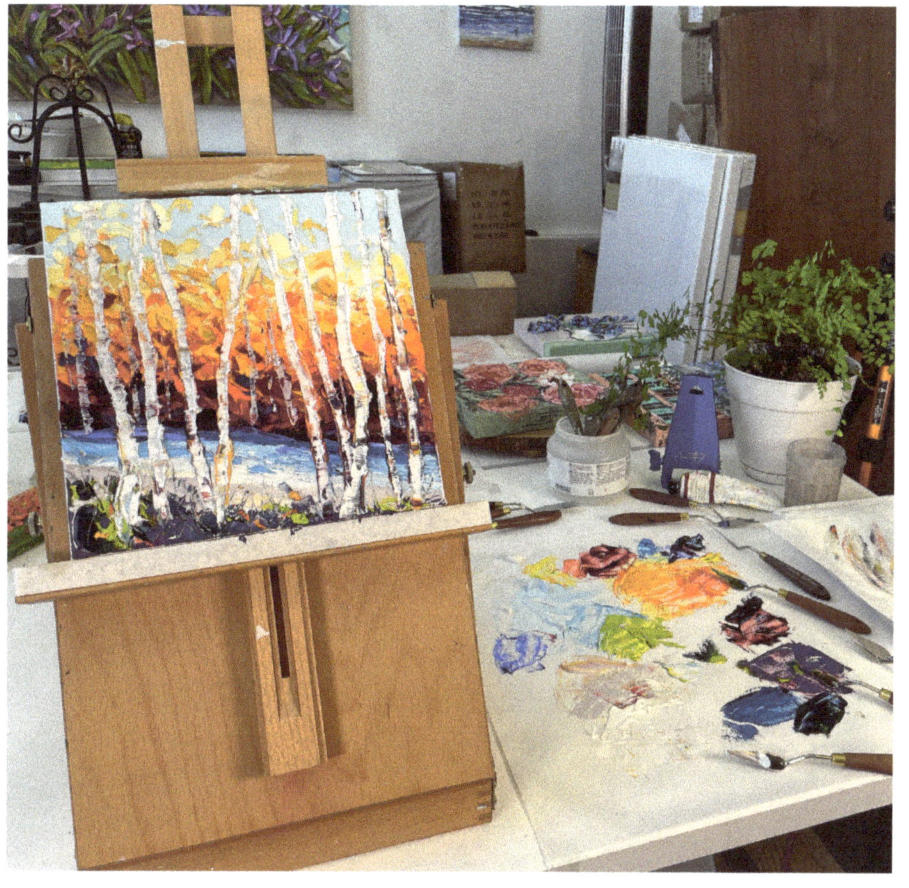

## SUMMARY:

## *Is Fall Your Favorite Season?*

These colorful fall tree paintings make me want to book a trip to New Hampshire! There's just nothing like the feeling of fall after a long summer, with crisp air and turning leaves.

You can create many different variations of this scene, large and small. If you make sure to follow the same steps, you can vary the color palette and composition. Just remember to always start with laying in your background before laying your trunks over the top. You can put mountains in the background, after the sky and before the foliage. You can also put another layer of trees like evergreens in the midground, over the top of the red foliage, and before the river. The possibilities are endless!

*"I'm so glad I live in a world where there are Octobers."*

—L.M. MONTGOMERY

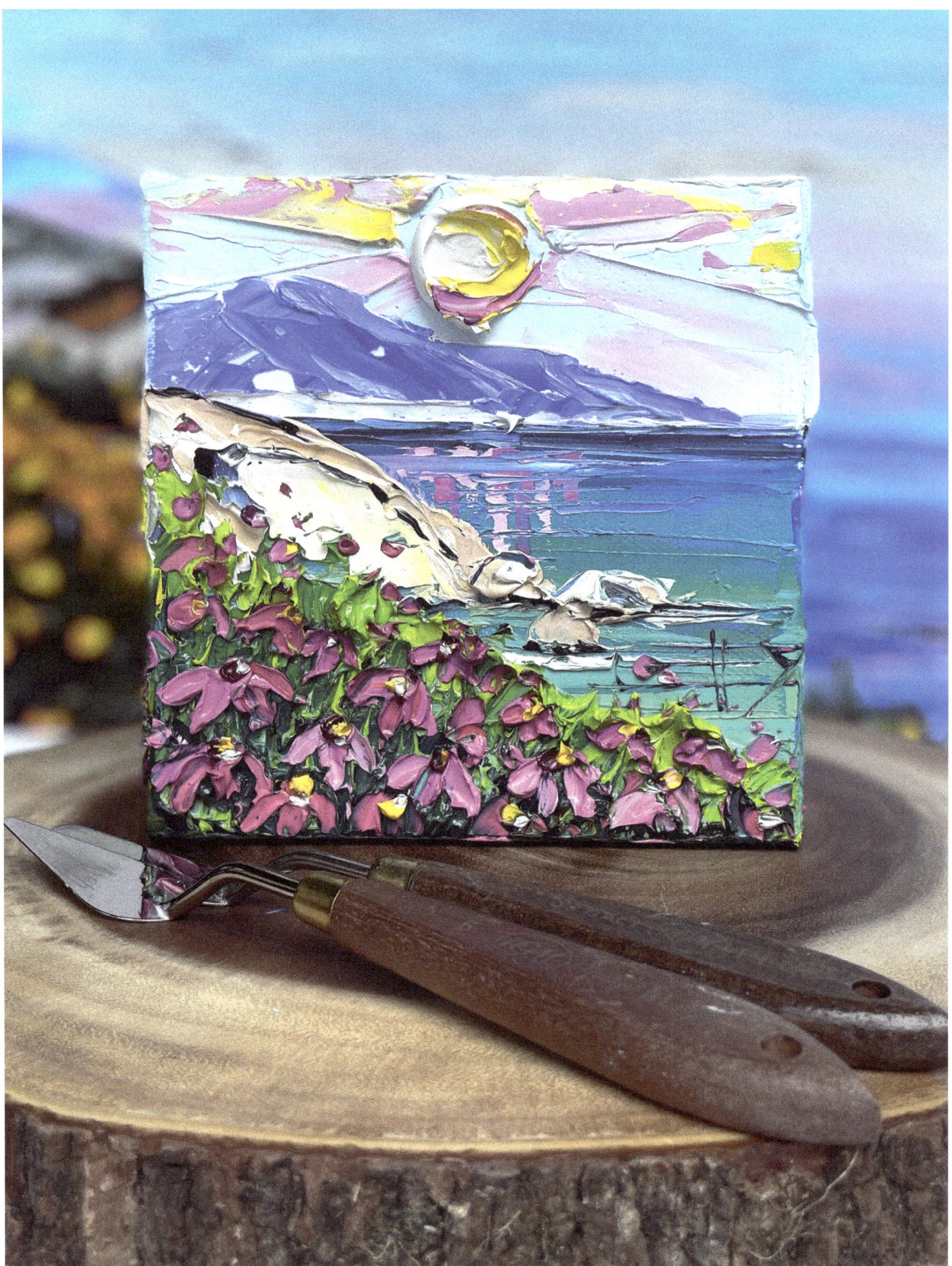

# COASTAL LANDSCAPE WITH WILDFLOWERS

### Tools & Materials

- Stretched canvas, size 6″ x 6″ with a 1½-inch depth
- Palette knife: medium size, teardrop shape with rounded tip
- Palette knife: small size, teardrop shape with rounded tip
- Palette knife: small round shape (optional)
- Palette knife: skinny tip (optional)
- Palette knife: small, long thin tip
- Lazy Susan or table easel
- Palette paper
- Paper towel or rag for wiping your knife

### Color Palette

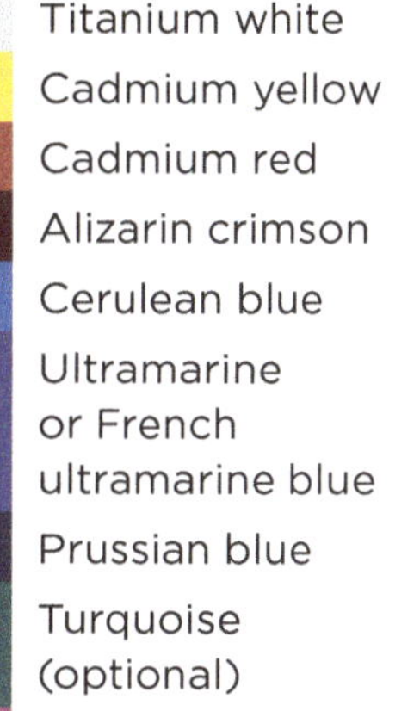

Titanium white
Cadmium yellow
Cadmium red
Alizarin crimson
Cerulean blue
Ultramarine or French ultramarine blue
Prussian blue
Turquoise (optional)
Magenta

### Difficulty Level

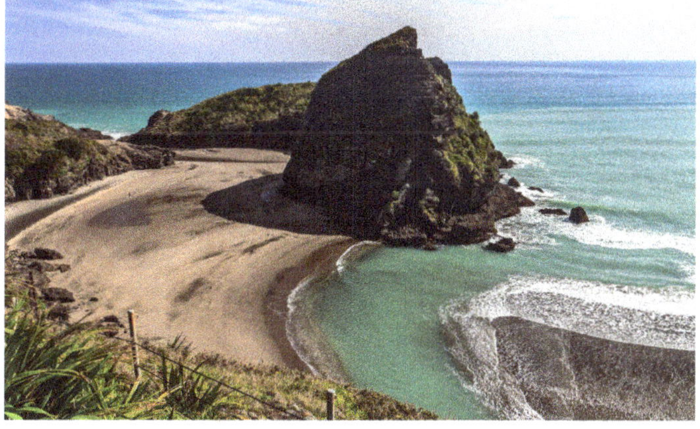

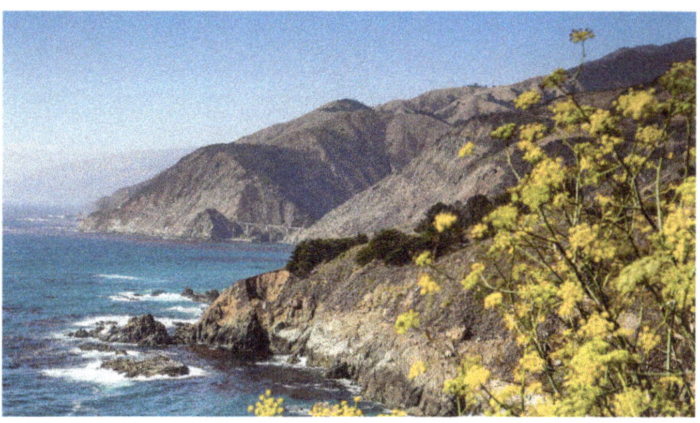

*Inspiration*

Landscapes are my happy place! I'm lucky enough to have grown up in New Zealand and now live in California, where the sweeping coastal vistas stretch for endless miles and offer amazing material for artists. In the following painting, I use a series of steps to complete a small landscape painting, starting with the sky and background mountains, before moving forward to the cliffs, water, and flowers. This can be scaled larger and the steps applied to any landscape scene. Start with your background and move forward, applying another layer as you go and ending with the most texture in the foreground. Another good rule to follow is to keep your brightest, most saturated colors in the foreground. This will add depth and really make your painting shine. Let's get started.

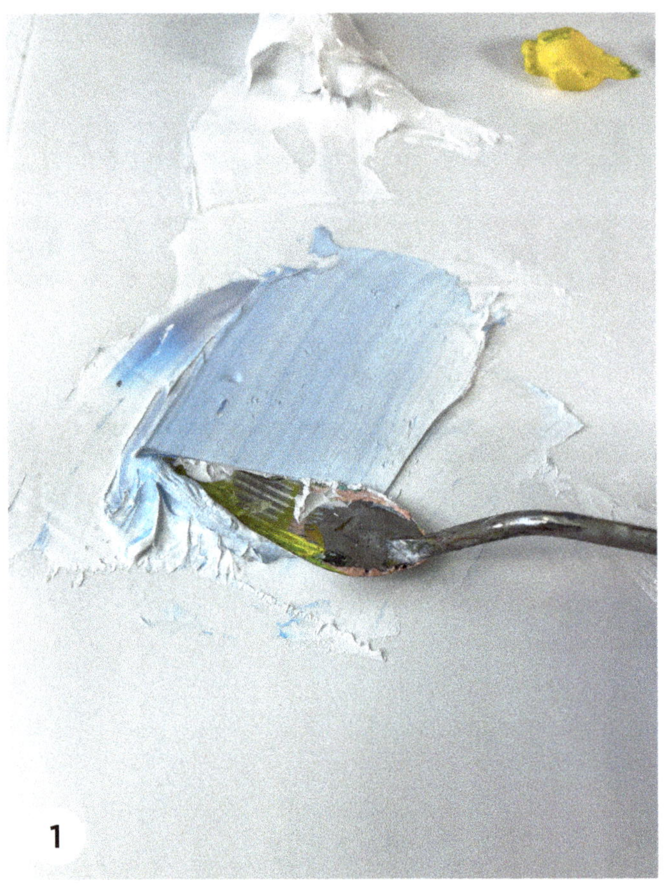
1

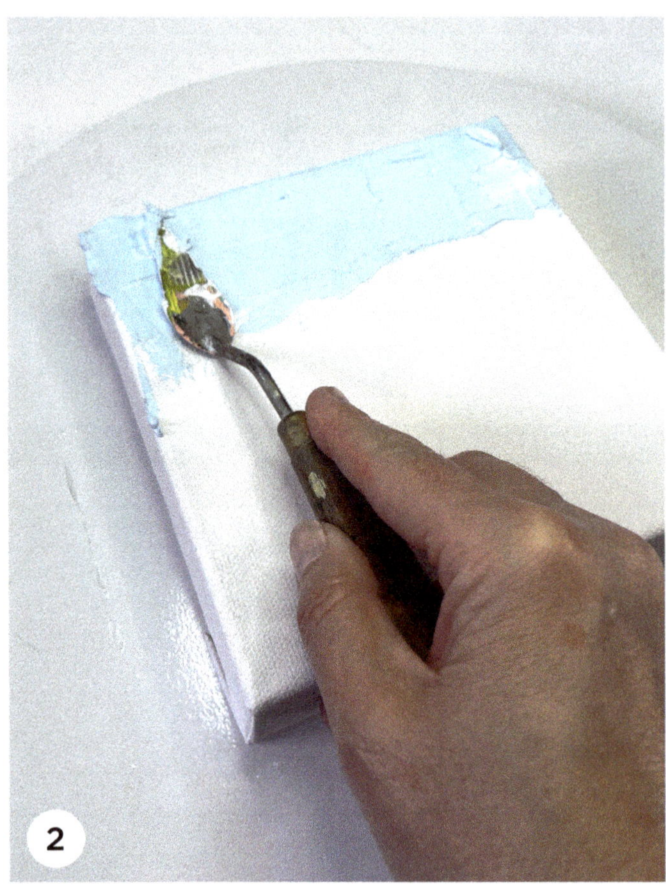
2

## Step-By-Step Instructions

**Step 1: Lay out your colors & mix your basic sky hues**

- Squeeze out a large portion of white paint, about the size of 2 heaped tablespoons on the top left of your palette. We are going to be blocking in the sky before placing in the sun and the colorful streaky sunset rays on this piece.
- Squeeze out around 1 teaspoon each of cadmium yellow, cadmium red, alizarin crimson, cerulean blue, ultramarine blue, Prussian blue, and magenta.
- Start by dragging down 1 tablespoon of white and ½ teaspoon of cerulean blue. Mix them together until very light blue. Then add a dot of orange mixed from red and yellow to dull it down a little.

**Step 2: Lay in your blue sky**

- Load your knife with 1 tablespoon of light blue, and starting at the top right of your canvas, start blocking in your sky with a large stroke side to side, right across the top of your canvas. Repeat this by reloading your knife with more tablespoons of blue, until you've filled in about 2 inches.
- Wipe your knife and reload with 1 tablespoon of white. We're going to create a slight gradient, right over the blue, to give emphasis to where the horizon line starts. Starting in the same position on the right, sweep your knife across, as far as you can go. Wipe and reload your knife, and repeat this from left to right. Then, using the middle portion of the blade, blend the line in the middle until it softens. We are actually going to be mostly painting over this portion with the mountains, but we need the white underlayer to peek through at the base of the mountain where the horizon shows.

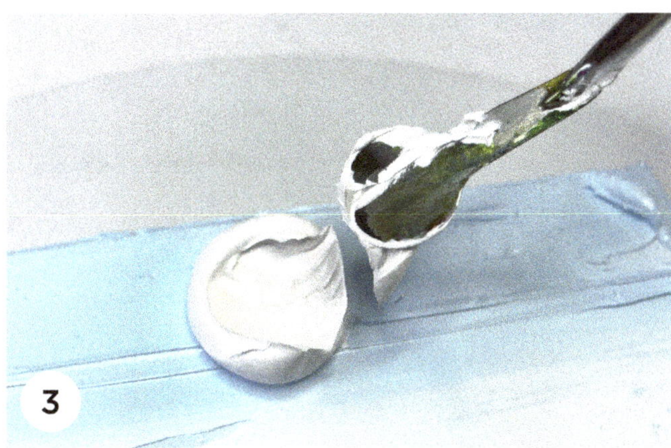


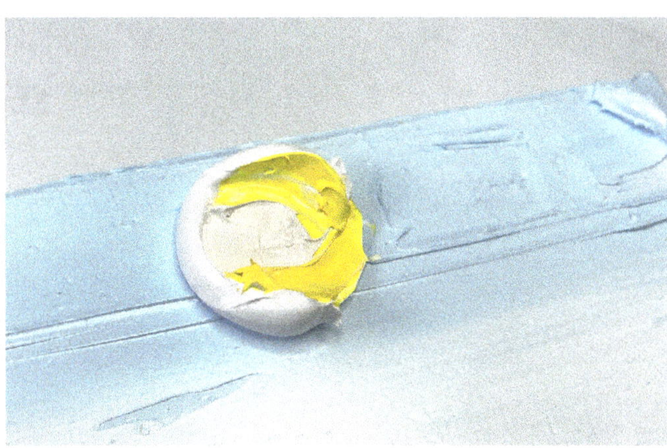

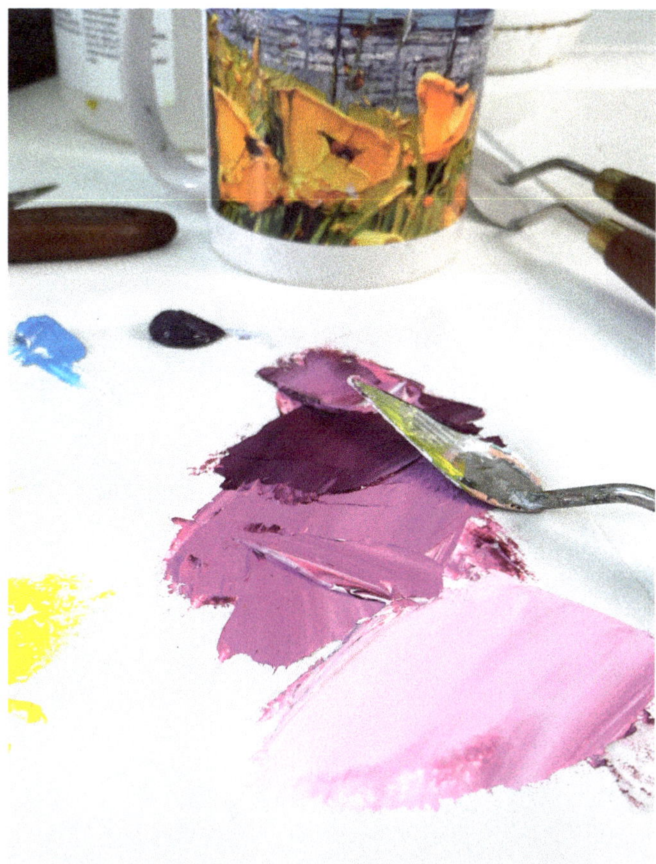

**Step 3: Lay in your sun & sunset**

- Now we are going to start on our super-textured sun.

- Drag down about 1 tablespoon of white, making sure to keep it clean and clear of other colors. Mix until it is pliable. Use your round palette knife if you have one. Otherwise you can do this step with your regular knife; you just have to use a more circular motion to lay the paint down in a round shape.

- Scoop up a blob on the bottom of your knife, about the size of 1 heaped teaspoon, and then flip your knife over and place the blob gently but firmly in the center of your sky. Apply gentle pressure until you feel it stick to the paint surface below, and slowly lift it up, pulling it slightly to the right as you lift it up, to make sure it's circular.

- Remember we're not going for perfectly round here, roundish is fine. Also, no going back and fiddling with it. If you really don't like how it turned out, scoop it off, reblend the blue underneath, and do it again. It's a good idea to practice on your palette first, so you don't waste any paint.

- We're now going to add some color. Drag down about 1 teaspoon of yellow and mix until it's pliable. Load the tip of the knife with a small streak of yellow, and sketch in a circular line partway around the sun. You can go three-quarters of the way around in a semicircle, but don't go all the way.

- Now we'll add some magenta, and the sunset will start to take shape. Drag down about 1 teaspoon of magenta and mix until pliable. Add a little white to it and have several shades ready to go on your palette. Using the very tip of your knife, dot some darker magenta on the tip, and sketch in another semicircle line around the edge of your sun.

- Now we'll move on to some sunrays. Mix a little white into your yellow, and load about ½ teaspoon on your knife. We're not really going for texture with this portion, but rather skimming the knife over the underlayer of paint to create a blended streak, which gives a lovely impression of a colorful sunset sky.

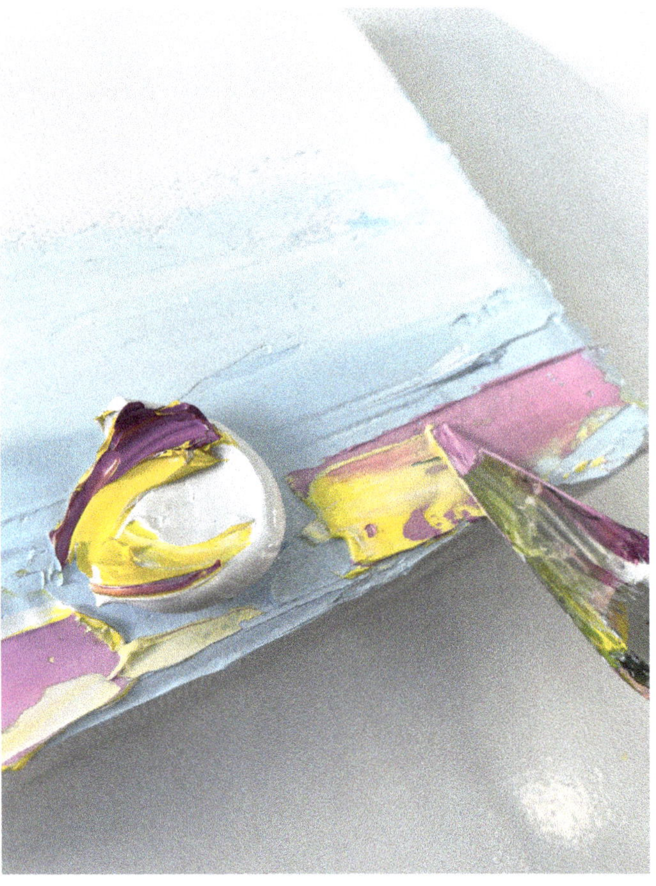

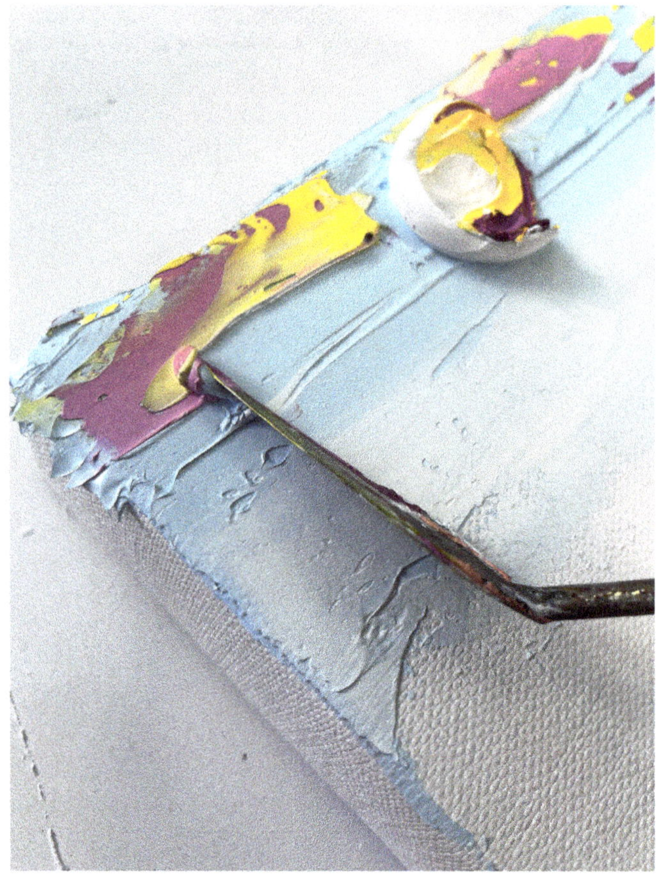

- Starting on the right side of my sun, and right at the top, I place a streak moving left to right. I then swivel my lazy Susan upside down to complete the next streak in the same manner. I'm right-handed, so it feels better to flip it upside down.

- Now let's add some delicious magenta streaks. With a clean knife, load a little midtone magenta, and add a streak right over the yellow, applying gentle pressure, but not so much that you scrape off the layer of yellow paint underneath. We want our yellow to peek through here.

- Rotate your canvas upside down and repeat this on the other side, starting at the sun and moving the knife off the canvas in a long sweep.

- I decided at this point that there was now a bit too much pink, so I went ahead and swiped some off with the tip of my knife.

- Now I want to create some rays moving downward toward the horizon line, so I load a little magenta on my knife and sweep it down on both sides at an angle toward the edge of the canvas.

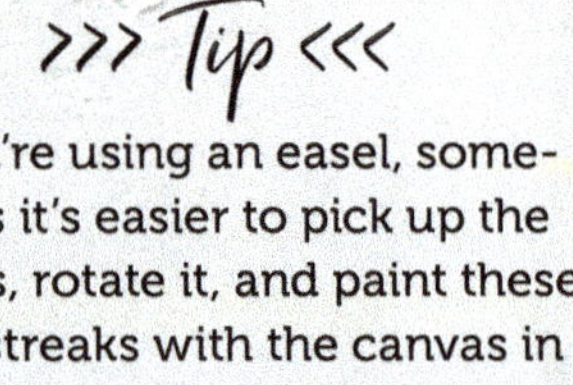

### >>> Tip <<<

If you're using an easel, sometimes it's easier to pick up the canvas, rotate it, and paint these little streaks with the canvas in your hand, rather than trying to move all around your easel.

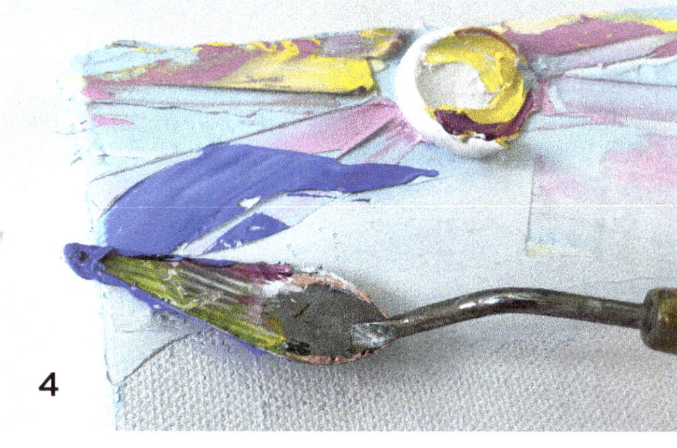


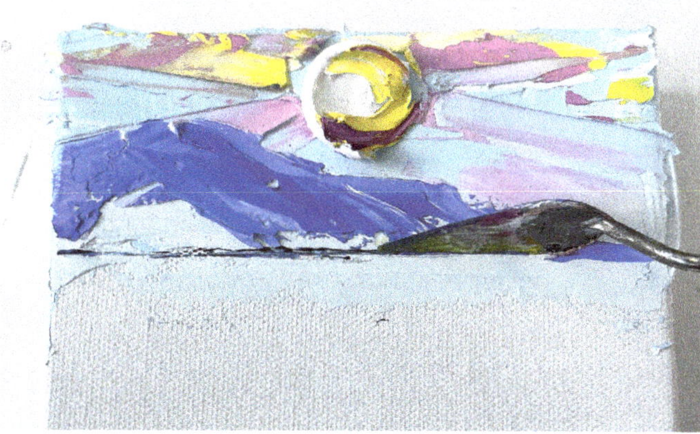

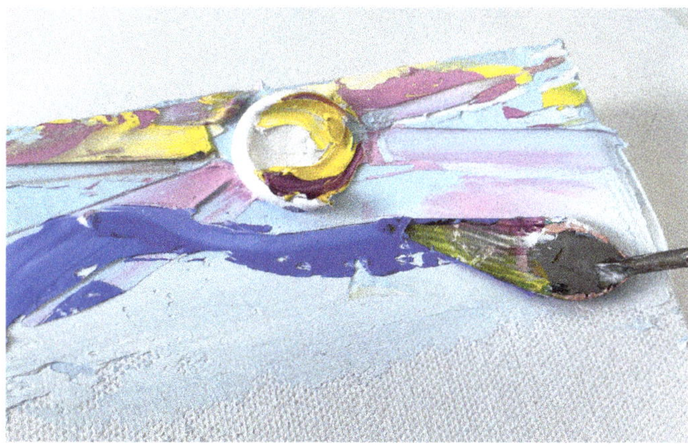

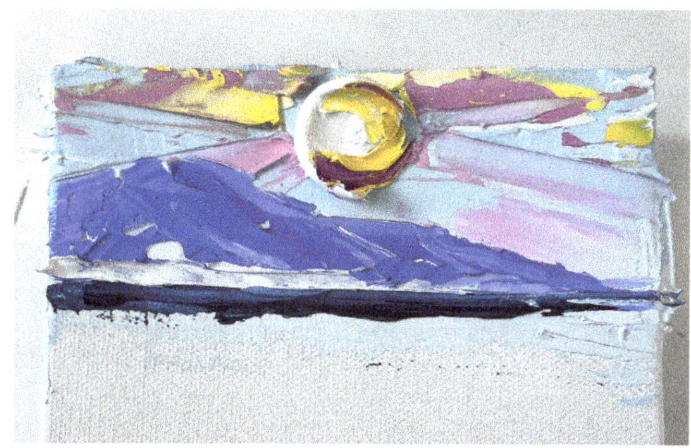

**Step 4: Sketching in the mountain**

- The next step is to add our gorgeous blue mountain in the background, so go ahead and drag down 1 teaspoon of ultramarine blue. Mix with a pea-sized amount of white. It's OK here for it to be streaky, as mountainsides have many inconsistencies. Because we want to keep it interesting, keep a few flecks of darker and lighter blue.

- With a clean knife, I load about 1 teaspoon, and starting on the left about ½ inch down from the top of the canvas, and slightly indented, I start laying in my mountain with one swipe from right to left off the canvas. This is where our mountains slopes down slightly on the side.

- Reload your clean knife and repeat this on the other side, starting just under the sun and moving right, trying to do this in as few strokes as possible and gently drawing the paint across the top of the underlayer so that it sticks.

- Now I'm filling in the rest of the mountain using a similar motion. Load your knife and gently place the paint pulling downward.

- This portion is very gestural, so don't worry about making it look exactly like mine, and remember, palette knife painting is hard! Sometimes when I'm asked to repaint a piece as a commission, it can be a challenge to repeat my own steps!

- Now we're going to add the horizon line, which will help line everything up. Load a sliver of Prussian blue on the edge of your knife, and draw in a straight line from left to right.

- Lastly, we want to add a little lighter color just above the horizon line, so load a thin portion of white on the edge of your knife and run this along the top of the dark line, being careful not to smudge the line underneath. If you do go over the line, which is easy to do because this is tricky, load a little Prussian blue on the edge of your knife, and go back over the dark area underneath.

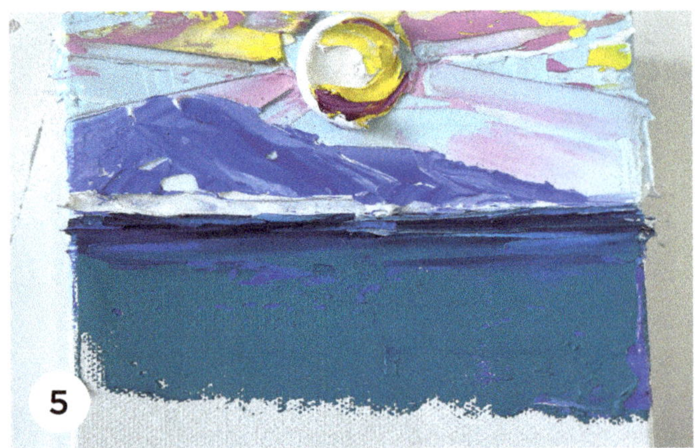

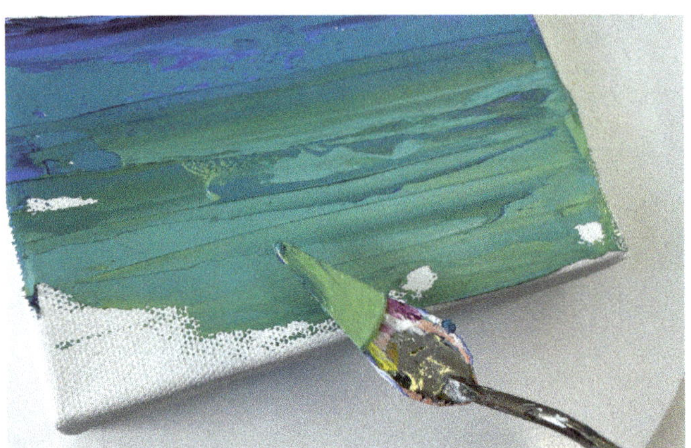

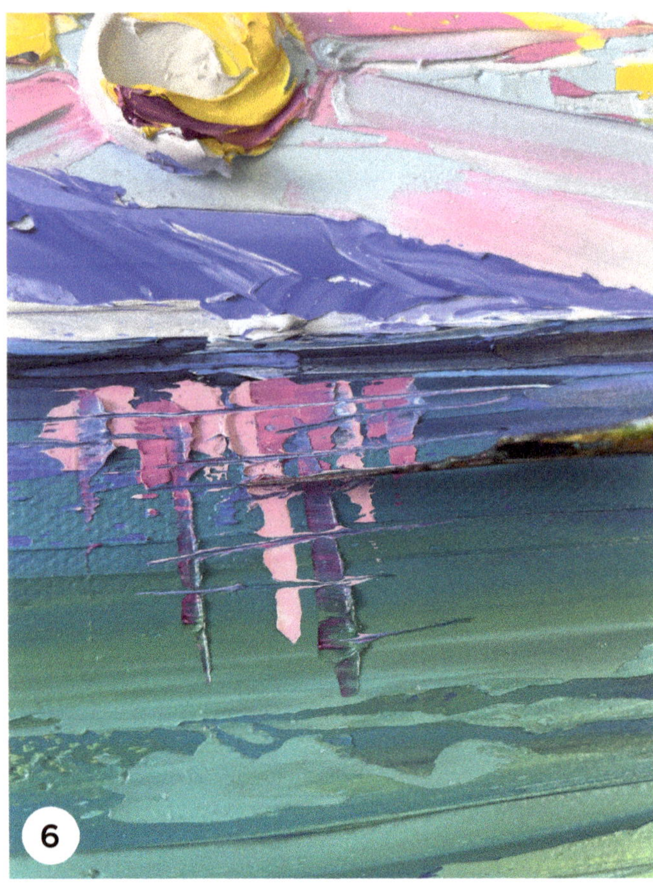

**Step 5: Adding the water**

- With a clean knife, drag down 1 tablespoon of ultramarine blue, and start laying in your ocean by sweeping left and right in long strokes, similar to your sky. Drag down 1 teaspoon of turquoise if you have it, or mix equal parts yellow and cerulean blue, and then start laying in your lighter blue, moving lower down the canvas.

- Now add a little more yellow and add another strip below to make a gradient, ending at the bottom of the canvas. Don't worry about covering the bottom-left corner, as this is where our flower field is going to sit. Draw your knife side to side and you'll see the underlayer of paint peek through, creating ripples and a waterlike effect. Don't blend this perfectly. It will lose all the natural waves and ripples. Stop when you've created a nice gradient.

**Step 6: Adding the reflections**

- Load your knife with a sliver of medium value magenta on the right edge, and gently start placing in a few thin strips vertically down the canvas, starting at the horizon line. Make sure to stagger the length of them. Once you've done a few, load your knife with darker magenta and do a few more strokes over the top. Wipe your knife and use the edge of the blade to drag some thin lines horizontally through the vertical lines. It's important to break up these lines.

**Step 7: Laying in the cliffs**

- Our next elements to add are the dreamy pink cliffs. Drag down 1 tablespoon of white, and then add 1 teaspoon of yellow and 1 teaspoon of cadmium red. Mix well until you have a sandy color. Titanium buff is an excellent color to use here if you have it, but you can easily make a variation of this by adjusting the yellow and cadmium red and adding a dot of greeny-blue if needed, to dull it down.

- Load your knife with about 1 tablespoon of the sandy color and starting on the left, just above the horizon line, start with a stroke from left to right. Apply gentle pressure so that the paint sticks, pulling the knife down and across the canvas

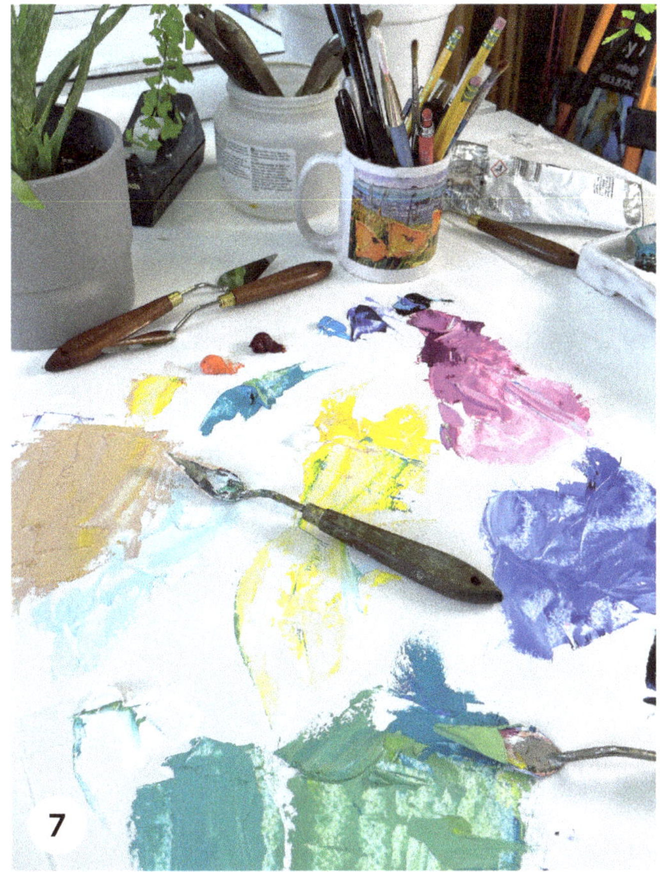

7

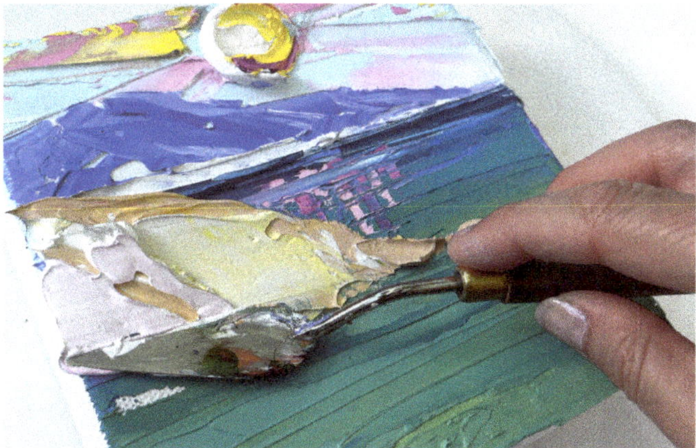

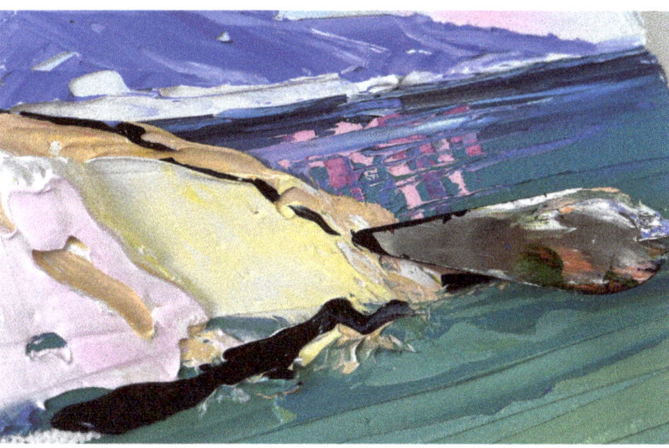

to end about halfway across. Be careful not to go over your reflections or too much of the water. Do another stroke with a clean, reloaded knife, bringing the cliff downwards. Remember we want to create movement here and cliffs have steep areas, so by dragging the knife across and then down, we create a natural drop-off on the cliff face. Cover up as much of the blue underneath as possible, as the blue should not be peeking through the cliff. I also added a little white to my sandy color, leaving it streaky, as the cliff face should not be all one color and should be reflecting the sunset colors as well. Also add a couple of little blobs right where the cliff bottom meets the ocean, as there are usually rocks here protruding from the water.

- Fill in all this portion with texture. A good rule to remember is that lighter colors always will need more texture, so go heavier here. I also decided to include some yellow and added another sweep right over the top of the sandy color, adding more texture. I then added some very light magenta as well, reflecting the sunset colors nicely. I did this by lightly skimming the knife over the sandy color paint.

- You should now have a fairly even-looking cliff, ending with a straightish line on the bottom that we'll go ahead and add a little definition to.

- Mix together a little Prussian blue, cadmium red, and alizarin crimson, and using the tip of your knife, sketch in a line under the cliff and rocks, at the water's edge.

- Also sketch in a thin line gently on the top ridge of the cliff, moving down. Don't go all the way here, though. Leave a portion incomplete, and keep it very loose and curvy, going with the natural movement of the paint.

- Now load a little white on the tip and edge of your knife and add a thin white line directly under the black lines at the water's edge.

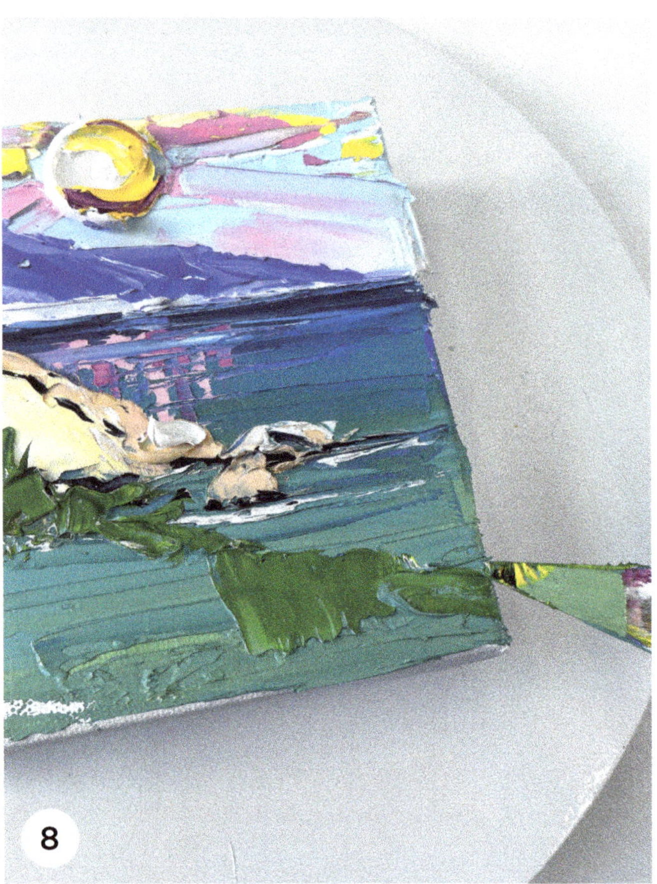


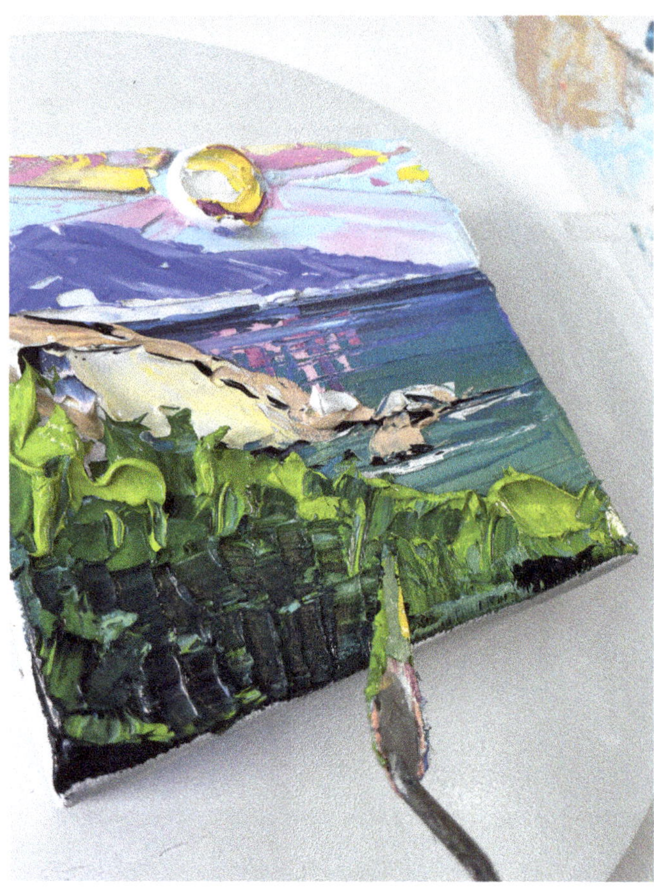

**Step 8: Adding the grass & flowers**

- Let's wrap it up! Every layer we add here has been adding depth and dimension, and once we get the grass and flowers in the foreground, everything else gets pushed back, creating a gorgeous multilayered effect.

- Drag down 1 teaspoon each of cerulean blue and yellow, and mix until you have a nice, vibrant green. Keep some of the mixture lighter and add Prussian blue to make a darker version.

- Load your knife with 1 tablespoon of yellow-green, and start laying in your foreground grass, starting about midway up the cliff. Use an up-and-down vertical motion for this portion, as we want to suggest the movement of the grass, so side to side won't work well here. This portion is going to be quite textured, so go ahead and be generous with your texture as well.

- Move down the canvas at a diagonal angle, placing in the grass strokes, being careful not to cover up all your cliffs. Go all the way to the edge of the canvas, ending the grass just above the corner, but not exactly on the corner, as this creates poor composition.

- Make sure you vary the size and direction of your grass strokes to keep the vegetation looking untamed. Using a slightly darker shade of green with Prussian blue added, start filling in the rest of your grass, getting darker as you go down and ending with the darkest portion along the bottom of your canvas.

- Now, if you have a skinny knife, go ahead and create some grassy strands in the same direction, pulling the paint upward and outward. If you don't have this knife, you can use your regular one by flipping it sideways and using the sharp edge.

- Drag down 1 tablespoon of magenta, and mix in about 1 teaspoon of white very loosely. Also drag down 1 teaspoon of cadmium red, and mix a portion of this into some magenta. Keep it to the side, ready to go.

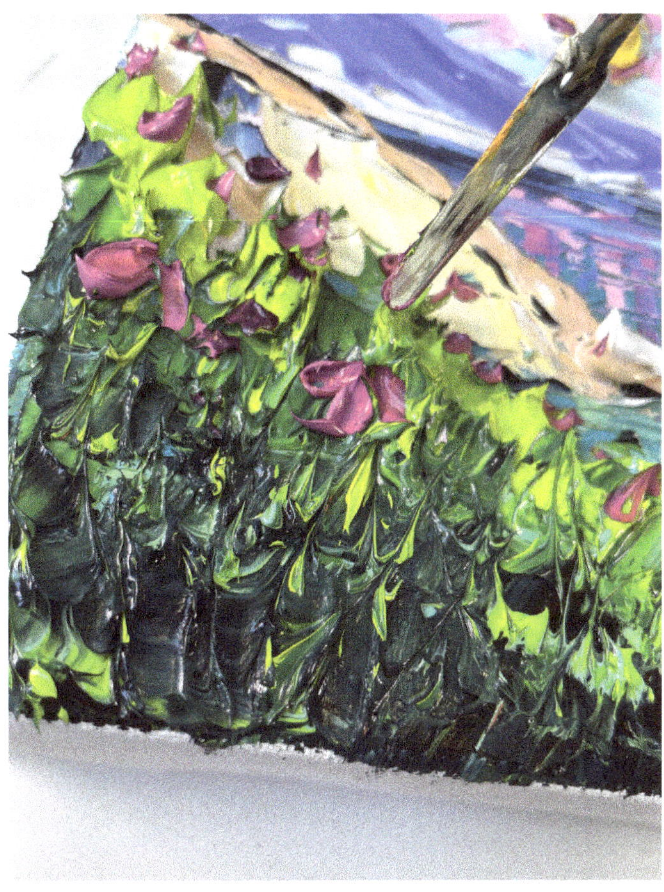

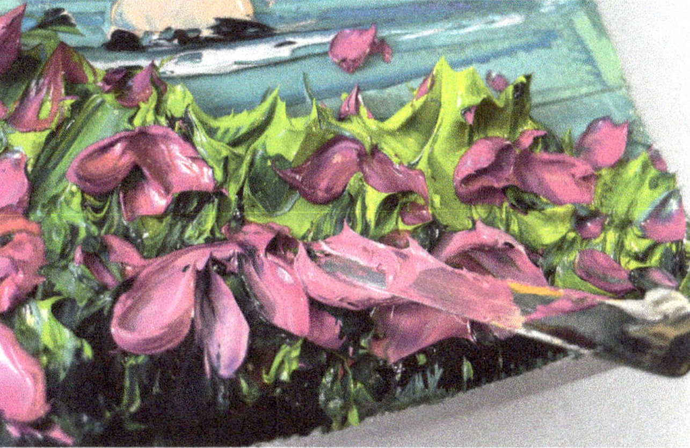

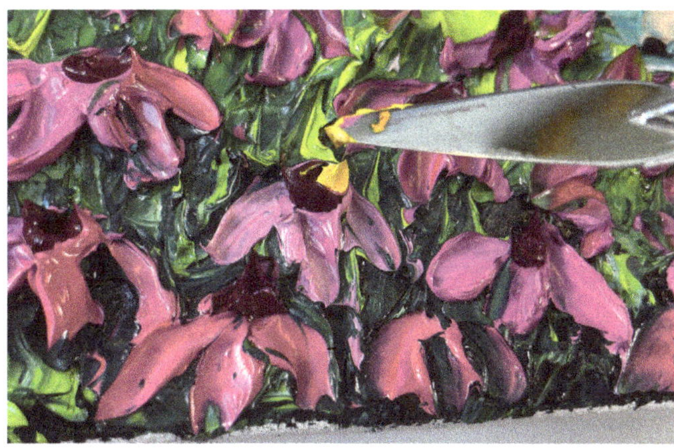

- I'm now going to be using my thin knife with a rounded tip. (You can use your regular knife here if you have to). This knife is great for longer-shaped petals, such as these coastal daisies.

- Load a portion of any hue of your magenta on the tip and start placing in the tiny flowers where the grass meets the water. These are going to be the smallest, and we want them quite loose and unformed, getting larger and more detailed as we move down the canvas.

- Once you've covered the area where the grass meets the water, start making the flowers underneath slightly bigger, and form loose petals by starting at a central point and placing little strips downward and outward, pulling up the knife. Start using lighter magenta as you move down the canvas. The grass is getting darker, and so we want our flowers to pop against the dark, so using lighter pink will work better. We also want it to be streaky and inconsistent, so using your pink with cadmium red for some petals will add variety and interest as well.

- Moving further down, repeat this process, making larger petals with more definition. Fill up your canvas, placing the largest flowers at the bottom of the canvas. For these larger flowers, I'm placing in three or four petals, starting at a center-top point and moving down and outwards.

- Lastly, we want to create a little definition in the center of the flowers, to anchor them, and at this point I switch to my smaller knife.

- Add a dot of alizarin crimson to each of the flower centers. Then go ahead and add a dot of yellow to each of the flower centers, just off to the side of the red. Do this with every flower that has a more formed shape, but not for all the tiny ones at the water's edge.

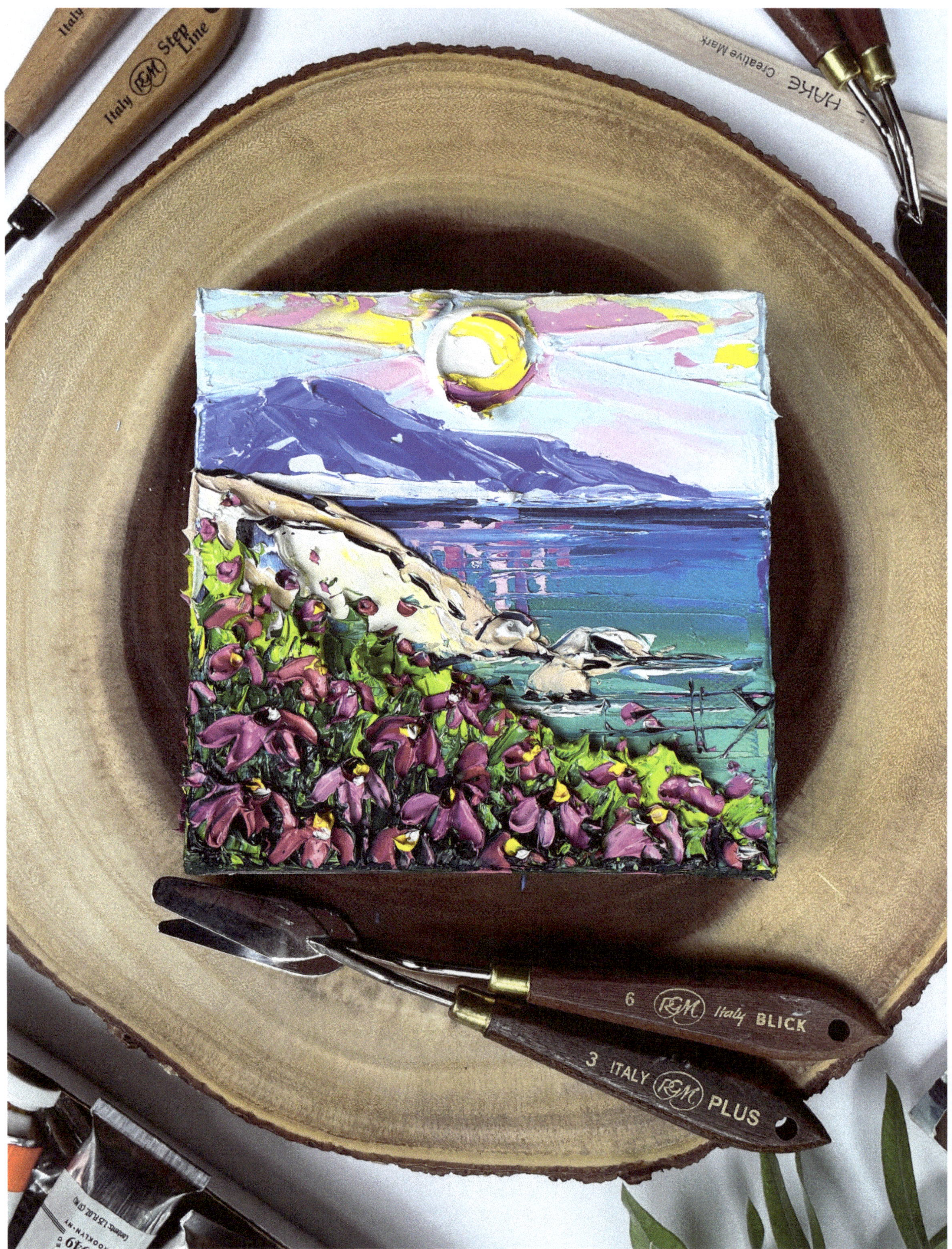
Italy RGM Step Line
6 RGM Italy BLICK
3 ITALY RGM PLUS

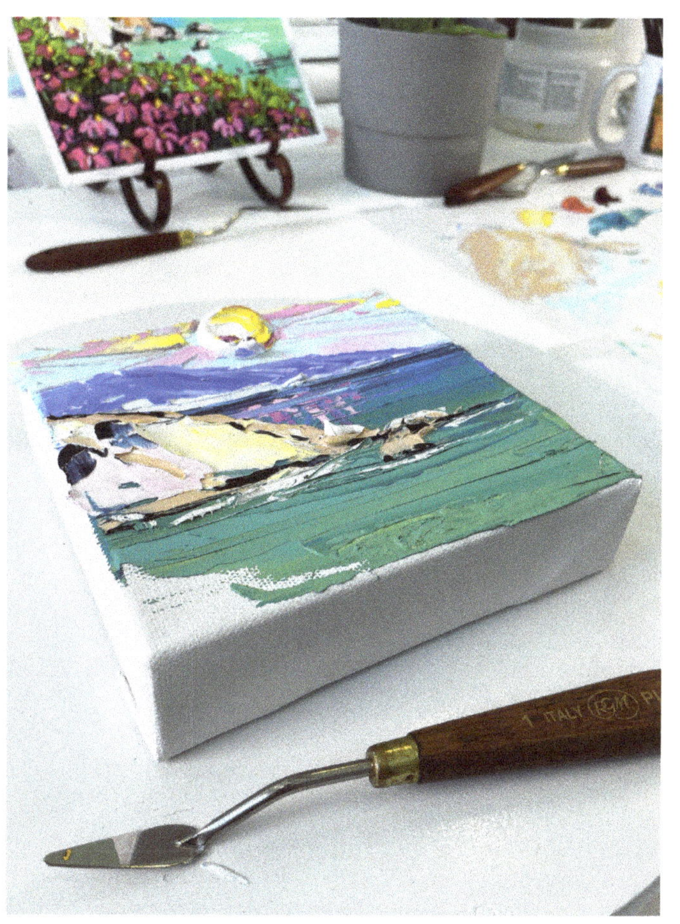

## SUMMARY: *Using Landscapes to Explore Different Aesthetics*

Once you've learned the steps for a landscape palette knife painting, you've opened up another world of possibilities for painting material and your paintings will really start to improve and become more complex.

This technique can be scaled much larger, with more details. Just remember to always keep in mind the order of where the elements sit in the background, mid, or foreground.

As always, I'm aiming for my sweet spot, the marrying of good technique with just the right amount of flair, texture, and a touch of whimsy. I like my landscapes to be somewhat representational, but colorful and interesting, drawing the eye in and roving around the canvas and telling a story. Some other ways you can explore landscape painting are by capturing changing seasons, showing a specific vantage point, exploring perspective, and by creating an abstracted view of nature. The possibilities are endless!

*"If the ocean can calm itself, so can you. We are both saltwater mixed with air."*

—NAYYIRAH WAHEED

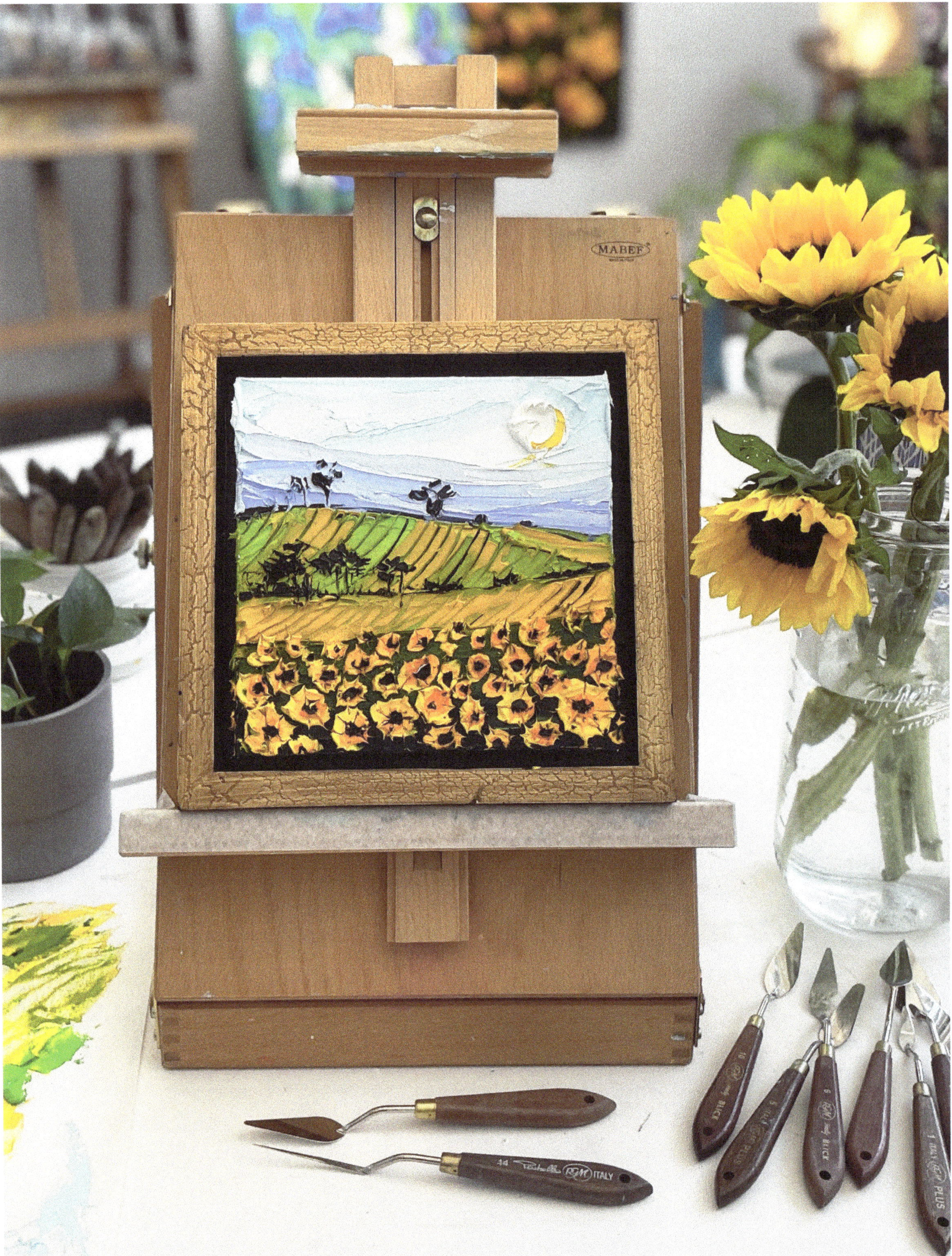
MABEF
ITALY

# TUSCAN VINEYARD LANDSCAPE WITH SUNFLOWERS

**Tools & Materials**

- Stretched canvas, size 8″ x 8″ with a 1½-inch depth
- Palette knife: medium size, teardrop shape with rounded tip
- Palette knife: small size, teardrop shape with rounded tip
- Palette knife: small round shape (optional)
- Palette knife: skinny tip (optional)
- Lazy Susan or table easel
- Palette paper
- Paper towel or rag for wiping your knife

**Color Palette**

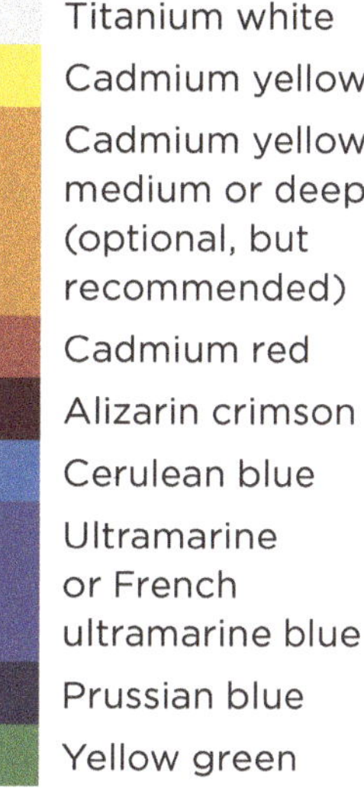

- Titanium white
- Cadmium yellow
- Cadmium yellow medium or deep (optional, but recommended)
- Cadmium red
- Alizarin crimson
- Cerulean blue
- Ultramarine or French ultramarine blue
- Prussian blue
- Yellow green

**Difficulty Level**

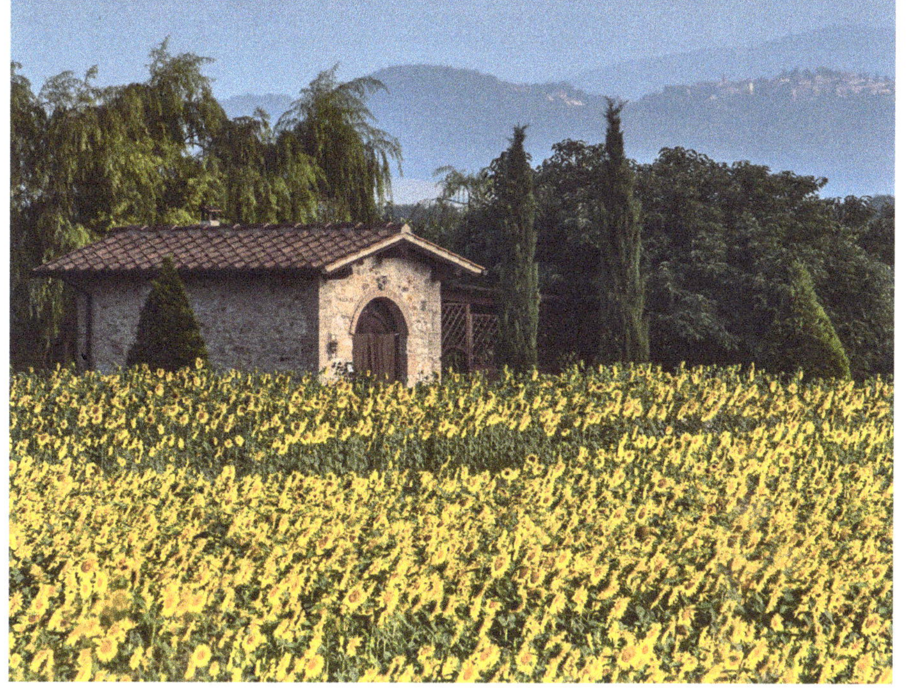

## *Inspiration*

Who doesn't love the idea of the sun-drenched hills and valleys of Tuscany in the summertime? Vineyards and sunflowers capture the essence of Italy and provide endless inspiration for artists. Add a touch of Van Gogh–inspired texture and big movement in the skies and fields, and you have a gorgeous, colorful painting that really personifies *la dolce vita!*

Like the previous landscape, this piece comes together from the background moving forward, adding texture as we go, and finishing with a crescendo of sumptuous sunflowers right in the foreground, leaping off the canvas.

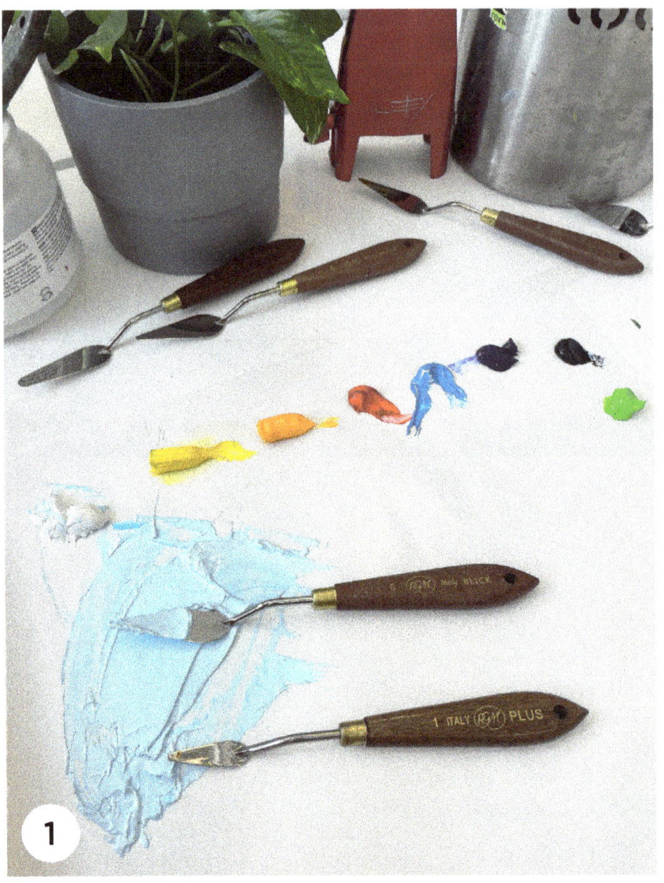


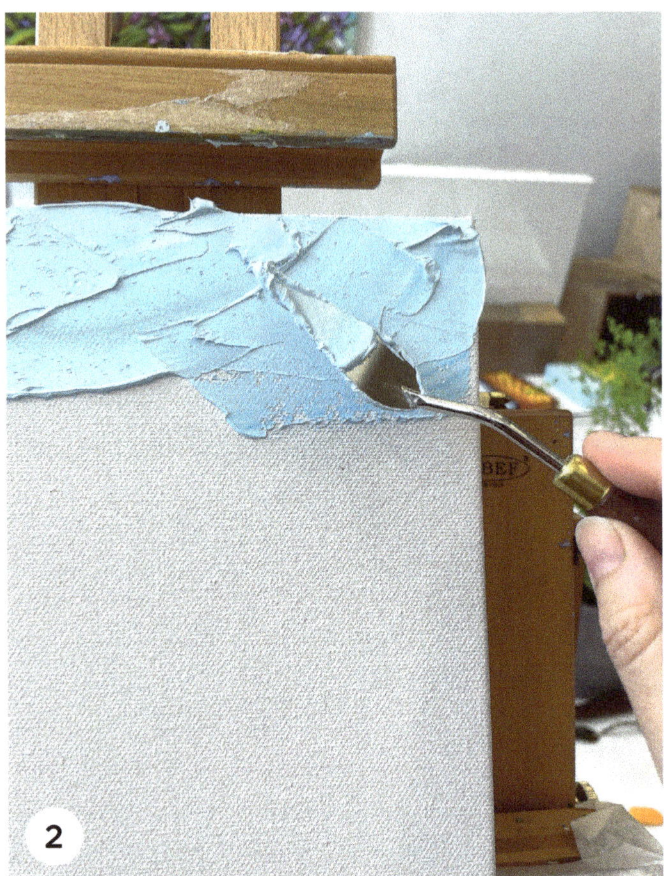


## Step-By-Step Instructions

**Step 1: Lay out your colors & mix your basic sky hues**

- Squeeze out a large portion of white paint, about the size of 2 heaped tablespoons on the top left of your palette.
- Squeeze out around 1 teaspoon each of cadmium yellow, cadmium yellow medium (more like orange), cadmium red, cerulean blue, ultramarine blue, Prussian blue, and yellow green.

* If you only have one lighter shade of yellow, you can make the deeper orange shade by adding a little cadmium red.

- Start by dragging down 1 tablespoon or so of white, and ½ teaspoon of cerulean blue. Mix them together until light blue. Then add a dot of orange to dull it down just a little.

**Step 2: Lay in your blue sky**

- Load your knife with 1 tablespoon of light blue, and starting at the top right of your canvas, block in your sky with large curved strokes side to side, right across the top of your canvas. Reload your knife and repeat this motion from left to right, filling in the canvas as you go. As usual, we want movement in the sky, so move the knife in the direction of the sunrays, which will emanate from the sun we are about to place on the right. Stop when you've gone about a third of the way down your canvas.

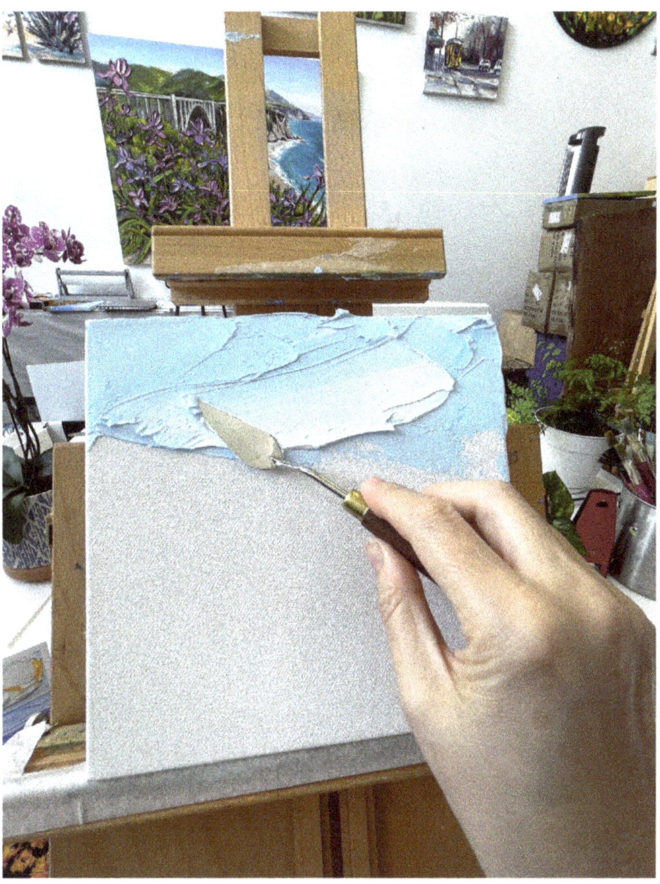

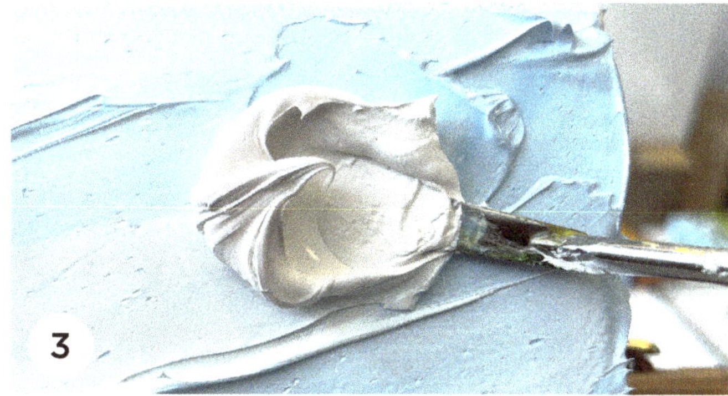


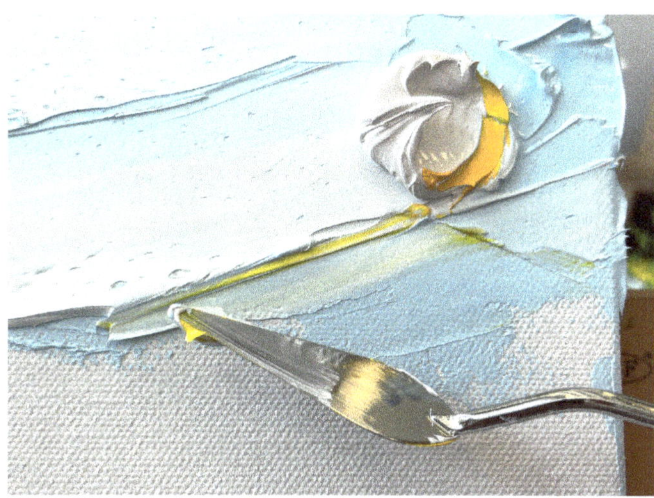

- Wipe your knife, and reload with 1 tablespoon of white. We're going to start creating the vast movement in the sky. Starting on the right, just below where your sun will sit, sweep your knife across, as far as you can go, curving downward slightly. Wipe and reload your knife, and repeat this from left to right at the top, creating another white overlayer.

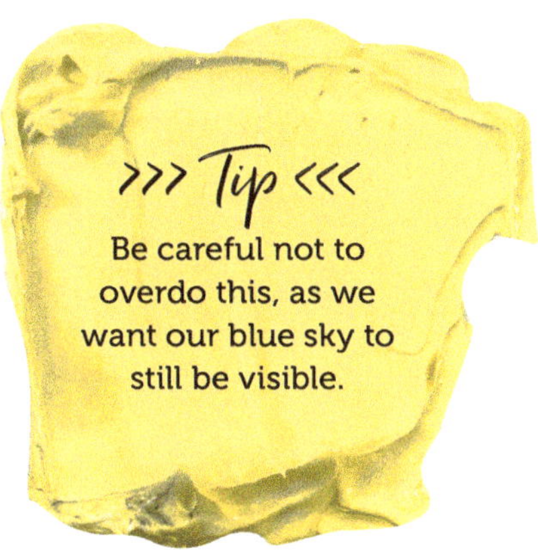

>>> *Tip* <<<

Be careful not to overdo this, as we want our blue sky to still be visible.

**Step 3: Lay in your sun & sunset**

- Moving on to our textured sun, drag down about 1 tablespoon of white, making sure to keep it clean and mix until it is pliable. Use your round palette knife if you have one. Otherwise you can do this step with your regular knife, using a more circular motion to lay the paint down in a round shape. This usually takes two strokes on either side with a regular knife.
- Scoop up a blob on the bottom of your knife, around the size of a heaped teaspoon, and then flip your knife over and place the blob gently but firmly in the right corner of your sky. Apply gentle pressure until you feel it stick to the paint surface below, and slowly lift it up.
- Now for some color! Drag down about ½ teaspoon of yellow and mix until it's pliable. Load the tip of the knife with a small streak of yellow, and sketch in a circular line partway around the sun.
- Wipe and reload your knife tip with a small amount of yellow, and now create a ray emanating from the bottom of the sun, moving down to the left.

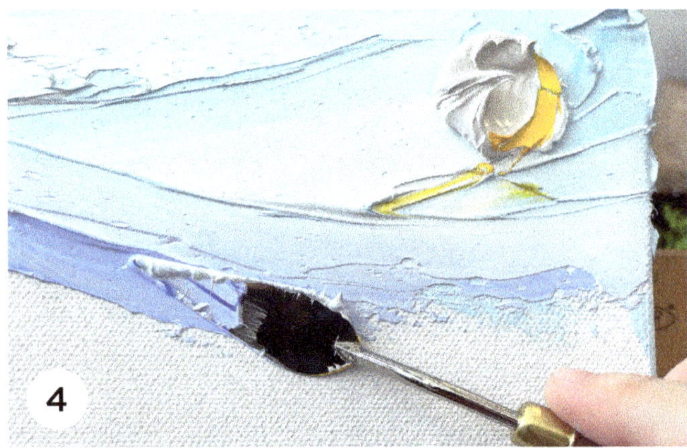


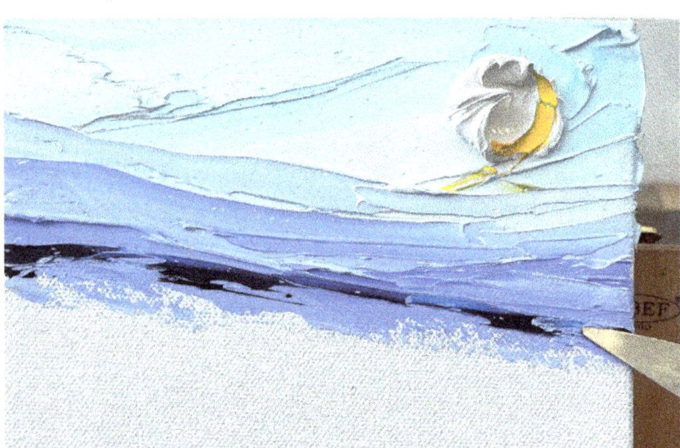

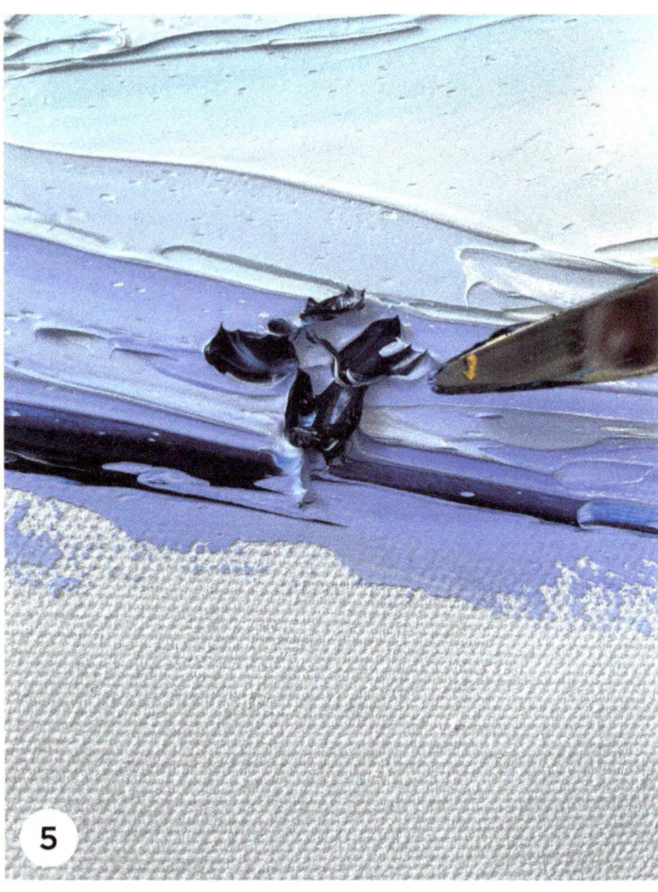


**Step 4: Sketching in the mountain**

- Drag down 1 teaspoon of ultramarine blue, and mix with a teaspoon-sized amount of white until it's fairly light. To create depth in the background, we start lighter and move forward with darker values. So load about 1 teaspoon on your knife, and starting on the left about 2 inches down from the top of the canvas, start laying in your mountaintop with one swipe from left to right. Keep this a little curvy, imagining your mountaintop as you go. Mountaintops aren't straight, so wavering here is good. Compositionally, I like to balance out my blobby sun with a taller peak on the left.

- Our next step is to create another mountain ridge moving forward a little, so we'll go ahead and darken up our blue just a little. Add a touch of ultramarine to your light blue, making sure it's visibly darker than the light blue. Repeat this motion with another mountain ridge below the first one, starting on your left and pulling the knife right across the canvas. Add a little darker blue to the right side of the canvas as well.

- Now make a slightly darker blue and repeat another stripe underneath, wavering along as you go.

- With a clean knife, drag down 1 tablespoon of ultramarine blue, load, and start laying in your last hilltop by sweeping left to right across the canvas in a gentle arc. This hilltop is moving forward into the midground, and you can see how much further forward it is looking already.

**Step 5: Adding the ridge of trees**

- Drag down 1 tablespoon of Prussian blue and mix until pliable. Using your small knife if you have one, dot some blue on the tip, and start loosely sketching in your tree line by dotting portions of paint in little blobs, attached to a trunk. Repeat this a couple of times along the dark ridge. Don't worry too much about the form here. They are more of a shadowy suggestion than detailed trees.

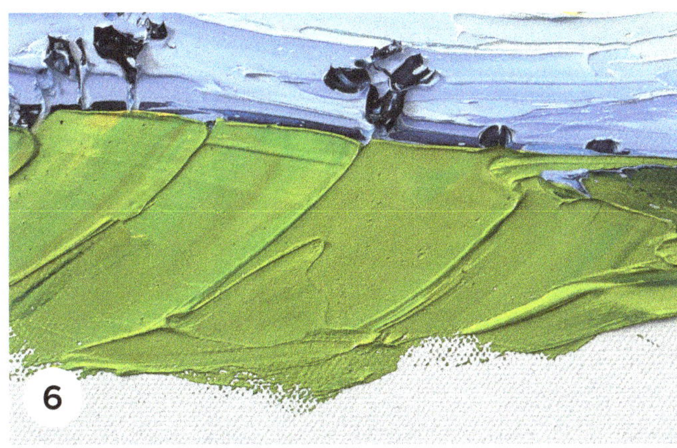

6

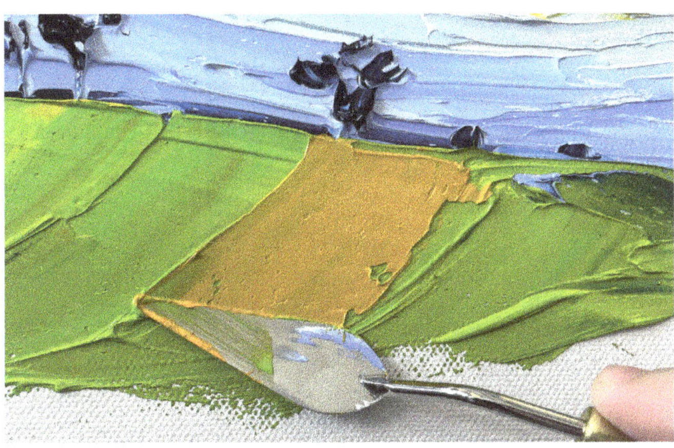

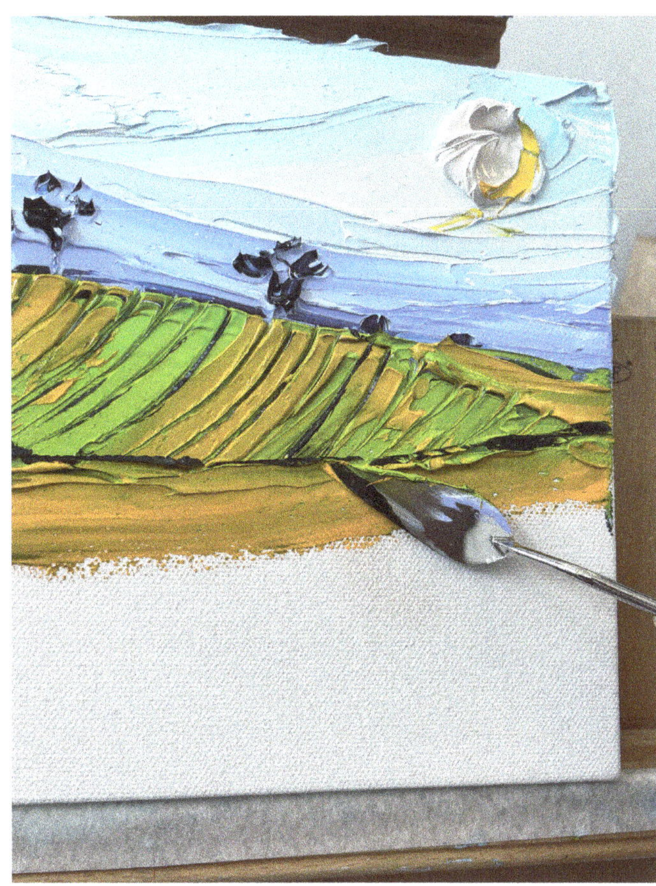

**Step 6: Adding the vineyard rows**

- Drag down 1 tablespoon each of medium yellow and yellow green, and mix. Load your knife with a tablespoon using the right edge of your blade and start laying in your vines by swooping the movement to the left. Continue with strips of green in the same direction until you've filled in the entire field. If you've gone down farther, don't worry. We'll paint over it with the next field that moves forward from the background.
- Now let's break up all the green. Drag down some medium yellow, mix loosely, load your knife, and skim it across the top of the green paint lightly with very slight pressure so that it catches but does not scrape the layer below. Continue this a couple more times, so that there are stripes of yellow and green.
- Now we're going to carve out the vines! Clean your knife thoroughly and draw the edge only through your Prussian blue paint until you have a thin sliver on the left edge. Place the tip of the knife right on the tree line, pivoting it sideways so that the thin edge is facing down. Now draw your knife through the paint in a gentle arc, pulling up at the end of the green. The knife has a natural flexibility, so by applying a little pressure as you go along, you can create an organic curve. Some of your Prussian blue paint will be left behind, and in other areas you'll carve out the paint, exposing the different-colored underlayer. Keep going, all the way to the end of the canvas on the left, and keep it gestural. Also, go back and place in a few suggestions on the right by dragging your knife through the ridge of paint on the right.

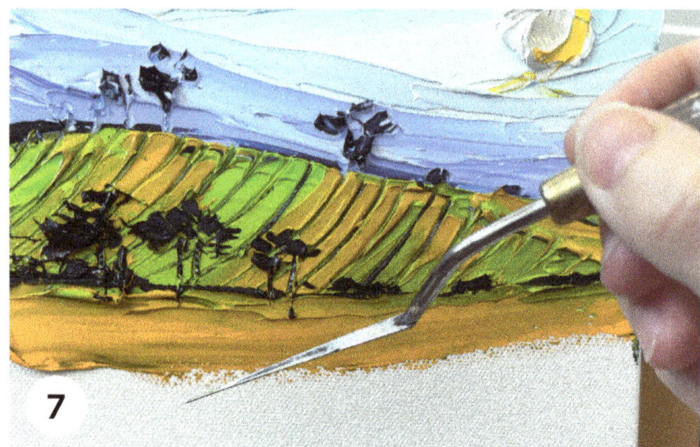

7

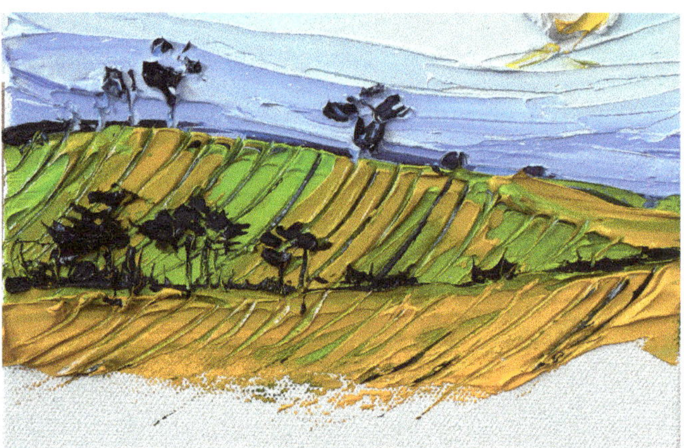

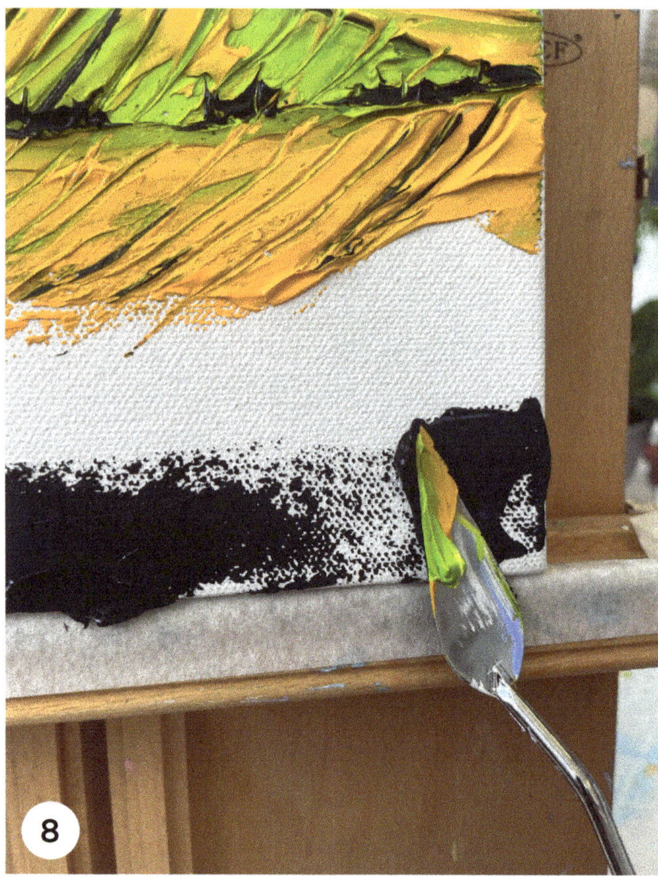

8

**Step 7: Laying in the midfield**

- Our next element to add is the midfield, which does a beautiful job of breaking things up and adding dimension. Wipe your knife and load a sliver of Prussian blue on the right edge. Starting on the left, sketch in a line dividing the field, close to the bottom.
- Wipe your knife and load with medium yellow. Starting on the left, under the dark line, lay in a swipe of yellow from left to right, all the way across.
- Now we'll place in some more trees, slightly larger this time, and with a little more definition, which will bring them forward. Using your small knife, load a portion of Prussian blue on the tip, and dot in some trees starting on the left and moving right. Also place some smaller dots at the dark line to look like bushes and to break up the line a little.
- Using your skinny or regular knife, scrape out some grass strands by pulling the knife up through the paint right on the blue line where the bushes are. This also helps to break up the line and create more movement.
- Lastly with this field, we're going to put in some vines, in a similar way to the top field. Load your knife with a sliver of Prussian blue, and place the tip at the top, drawing the sharp edge through the paint in a slight arc. Repeat this process all the way across the field.

**Step 8: Adding the grass**

- Using Prussian blue, start blocking in the bottom edge of the canvas all the way across. We want this portion very dark to accentuate the yellow sunflowers.
- Now we're going to join up the colors by placing in some green. Add a little medium yellow to your Prussian blue and blend until it's a medium green. Load your knife and add a strip from left to right. Then using the middle flat portion of your knife, go ahead and blend these together until you have a nice gradient between the dark and lighter colors.

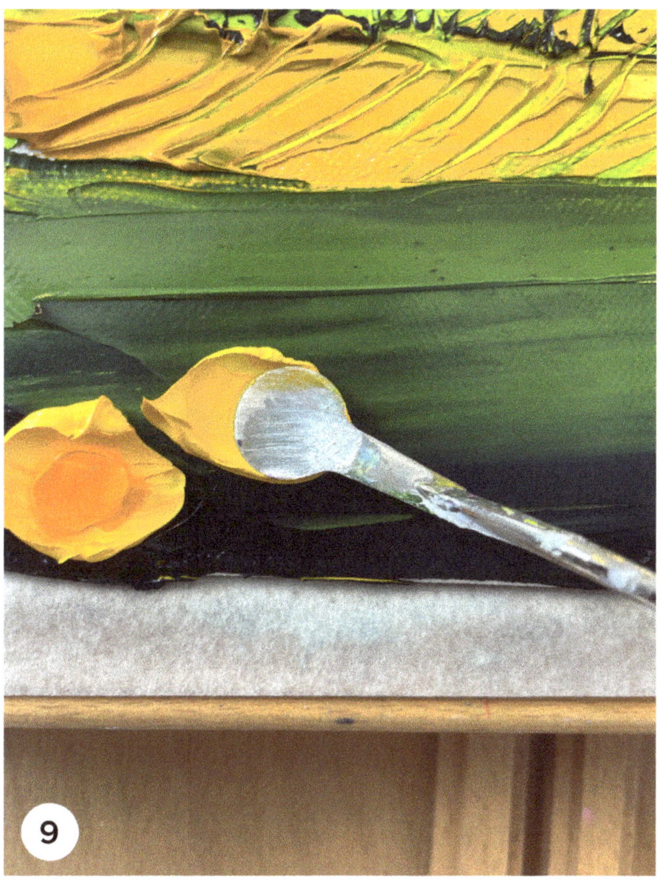


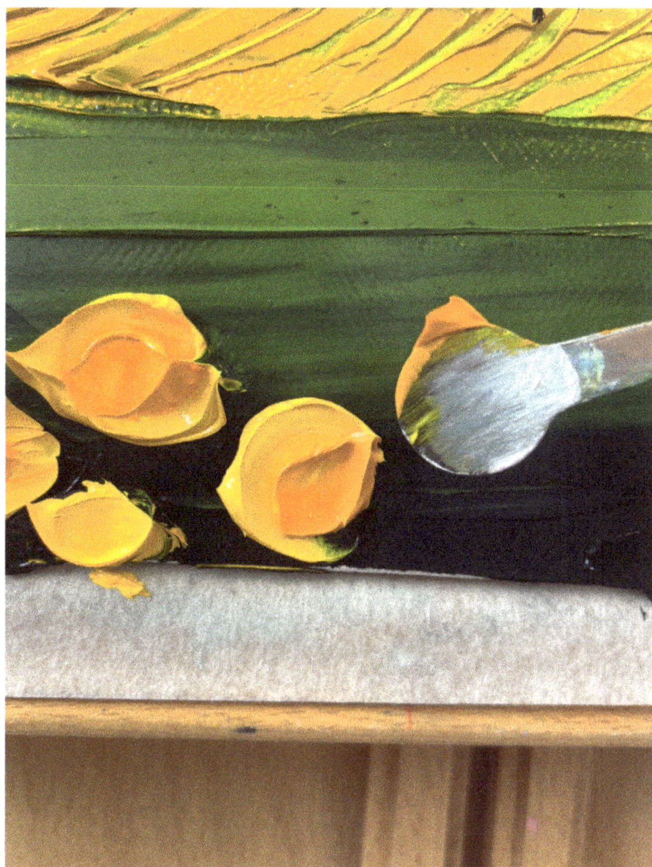

**Step 9: Finishing with the sunflowers**

- Let's add some drama! For this portion, we're going to be using the round palette knife, but you can easily use your regular one as well. Load about a heaped teaspoon on the bottom of your knife by flipping it upside down and scooping up a good-sized blob.

- We're going to start placing flowers at the bottom, and then fill out the rest of the field up to the vines. It's easier to gauge the composition of this final portion if we place in the foreground flowers first. This way, we make sure they are the size we want, with the biggest ones at the bottom of the canvas.

- Place your first flower at the bottom left, applying gentle pressure and pulling up. Use the same motion with your regular knife, but with more of a circular motion, and it won't be quite as round, which is OK.

- Wipe your knife and reload with darker yellow and a smaller amount, around ½ teaspoon. Dot this in the center of your flower, in the same way, making sure it's not bigger than the underlying yellow.

- Wipe your knife and reload, and continue placing in the medium yellow flowers across the bottom of your canvas. It's important to vary the sizes a little here. Try not to make them all the same, and wherever you see a gap, place a smaller flower in there. We want to maintain the color-blocked effect, keeping the dark layer visible underneath. Some of the yellow flowers can be touching, but try to be mindful of overdoing the yellow flowers, which is easy to do because this part is fun!

- Placing in the smaller blooms gives the feeling of their receding into the background and makes the piece very striking. I'm also starting to break them up a little, and I vary the colors so that some of them are only the deep yellow. As we go smaller, they are less defined and slightly less textured.

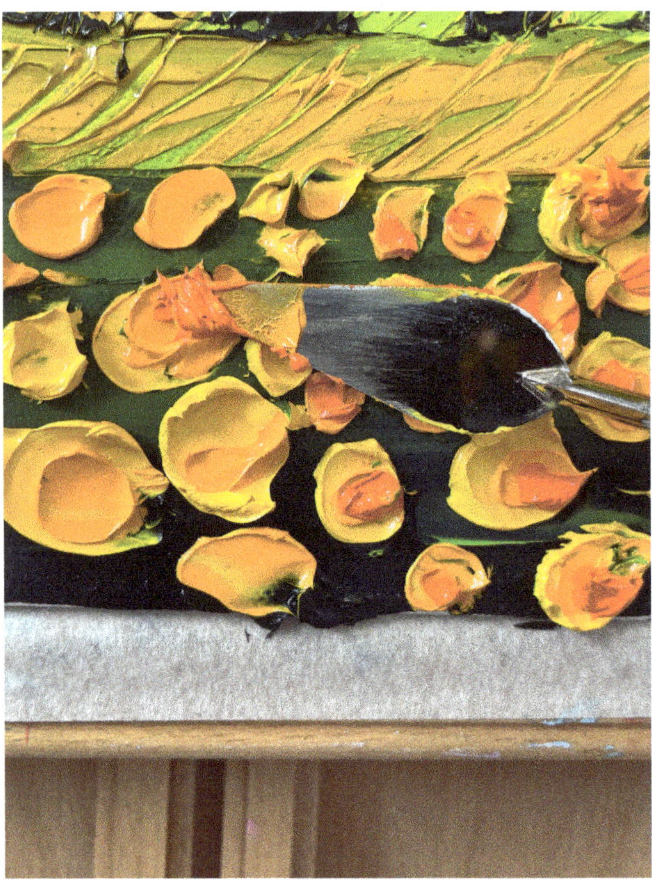

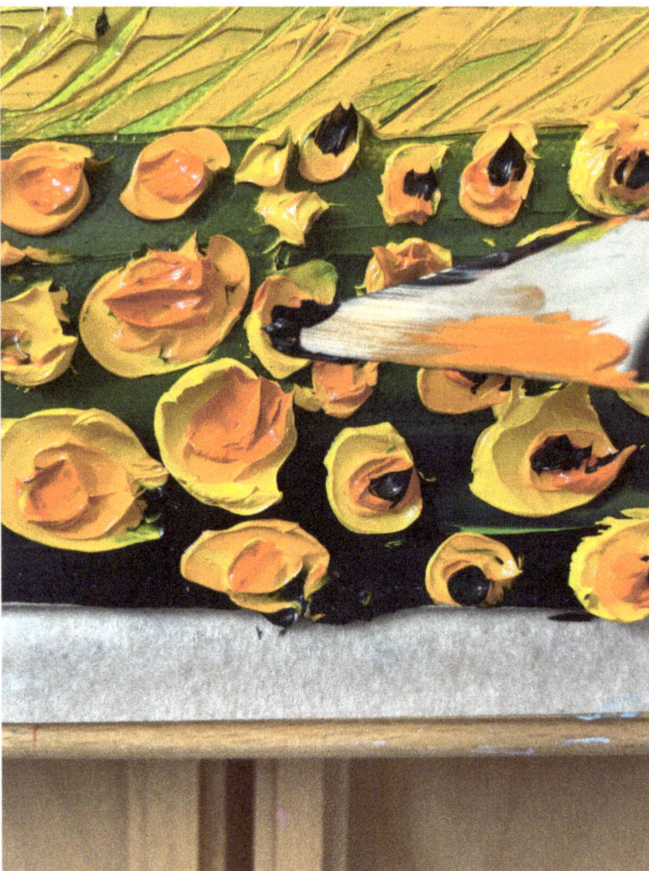

- Continue with this technique, getting smaller and smaller as you near the vines.
- When you get to the last strip below the vines, dot in a few small and haphazard flowers to fill in the space.
- Our final touch is to detail the flowers a little to give them some definition, especially the larger ones in the foreground.
- Drag down ½ teaspoon of cadmium red and mix with your medium yellow to create a rich, saturated orange.
- Using your regular knife now, load a blob on the tip, and loosely dot a small, textured portion in the center of the flowers. Make the dots larger for the big flowers and smaller for the little ones.
- In a similar manner, scoop up a little of your darkest blue, and dot in a smaller center for each flower here, making sure not to make it larger than your underlayer of orange.
- It's important to keep all of these gestures very loose and not finicky. The more you fuss here, the more contrived it looks, and we want a beautiful flow of natural creativity, rather than a controlled and symmetrical look. One of the reasons I don't use a smaller knife that often is so that I can't get pulled into the details and fuss over things.
- Our very last detail is to just give the round flowers a little more of a sunflower shape and drag some petals outwards. Using your skinny knife or regular knife, gently drag out a few lines from the center of your flowers.

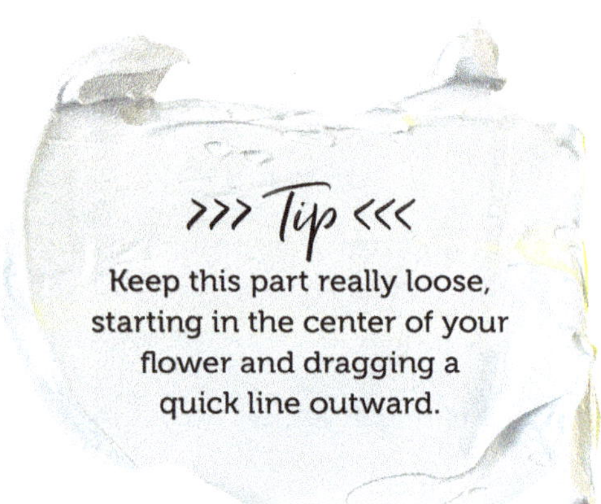

>>> Tip <<<

**Keep this part really loose, starting in the center of your flower and dragging a quick line outward.**

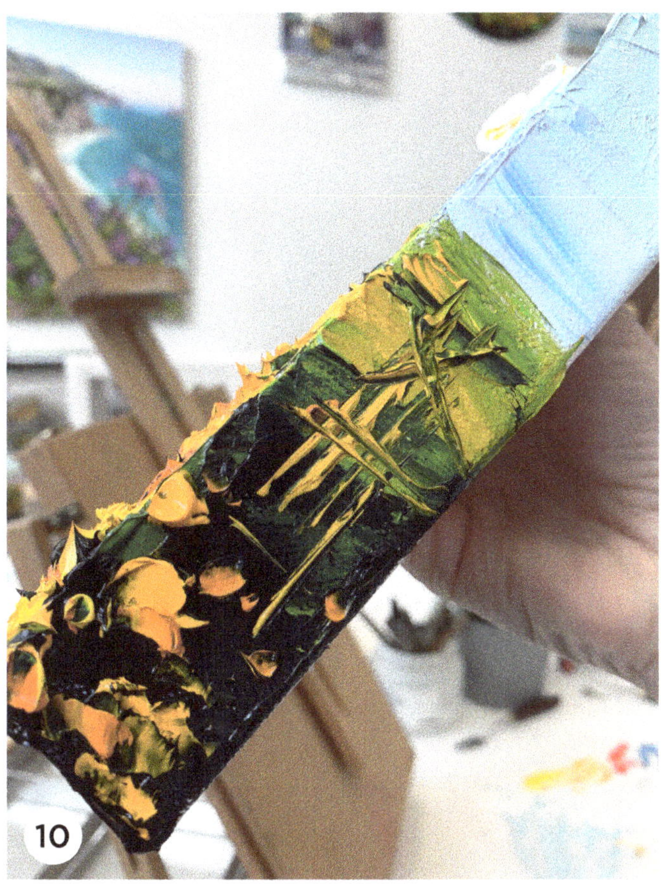

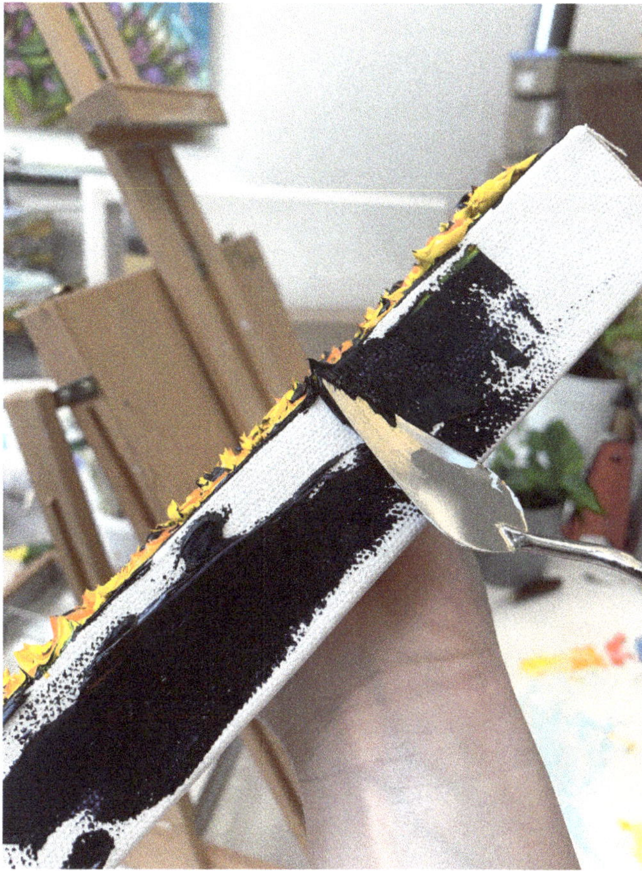

**Step 10: Signing your piece & painting the edges**

- I signed my piece on the edge this time. There was no space with the blobby flowers, and I didn't want to break up the continuity of the field above, so using leftover yellow, I signed it on the right edge. I also dotted some loose flowers around the edges.
- Using up the paint you have on your palette, start with blocking in your sky color on your top edges, before moving on to your remaining darker colors of green on the sides, loosely matching it up with the fields on the front. Lastly, pick up your canvas and complete the bottom edge, using up all your darker paint.

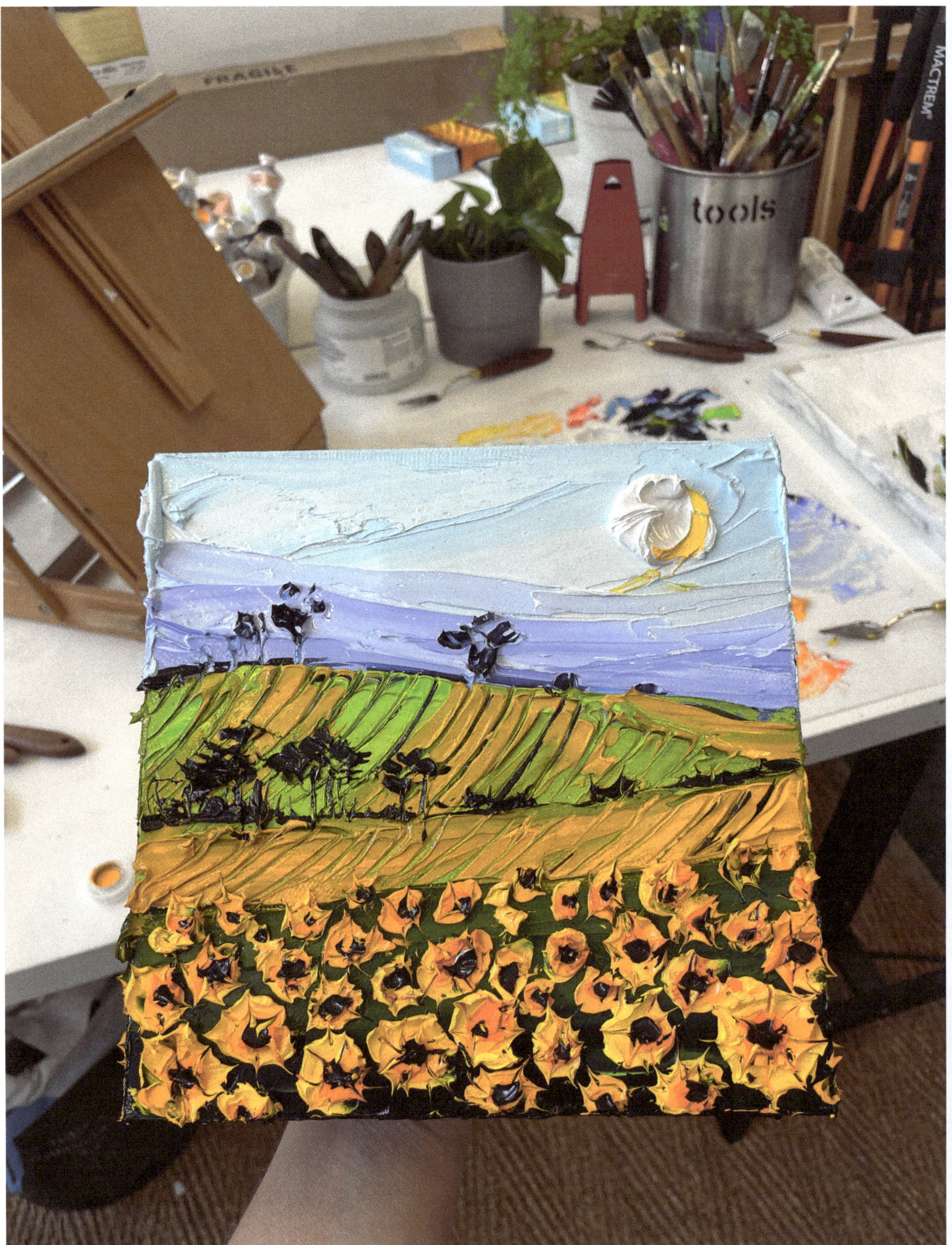
FRAGILE
tools
MACTREM

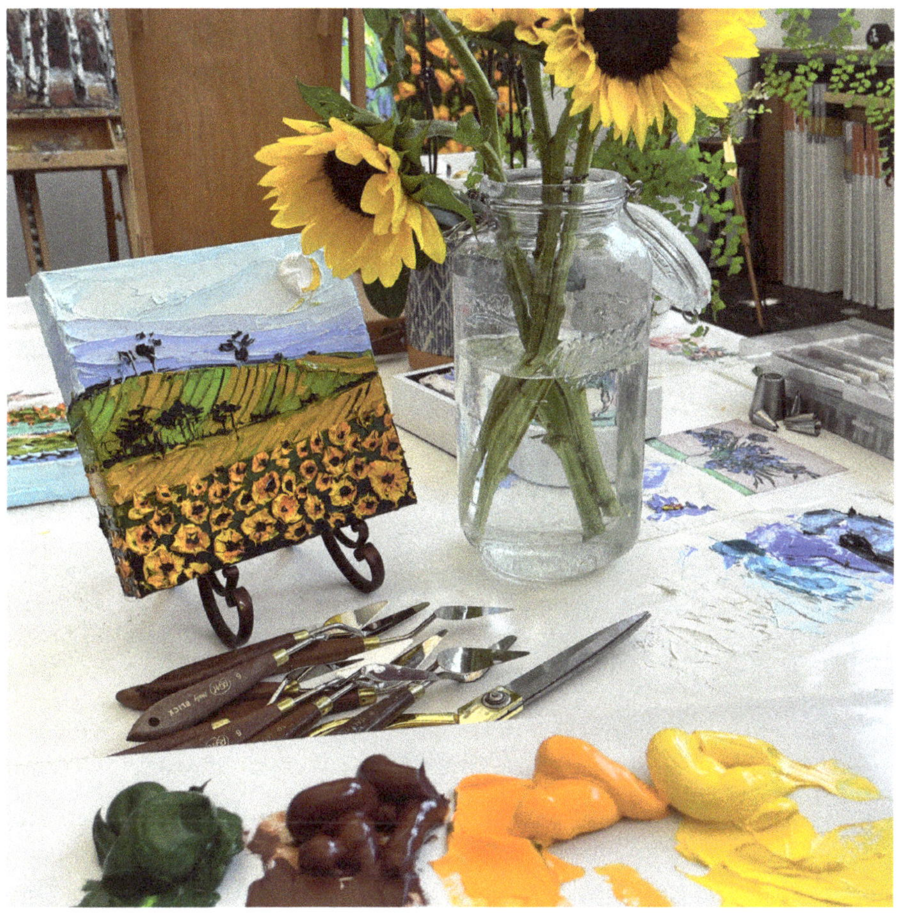

## SUMMARY:
## Let's Book a Trip to Tuscany!

It's tempting, isn't it?! Sunny afternoons strolling through the fragrant vines, enjoying the slower pace of life sounds divine, but in the meantime, it's a wonderful feeling of creativity to paint the places you've been, or wish to visit, reliving the memory or the excitement and anticipation of making a new one.

Art is emotion, and when you feel like you've conveyed emotion in your piece, you've done your job, regardless of how good you think the end result is. Remember, art is subjective, so someone else will see and feel entirely different things when looking at your art, and that's the beauty of it!

"If you could say it in words, there would be no reason to paint."

—EDWARD HOPPER

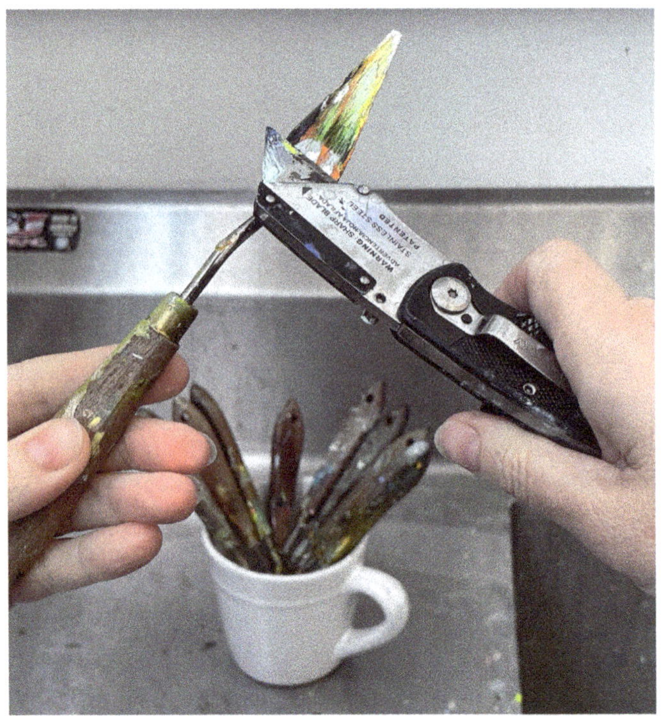

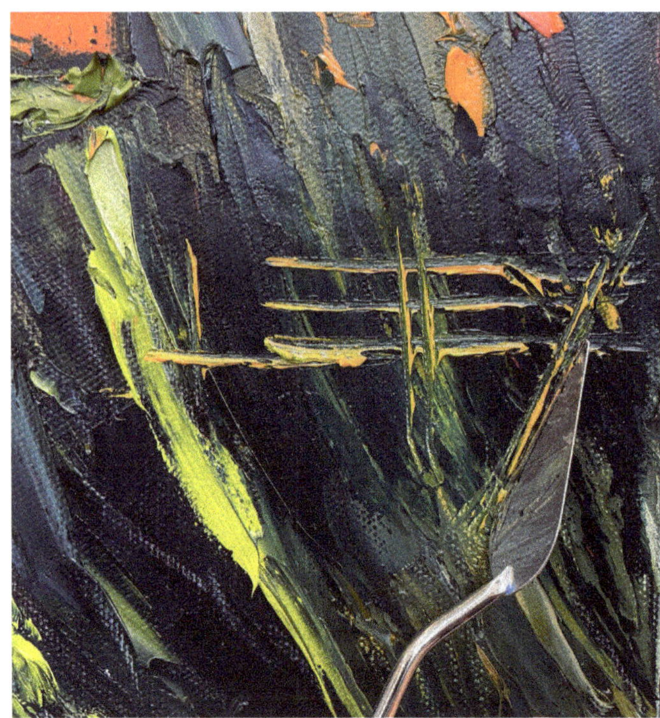

## CLEANUP & CARE

One of the advantages of palette knife painting is the easy cleanup. Just wipe your knife and you're done! There's no need to clean mucky oil paint out of brushes.

However, oil and acrylic paint residue can build up on your knife over time. Some people prefer the extra layer of paint on the metal blade, but I really like the clean and sharp feel of the blade, so I try to keep mine clean.

Here are a couple of tips. Don't get the wood handle wet, as this will affect the patina of the wood and will damage it. Use water with acrylic paints, or if you prefer oil paint, try a little bit of odorless mineral spirits (you can find this at hardware stores). You want to wipe off the paint that accumulates and dries in the crevices, particularly around the neck and widest portion of the blade. Also, if your paint dries and accumulates like mine does, just boil some water and pour it into an old coffee cup. Dunk the palette knives in there and leave them for about 10 minutes.

This method works beautifully to soften the paint, and then you can scrape it off with a razor blade or box cutter. This does not damage or scratch the blade, and it really gets the built-up paint off effectively.

When you're done, lay the knives on an old dish towel, make sure they're dry, and store them any way you like, upright or flat, preferably out of direct sunlight if you would like to preserve the wood finish. It's so easy!

## SIGNING YOUR ART

It took me several years to arrive at my unique signature, and now I love it so much! Signing your piece not only identifies it as yours, but it's also your final chance to infuse it with all your pride!

It feels great to finish a piece, and I love signing mine. For many years, I signed my palette knife paintings with a brush and a cursive style, until one day I thought to myself, "Wait a second...why am I signing this with a brush? I didn't paint it with a brush; wouldn't it be far more authentic and easier to sign it with a knife?" So I started scraping out my signature with the tip of the knife in the same cursive style. This only works on areas with very thick paint, however, so I started playing around with the edge of the knife. I really liked the geometric and more modern look of the letters formed with the straight edge of the blade, and I was delighted when I arrived at my current iteration. It was exactly that—an iterative process—so keep going, trying different shapes and playing around until you find something that feels right for you.

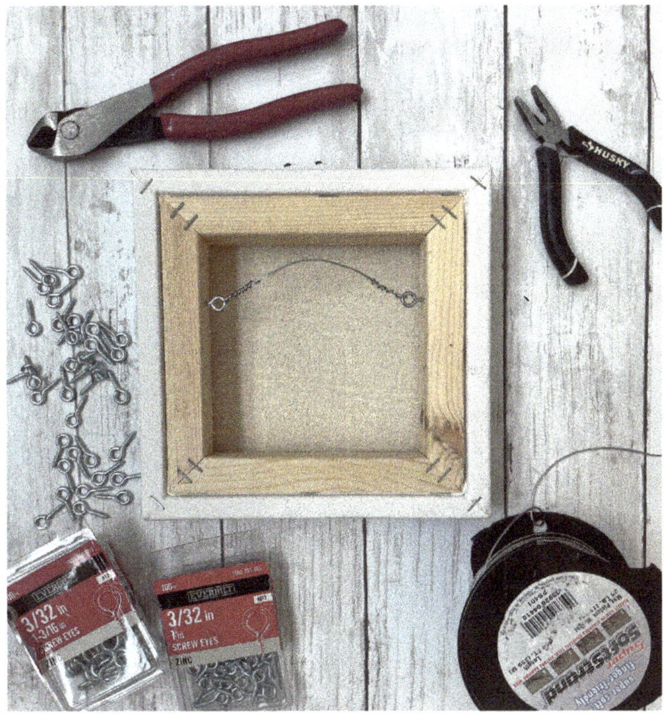


## WIRING A PAINTING

Wiring a painting and getting it ready to hang is also an easy step, and it really makes a difference if you sell your work. Here's what to have on hand:

- A small electric drill with thin bits (not jewelry-making bits—they're too small) or a manual push drill to form pilot holes for your screw loops
- A good pair of wire cutters (you can use the jewelry kind, but the larger ones will cut and feel better)
- Vinyl-coated, flexible, picture-hanging wire
- Screw loops in several sizes

Use your power or manual drill to make a small pilot hole about 1 or 2 inches down from the top stretcher bar, on the side of your canvas. Repeat on the other side.

Screw in both of your loops and thread through the wire, leaving about 1½ inches to spare, and twist the end around itself to secure. Repeat this with the other side, making sure to keep some slack in the wire and not to tighten it. If the wire is too tight, it makes it difficult to hang. Done!

## VARNISHING

The final piece of the puzzle is adding a lovely coat of varnish, which will protect your piece against UV light, dust, and damage. Varnish also adds a nice sheen, the level of which is entirely up to you and depends on whether you choose matte, satin, or glossy varnish.

I usually go for a gloss finish, as I like the shine and the way that it reflects the light. Varnishing over a thick texture can be tricky, timing-wise. How do you know when it's dry enough? Well, very thick paint will not dry for many months, and it must be dry for you to apply the varnish.

If you have a commission or time-sensitive piece, or you just don't want to wait, a "retouch" varnish is a great compromise. This is basically a diluted varnish, which will provide protection and still let your oil paint breathe and cure. Many major brands make a version of retouch varnish, including Utrecht and Winsor & Newton.

Apply a light coat in a well-ventilated space (outside if you can) and using a large 1- or 2-inch brush, move loosely around in the same direction as the movement on your painting. You don't have to be exact here; just make sure not to use too much on as it can bubble and pool. If you like the idea of a spray varnish, Krylon makes an excellent spray varnish that can be used on not fully dry oil paintings. It's more expensive, but it's very convenient. Most of these modern varnishes are also designed so that they can be reapplied or removed and redone at some point.

When varnishing acrylic, it's best to use an "isolation coat" first if you can, as you cannot remove varnish from an acrylic painting without this protective coat. Golden makes a great one. Then simply apply any water-based polymer varnish over the top after an hour or so of drying time. One of my favorites is Liquitex. Before varnishing, I also like to "dust" the surface first with a soft, dry brush to remove any contaminants.

## PRESENTING

Presentation is important too. Great photography can be easily achieved with a smartphone now, and I like to use floater or plein air frames (for panels) to stage my work. A floater frame has no glass and an open area where the canvas sits in the frame with the edges visible. Because you've already wired your piece, you can hang it straight on the wall like this with no extra work. Plein air frames also have no glass and are good for panels. Both types of frames can be found on any art-supply website.

# ABOUT THE ARTIST

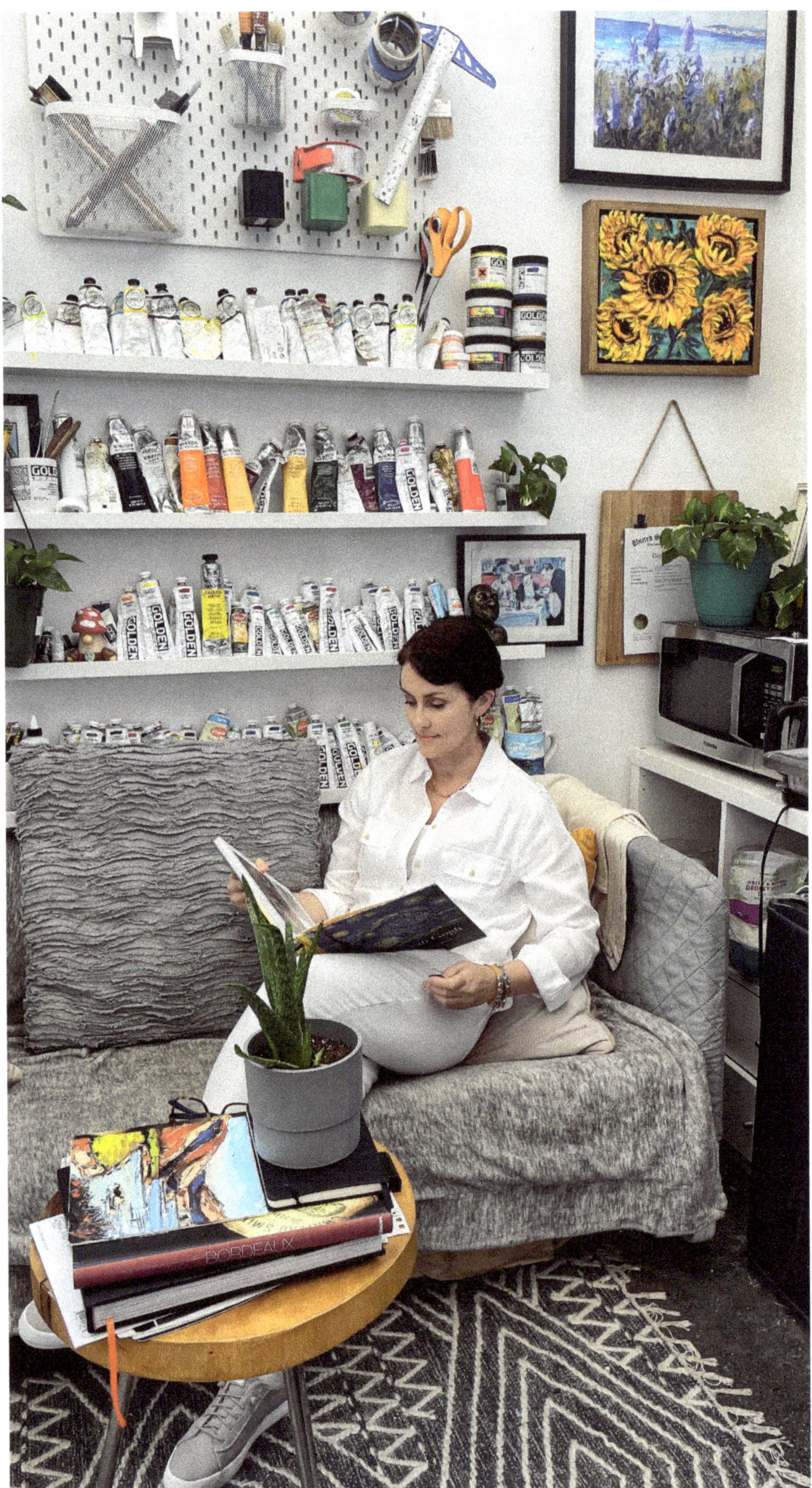


**LISA ELLEY** is an award-winning professional artist working from her studio in the San Francisco Bay. Her signature deep impasto technique utilizes palette knives to create unique paintings with incredible texture, dimension, and movement. Art reflects personality, and Lisa's passion and playfulness are infused in her colorful and uplifting paintings.

Mostly self-taught, Lisa has honed her skill over the years with perseverance and daily practice. Her story starts on a little farm in idyllic New Zealand where she was surrounded by rolling green hills and sweeping vistas. After traveling the world and settling in the United States, Lisa has continued to find inspiration in the coastal California landscape. She always strives to connect with the deeper world around us via her art.

Lisa's art is available on her own website, and she now offers online courses for all skill levels of palette knife painting. Active on social media and with a large following, she shares inspiration and tips and has millions of monthly views across her online platforms. With over a decade of experience exhibiting, Lisa shows at select international online and brick-and-mortar art galleries, corporate and public art installations, and vineyard tasting rooms. Her career has explored many creative avenues including licensing, wine labels, magazine press, live painting, guest speaking, and collaborations with major brands, large retailers, and interior designers.

To learn more about Lisa, her online courses, and her vision with her art, visit her website at www.lisaelley.com

www.ingramcontent.com/pod-product-compliance
Lightning Source LLC
Chambersburg PA
CBHW051216180526
44690CB00005B/6
*9780760382165*